LIVING ON THE MA

Undocumented mi{
in a global cit}

Alice Bloch and Sonia McKay

P

First published in Great Britain in 2017 by

Policy Press
University of Bristol
1-9 Old Park Hill
Bristol
BS2 8BB
UK
t: +44 (0)117 954 5940
pp-info@bristol.ac.uk
www.policypress.co.uk

North America office:
Policy Press
c/o The University of Chicago Press
1427 East 60th Street
Chicago, IL 60637, USA
t: +1 773 702 7700
f: +1 773-702-9756
sales@press.uchicago.edu
www.press.uchicago.edu

British Library Cataloguing in Publication Data
A catalogue record for this book is available from the British Library

Library of Congress Cataloging-in-Publication Data
A catalog record for this book has been requested

ISBN 978-1-4473-1937-5 paperback
ISBN 978-1-4473-1940-5 ePub
ISBN 978-1-4473-1941-2 Mobi
ISBN 978-1-4473-1938-2 ePdf

The right of Alice Bloch and Sonia McKay to be identified as authors of this work has been asserted by them in accordance with the Copyright, Designs and Patents Act 1988.

Policy Press works to counter discrimination on grounds of gender, race, disability, age and sexuality.

Cover design by Hayes Design
Printed and bound in Great Britain by Clays Ltd, St Ives plc
Policy Press uses environmentally responsible print partners

Contents

List of tables

Acknowledgements

There are many people who have been involved in this project over the years and we would like to thank them. First, thank you to the Economic and Social Research Council (grant reference ES/1037490/2), who funded the research project on which this book is based. Thank you to the 55 undocumented migrants and the 24 migrant entrepreneurs who were willing to share their experiences and whose lives form the empirical basis of this book. Salwa Chowdhury, Ozlem Galip, Tom Lam and Ansar Ahmed Ullah carried out the field work interviews with undocumented migrants and translated and transcribed the interviews. Their hard work, skills and knowledge helped to shape the project and we are grateful for their insights and input. Thank you to Jawad Botmeh, who worked with us during the first year of the project. We also had a great deal of support from others who enabled the relatively smooth running of the project within our institutions, notably Linda Butcher, Andrea Tinson and Gillian Whitworth and we would like to thank them for their help. We also received invaluable advice from members of our Project Advisory Group and some even acted as gatekeepers, facilitating access to interviewees and providing interview space. Finally, thank you to John Broadbent, who literally walked the streets of east London talking to people and cold calling in businesses to help us to find interviewees.

Alice would like to thank the following colleagues who have helped in one way or another even if they don't know it. Claire Alexander, Suki Ali, Leah Bassel, Wendy Bottero, Bridget Byrne, Kirsten Campbell, Milena Chimienti, Allan Cochrane, Giorgia Dona, Brian Heaphy, Shirin Hirsch, Vanessa May, Kate Nash, Sarah Neal, James Rhodes, Liza Schuster, John Solomos, Fran Tonkiss, Amal Treacher, Judy Wajcman and Frank Webster. Finally, thank you to Sonia McKay, who has not only been a fantastic colleague, over the years we have worked together, but a great friend too.

Sonia would like to similarly record her thanks to colleagues at the Working Lives Research Institute, Anna Paraskevopoulou, Nick Clark, Eugenia Markova, Cilla Ross, Leroi Henry; to Sian Moore and Tessa Wright for the insights they have provided in previous projects; to Rosa Crawford, Don Flynn and to the too numerous friends, colleagues and activists who fight to make sure that migrants get a fairer deal and are not the scapegoats for governmental failures. Sonia too needs to end this small piece by thanking Alice, not only a great colleague and supportive friend, but someone who can always be relied on to get a job done. This book itself is a tribute to that determination.

Both Alice and Sonia reserve a special thanks to Leena Kumarappan, who worked as a Research Fellow for the duration of the project and who was a vital member of the research team. Not only did we have the privilege of working with Leena but we had the joy of welcoming Leena and Murad's wonderful daughter, Anisa.

ONE

Introduction

"I had a passport prepared by the snakeheads ... We followed the snakeheads like fools. We didn't speak any English and didn't know where we were, how far we had travelled and so on. We were smuggling ourselves out of China ... I have been here for over 12 years ... I didn't do anything bad. People like us go about our business with a sense of honesty. We are hard working people. Each day we'd be happy as long as we've done our job ... if you let people like us work like all the others, we can just pay tax contributions. It's our duty to pay tax contributions. All you need to do is give us the rights to work ... We don't have any excessive wants. But the current situation doesn't give us much freedom; and the authorities crack down hard on illegal workers. They are rounding up illegal workers ... Our plight is the worst of all. We'd be locked up if we were caught. We are the unluckiest of all." (Lok, male, from China)

Lok is 46 years old and comes from Fujian Province in China where he had worked on a building site doing repairs. He entered the United Kingdom (UK) on a fake passport with a fictitious name. He moved for livelihood reasons after his divorce, leaving his children in China. Since he has been in the UK his contact with family and friends has gradually reduced to almost nothing except for the money he still sends to his parents. In the UK his social networks are small and consist of others from the same province in China, mostly due to language barriers. His friends offer important support, in the absence of any statutory welfare provision, and during periods of ill health – and therefore no income – he has been able to stay with them rent free. Lok has worked only in the kitchens of Chinese restaurants and take-away shops while in the UK, starting as a kitchen porter doing the most menial labouring jobs and gradually working his way up to a chef. He works long hours and has little time off, describing his daily routine as one of work and sleep. Lok's experiences are not dissimilar to those of other undocumented migrants in the UK and elsewhere.

Life is work within ethnic enclaves or for co-ethnic employers, narrow but necessary co-ethnic social networks, and being forced into the periphery of society by the restrictions of status and the fear of being caught, incarcerated and deported.

This book is about the everyday lives of undocumented migrants in London, a group that by the very nature of their immigration status finds itself for the most part living on the margins of a global city. Our aim is to present the realities faced by undocumented migrants in London, who live under the constant shadow of insecurity and the fear of being caught and deported. The experiences we present are not unique to undocumented migrants in London, but are mirrored among undocumented migrants all over the world who are living and working in cities, on farms, in towns and in villages. Undocumented migration and undocumented migrants are a global phenomenon and almost universally they lack rights, are marginalised and excluded, and their labour is exploited.

In November 2014 President Obama announced executive actions on US immigration policy noting, that the immigration system was broken and that routes to regularisation were about 'who we are as a country, and who we want to be for future generations'. Obama went on to argue that changes would enable people to 'come out of the shadows' and that when it comes to discussing immigration,

> We need more than politics as usual … we need reasoned, thoughtful, compassionate debate that focuses on our hopes, not our fears.

While the scale of undocumented migration in the US far exceeds the numbers in the UK, the issues both politically and in terms of lived experiences of low-paid work, marginalisation and divided families are not qualitatively different. Our concern in this book is to present the voices of undocumented migrants in order to convey how being undocumented shapes experiences, from the initial reason or reasons for migration right through to everyday lives at the time of the interview. In the different chapters of this book we consider what drives migration, why people come to the UK, what their journey was like and how they became undocumented, how work is found and experienced in the labour market, the building and use of social networks, what migrants' lives are like outside of work and the consequences of being undocumented in relation to access to and exclusion from services, resources and justice. However, this book is not only about undocumented migrants; we also consider the perspectives of ethnic enclave employers who own businesses that exclusively or largely employ people from the same ethnic group and who, in some cases, rely on the low-cost, flexible labour offered by undocumented migrants (Waldinger and Lichter, 2003; Jones, Ram and Edwards, 2006; MacKenzie and Forde, 2009). The views and positioning of ethnic enclave employers within enclave economies and in relation to government policies are a central part of undocumented migrants' experience, due to their dependence on these employers for work. Central to understanding the experiences of undocumented migrants and ethnic enclave employers is diversity; we found intersections with gender, class, reasons for migration and country of origin. These intersections result in different obligations and power relations that in turn frame experiences and strategies.

This chapter, in conjunction with Chapter Two, provides the overall context for the book. While Chapter Two focuses on immigration policies and regimes, international law and the related human rights, here we present our theoretical framing and concerns, in particular the relevance of the existing theoretical ideas in relation to undocumented migrants and their employers. First we will focus on the reasons for undocumented migration within the broader theoretical paradigms that consider economic, structural and migration systems, as drivers for international migration as well as the structural and state-based factors that result in irregular migration. Second, and central to our analysis, is the concept of social capital in the form of networks. These networks on the one hand can act as a trap, while on the other hand they serve as a mechanism for securing some, even if extremely minimal, resources. In this overview we will offer a critical assessment of the literature in relation to social capital and social networks and their linkages with the ethnic enclave. Third, the literature on labour market experiences and strategies among undocumented migrants will be examined, alongside those of ethnic enclave employers, including their preferences for certain types of workers who are often from the same ethnic group and perceived to be hard working and compliant. Throughout we will address the main cleavages of gender, class, power and status that frame the analysis in the empirical chapters.

Theoretical understandings of undocumented migration

Migration and any decisions to migrate are complex. Early theoretical analysis focused on the economic reasons for migration, looking for example at wage differentials as a push factor or the world economy as a system to meet the needs of capital, including its need for unskilled workers labouring in the service sectors of global cities (Arango, 2000; Sassen, 2001; Wills et al, 2010). These economically focused paradigms failed to consider the non-economic motives for migration, including the relationships between sending and receiving countries in creating and maintaining flows of migrants, and immigration politics and policies that dictate – in theory – who may enter and who can stay, as well as under what conditions and with what rights (Arango, 2000; Castles, de Haas and Miller, 2013).

The reality of migration is that any decision to migrate can be multifaceted, with more than one initial driver. For example, in states where there are human rights' abuses, generalised conflict and/or civil war, there are generally poor economies and a lack of livelihood opportunities (Castles, de Haas and Miller, 2013). Migration and migration destinations can be driven by linkages between individuals, households, communities and countries, including former colonial relations, and the social networks that facilitate flows and systems that result in exchanges, including of information (Bakewell, 2015). What is sometimes termed 'globalisation', together with technological developments, are key components of contemporary migration and migration systems where different levels of analysis – micro, meso and macro – and their linkages need to be considered (Faist, 2000). Micro refers to the individual and small-scale values and desires, meso to the intermediate levels such as social networks and collectives, and macro are the large-scale structures including the political economy, social structures and the migratory regimes established by national-states to control and manage migration.

While there has been a long history of academic work on migration more generally, in different academic disciplines (Brettell and Hollifield, 2007) theoretical work addressing the position of forced migrants is more recent. Initially research focused on refugees – that is, people who are recognised as refugees under the 1951 UN Convention definition as having a well-founded fear of persecution, on the basis of one of the stated Convention reasons (race, religion, nationality, membership of a particular social group or political opinion), and have crossed an international border. Now the focus tends to be more generally on 'forced migrants' as a way of including other groups that are also persecuted or vulnerable, such as asylum seekers; internally displaced people who have fled from generalised conflict and civil war, development projects, environmental disasters or changes; undocumented migrants and stateless people. The reasons posited for the more inclusive terminology are recognition that the bureaucratic categories such as refugee, stateless person and undocumented migrant do not reflect the reality of migration, with migration drivers often being complex and mixed, and protection needs being variable (Cohen, 2007; DeWind, 2007; Zetter, 2007). However, concerns remain that the more inclusive focus of forced migration could potentially compromise refugee protection (Hathaway, 2007; Crisp, 2008).

While the United Nations High Commissioner for Refugees is concerned largely though not exclusively with refugee protection there is acknowledgement of the complexity of migration, which means, argues Crisp, that:

> stakeholders, especially states, increasingly regarded the movement of refugees, asylum seekers and irregular migrants as part of a single (and often unwanted) phenomenon. (2008: 9)

Though we recognise the specificity of the protection needs of refugees, in this book our concern is with the broader and more inclusive concept of forced migration, where the analysis includes refused asylum seekers, migrants who move for economic reasons and undocumented migrants. We also recognise the mixed flows, multiple reasons for migrating and survival migrants who are outside of their country of origin because of threats to their basic rights but for whom there is no domestic/home-country solution (Betts, 2013). This wider application reflects some of the main patterns in contemporary human mobility and mirrors the experiences of the undocumented migrants in our study. Key to contemporary migration and mobility are globalisation, global inequality and social transformation (Castles, 2003; 2005; 2010; 2013). These elements of migration and social and economic structures reflect uneven opportunities to migrate, with border controls aimed at excluding some groups while the global elite can move freely; the growth of forced migration as a consequence of North/South relations and the needs of capitalism for low-paid and often precarious workers; and the social change that occurs, in both sending and receiving countries, as a consequence of migration.

There is no one theoretical framework that focuses on undocumented migration, because, as with other forms of migration, motives are often mixed and experiences vary. Moreover, there is no one term used to describe this group of migrants; 'undocumented', 'irregular', 'illegal', 'clandestine' and 'unauthorised' are all terms used to categorise people who are residing in a country without authority to do so. Governments favour the term 'illegal' as a means of framing some migrants as a threat. 'Irregular' and 'undocumented' are preferred by many non-government actors, including some academics, as they better reflect the reality of an individual's situation and move away from the idea of an individual as 'illegal' (Flynn, 2014). Critics of the term 'irregular' argue that it suggests a dichotomy with 'regular' that fails to convey the real complexities of status. The term 'undocumented migrants' is also criticised because migrants often have documents, though they might well be bought, borrowed or constructed (Vasta, 2011; Reeves, 2013) and so in the North American context some academics use the term 'non-status' or 'precarious legal status' as a better representation of reality (Goldring, Berinstein and Bernard 2009). We will use the term 'undocumented' with an awareness of the problematic nature of terminology and that the terms used are both contested and political (Anderson and Ruhs, 2010a; Bloch, Sigona and Zetter, 2014).

To understand undocumented migration, any research and scholarship needs to contemplate the multifarious routes both of clandestine entries into a country and into becoming undocumented. Being undocumented is not an end state, routes are complex and varied, as Cvajner and Sciortino note when they argue that 'irregularity is a status that may be both attained and left behind in different ways' (2010: 214). Pathways to becoming undocumented are: being a refused asylum seeker who is not deported or cannot return, state bureaucratic failures in relation to processing and inefficient renewal of visas and permits, clandestine and/or irregular entry into a country or through being born to parents without status (Düvell, 2011a). These routes are linked to border control and immigration regimes, as it is these controls and regimes that *make* migrants 'illegal'. Thus, argues Düvell:

> irregular migration is not an independent social phenomena [sic] but exists in relation to state policies and is a social, political and legal construction. (2011b: 276)

Status is mobile, dynamic and responsive to changes in legislation and circumstances. McIlwaine (2014) notes in her study of Latin Americans how, in short spaces of time, people move from having a regular status to being irregular. This status mobility, coupled with the very nature of the population, who often try to stay invisible from authorities or have entered the country clandestinely in the first place, means that there is no definitive or accurate data on numbers. Instead there are a series of estimates that use slightly different definitions, meaning that comparisons are not methodologically robust. The International Organization for Migration (2010) estimated that, globally, undocumented migrants accounted for 10 to 15% of the world's migrants. In Europe the estimates made by the Clandestino Project (2009) gave a range of between 1.9 million and 3.8 million undocumented migrants in the 27 European Union countries, or a central estimate of just 0.58% of the total population, which is far fewer than the global proportion. In the UK Woodbridge (2005) estimated that the *unauthorised* resident population at April 2001 was between 310,000 and 570,000. Research by Gordon et al (2009) gave a higher range of between 417,000 and 863,000 undocumented migrants at the end of 2007, with visa overstayers thought to be the largest single category of undocumented migrants. Once in a country and undocumented, migrants experience the effects of stratified rights (Morris, 2002) and hierarchical citizenship (Castles, 2005). Castles notes that undocumented migrants 'lack nearly all rights except those guaranteed by international human rights instruments' (2005: 219), but, as we show in Chapter Two, even when these rights are in theory attainable, the reality for undocumented migrants is somewhat different (Rutherford and Addison, 2007; Bloch, 2010; Nash, 2015).

For undocumented migrants themselves, the impact of being irregular and, in particular, their 'deportability' (see de Genova, 2002) is the lens through which everyday life is experienced, negotiated and managed (Willen, 2007). It can be a constant strain to stay hidden, to avoid public places, public transport, town centres, too many social interactions or places where documents might be requested or insisted upon. However, being undocumented is situational and so the 'condition of illegality' has greater impact in environments where documents are checked, such as workplaces (Khosravi, 2010: 96). In the UK these checks have been extended as a consequence of the 2014 Immigration Act and includes more members of civil society in the immigration regime, such as private landlords.

Undocumented migrants, though susceptible to vulnerability, marginalisation and disadvantage, are not passive victims without any individual agency or power and this needs to be incorporated into any analysis (Anderson and Ruhs, 2010a). For example, acts of individual and collective resistance, such as identity stripping by destroying documents to avoid deportation (Ellerman, 2010), group solidarity over wages (Cleaveland and Pierson, 2009) and job mobility to acquire new skills, better wages or improved working conditions (Bloch and McKay, 2013) are evident from research studies. Experiences are diverse and acts of resistance and strategies are dependent on what is at stake if one is found and deported. Where someone fears persecution in their country of origin or has large debts as a consequence of making their journey it is likely that the fear of being caught and deported will be greater than among those who do not face the same fears of persecution or financial pressures (Bloch, Sigona and Zetter, 2014). These fears and pressures will impact in different ways and can and do dictate social, community and economic choices and decision making, areas that we explore theoretically in the next two parts of this chapter.

Social capital and undocumented migrants

One of our aims in this book is to engage to some extent with the theory of social capital and to understand better its explanatory relevance (or not) in the lives of those who are undocumented. We hypothesised at the start of our study that undocumented migrants would be well networked, indeed that they would rely on and foster the building of networks to possibly a greater extent than would be the case for those who are indigenous and documented, whose networks (social capital) are part of the fabric into which they have been born, or upon which they are more able to build (Lancee, 2012) and in which they grow. For those who arrive as undocumented migrants, finding individuals and groups who may be able to assist them is a vital element in their survival strategies. We demonstrate in subsequent chapters, the ways in which those without documents actively engage in network building as a fundamental survival strategy; however, in measurable terms the results are not advantageous, nor do they represent 'the aggregate of the actual or potential resources which are linked to possession of a durable network of more or less institutionalised relationships of mutual acquaintance or recognition' (Bourdieu, 1986: 241).

Bourdieu's definition of social capital requires that it is decomposable into two elements: first the social relationship itself that allows individuals to claim access to resources possessed by their associates, and second the amount and quality of those resources. The acquisition of social capital requires deliberate investment of both economic and cultural resources, although, as Erel asserts, the latter should not be conceived through a 'rucksack' approach (2010: 643), which assumes that migrants arrive with their cultural and human capital and then merely determine whether it is usable or not, but rather, migrants shape and further produce such capital, as active agents in the destination country. Portes (1998), drawing on Bourdieu and focusing on migration, asserts that the concept of social capital consists of 'actual' or 'potential' resources requiring both a social relationship that allows individuals to claim access to resources and that the amount and quality of these resources must be sufficient to advantage those who possess them, so that social capital does not of itself give advantage merely by having a network or networks. Furthermore, any social capital which undocumented migrants may have or try to build after arrival can be quickly depleted where they are unable to reciprocate within community networks, other than through the offer of labour that is underpaid. Cederberg (2012) in particular presents a strong challenge to the application of Bourdieu's theory of social capital to migrant communities, pointing to the existence of inequalities on ethnic lines, which are obscured in a focus on social capital. Moreover, she questions the distinction between 'bonding' and 'bridging' capital, which 'fails to attend to internal conflicts and hierarchies and, more generally, intra-group differences', as well as to fully engage 'with the complexity of structures and processes of disadvantage' (Cederberg, 2012: 68). This leads us to suggest a focus on the notion of 'instrumental' social capital that may meet immediate needs but that does not amount to social networks of value, which may remain 'spatially dispersed' (Ryan et al, 2008: 684).

Ryan maintains that nationality is 'not enough to guarantee close bonds of friendship' (2011: 721), while Ryan et al (2008), in their study of social networks, social support and social capital explored through the experiences of Polish migrants, engage with the concepts of bonding and bridging capital, challenging the assertion that migrants invariably enter into dense networks with co-ethnic groups, pointing to a combination of distrusting outsiders alongside the tendency to exclude newcomers so that the relationships between newly arrived migrants and existing social networks are not linear. Instead Ryan et al (2008) suggest an approach that differentiates between social capital and social networks, where the latter may provide emotional, instrumental and informational support without offering the advantages of the former. These observations are offered primarily in the context of documented migration, so that in relation to our study, which focuses on those who are undocumented, a critical approach to the concept of social capital is even more necessary in a context where bonding capital may actually inhibit the development of bridging capital. In relation, for example, to the Chinese-origin migrants in our study their identification purely on the basis of nationality and as connected to the existing and long-standing Chinese community in the UK fails to take account of differences of class, history, language and location such that they did not bond with the established Chinese community and did not see themselves as connected through nationality. We can find similar points of differentiation between existing and newer Bangladeshi and Turkish/Kurdish communities in the UK.

Within the broad-brush notion of community and ethnic-minority solidarity there are in fact significant differences, which are often overlooked in describing these 'communities' and their operational rationale. In a study of migrants from the Caribbean, Reynolds (2012) found that underpinning intra-ethnic familial and community divisions are culturally prescribed notions of status, social morality and respectability, based upon migration patterns and intersected identities of social class, 'race'/colour and gender. Migrants from lower socioeconomic backgrounds were constructed by 'established' Caribbean individuals as lacking in social standing and respectability because they did not appear to conform to English cultural codes of behaviour, demonstrating distinctions between groups who share some co-ethnic elements but are differentiated as much by what they do not have in common as any by other facet, which, according to Erel, 'is not useful as it glosses over intra-group hierarchical distinctions and exclusions' (2010: 654). Therefore understanding the ways in which networks operate requires an understanding of context and intersections. As Ryan (2011) suggests, it is necessary to consider the social location of migrants in assessing the available and realisable resources that social networks can provide, such that 'a network made up of people from similar or lower socio-economic groups may further reinforce social marginalisation' (2011: 721), rather than overcoming it. This is likely to be even more so in the case of undocumented migrants than for others.

Thus, although much of the literature on social networks as a form of social capital focuses on ethnic minorities and new migrants, there is little attention to the ways in which undocumented migrants, whose structural position within society is qualitatively different, as a consequence of their lack of status, develop, engage in and perceive such networks within their everyday lives. Moreover, organisations are rarely funded to work with undocumented migrants, and so this will, for some, affect access to basic information and advice and community activities. The consequence is that undocumented migrants seek out alternative networks and routes to advice and support, but these are not always altruistic and can instead be contaminated by those seeking to profit out of the vulnerable situation of undocumented migrants.

Do social networks advantage?

Most proponents of social capital have ignored the relationship between actual, valuable resources and the creation of social capital. Putnam equates social networks with social capital so that, he argues:

> a well-connected individual in a poorly connected society
> is not as productive as a well-connected individual in a
> well-connected society. (2000: 20)

Moreover, Putman argues that social capital helps to surmount barriers based on race because some workers in ethnic enclaves get paid as much as white workers, and that 'social capital may help produce equality' (2000: 359). Rarely do undocumented migrants experience the type of networking advantages which Putnam (2000) describes, such as the networks found in the bowling clubs and groups of middle Americans whom he eulogised, as representing an era when things functioned simply because people came together, celebrating their common identities.

The undocumented migrants we interviewed spoke extensively of the networks they had created, but whether these provided real benefits was less certain and, for many, class and economic position, in conjunction with status, acted so as to effectively both exclude and isolate them. This reflects the assertion by Daly and Silver that:

> social network truncation translates, not into the lack of
> social capital based on relations of trust and reciprocity,
> but into a diminished capacity to gain access to resources
> controlled by larger social groupings. (2008: 99)

The literature on social capital has sometimes identified co-ethnic networks as a route to economic, social or cultural opportunities (Sanders, Nee and Sernau, 2002), although also as one that can limit opportunities (Datta et al, 2006; Phung, 2011; Holgate et al, 2012). These networks have been seen as paths to individual improvement; as ways of enriching migration outcomes; and overall as contributing to societal prosperity (Maroukis, Iglicka and Katarzyna, 2011). Ryan (2011) found evidence of network formation post-migration and of changes in the composition of networks. However, in relation to undocumented migrants, our study suggests that there is limited opportunity for such development, so that individuals can become stuck in early networks or, where they are developed, they tend to be composed of other undocumented migrants and so they remain rooted in the positions that they had on arrival or soon after arrival. Co-ethnic networks may therefore appear durable, but this is primarily because there is no alternative accessible network, even though the social composition of the network may result in those within it nevertheless perceiving themselves as outsiders, based on their class position and human capital held prior to migration. Kloosterman, van der Leun and Rath (1999) argue that through such networks migrants gain 'privileged' access to information, although Portes (1998) has cautioned about placing too much emphasis on the advantages of social capital, noting that:

> Social ties can bring about greater control over wayward behaviour and provide privileged access to resources; they can also restrict individual freedoms and bar outsiders from gaining access to the same resources through particularistic preferences. (1998: 21)

Undocumented migrants are thus conceptualised as making use of social networks to access ethnic enclave employment – that is, work within a location characterised by the clustering of people from minority ethnic groups – and as using these networks as a way of overcoming the barriers that otherwise they might face (Sanders, Nee and Sernau, 2002; Iskander, 2007; Ahmad, 2008a; 2008b). The result may be to restrict their employment opportunities to the ethnic enclave (Phung, 2011), and so networks can be both positive and negative. The assumption that social networks have a positive influence – from the perspective of the undocumented migrant – in assisting entry into work fails to take account of how that entry takes place, what obligations it imposes on the migrant worker and, indeed, what that work amounts to. An assumption that social networks have a positive effect suggests that there are advantages that are gained through the holding or acquisition of social capital in the form of such networks. In reality the effects of social networks are mediated by factors that include:

> the social valuation of the ethnic ties, both within and outside the ethnic category, the social location of the actor (for example their gender) and the social context. (Anthias, 2007: 788)

We recognise that these social networks exist and that they are seen as valuable in terms of the 'practical and emotional support' they offer (Cederberg, 2012: 63). Our contention is that these networks do not provide the 'capital' or 'resources' that social capital theory implies and that, as much as they are protective and supportive, they are also restrictive, because these networks are limited and constrained by status and therefore replicate disadvantaged positions.

Our view is that to theorise such networks as social capital in relation to undocumented migration is indeed to be 'parasitical' (Fine, 2010: 3). Instead, we suggest that the concept of social capital already sits uneasily within the study of migration generally, and in relation to undocumented migration its value is extremely limited in explaining the interconnection between high levels of networking and the few, if any, entitlements or resources that networks bring to those who are undocumented, including that they may equally restrict workers to specific sectors, occupations or types of employment (Reingold, 1999; McIlwaine et al, 2006; Ryan et al, 2008; Nakhaie, Lin and Guan, 2009). The networks explored in our work echo Granovetter in that they:

> not only insulate them [migrants] from the latest ideas and fashions but may put them in a disadvantaged position in the labor market where advancement can depend ... on knowing about appropriate job openings at just the right time. (1983: 202)

Strong ties to co-ethnics may prevent migrants from developing the 'weak ties' that might permit them to emerge from the constraints of their co-ethnic networks. Ryan (2011) suggests that the workplace may be a key locus that enables the establishment of weak ties, though this is less likely in relation to undocumented migrants, whose workplace is also delineated by their undocumented status. The inability to work outside of ethnic enclaves, or the possibility to do so only in the context of hiding identity and status, delivers additional challenges to the construction of weak ties. Even where it is argued that enclaves could be perceived as 'safe spaces', we have shown (Bloch, Kumarappan and McKay, 2015) that the targeting of minority-ethnic businesses by UK Border Agency raids demonstrates that they can also represent a trap for undocumented migrants and a risk for employers caught employing those without the legal right to work.

An essential component of social capital is trust. However, trust is a complex phenomenon; it does not necessarily indicate relationships of equality or even of choice. In the context of undocumented migrants there may be no alternative but to 'trust' or perhaps more correctly to 'hope' that the individual or organisation in whom trust has been placed will not betray. Thus, in examining trust it is equally important to reflect on mistrust as well as on the fact that trust and reciprocity can 'also contain less positive aspects, such as control' (Cederberg, 2012: 65), or operate as 'different layers of trust' that can actually include a wariness or suspicion of co-ethnic networks (Ryan et al, 2008: 679).

We find that the notion of 'mistrustful solidarity' (Levitt 2001: 118), where family and community ties are strong but are accompanied by a high degree of scepticism, provides a useful starting point as something that better captures the real meanings that undocumented migrants attach to 'trust' in the context of their employment.

As Roggeveen (2013) found, in her study of undocumented Brazilian migrants in Amsterdam, individuals might associate with one another, but there were only a few family and close friends or groups that they specifically affiliated themselves to who were regarded as trustworthy, and this too had a direct bearing on their acquisition of social capital. While trust is essential and co-ethnicity at one level generates trust (Reeskens and Wright, 2012), it did not overcome inequalities of class and gender and even of place of origin. Thus it is important that social capital is theorised and understood in relation to intersections and is not gender neutral (Ryan, 2011).

Throughout this book we attempt to address the subtle nuances of intersections and find that gender, migration patterns and different aspects of capital affect experiences. These are variable and, in reality, social capital may also increase social exclusion rather than alleviate it. While social ties to family and close friends may yield material support, this is usually accompanied by the 'lack of "weak ties" to other social networks that may be more valuable for obtaining scarce information' (Daly and Silver, 2008: 561). For migrants from lower socioeconomic backgrounds or who fear persecution based on behaviours, actions or opinions that are in a minority or socially unacceptable, there may even be a greater wish to disassociate from networks (Gill and Bialski, 2011; Bloch, Sigona and Zetter, 2014). Thus networks may represent a choice, but a constrained choice which will be obviated when possible. According to Anderson et al:

> In order to understand migrants' choices and agency one must then consider the options that are available, and how these constrain and/or facilitate choice. In understanding experiences and labour market outcomes, the particular circumstances and personal characteristics of individuals are important – age, gender, education, whether they have dependents or debts, for instance. These inter-relate to shape the range of options open to people. Immigration status is one such factor, but it cannot be understood in isolation. (2006: 104)

In relation specifically to ethnic enclaves it is recognised that while networks are conceived as offering work opportunities, for some the very decision to migrate can be premised on a desire to separate from a society of origin that is hostile or prioritises different values. Furthermore, living in segregated areas increases the risk of unemployment and lower economic returns (Khattab et al, 2010). This can result in the adoption of alternative strategies, including a chosen exclusion or distancing from a social network (McKay, 2009; Holgate et al, 2012; Bloch, Sigona and Zetter, 2014), and it is thus just as important to understand why individuals do not use networks as it is to explore why they do.

In summary, networks can and do foster social exclusion, as they set the boundaries of opportunity and, in the case of those in minority ethnic communities, whose own resources may be limited, the network can trap new arrivals into a position at the bottom of a cycle of poverty that is resource poor, where community relations can be conflictual or where there are historical and generational differences which exclude new arrivals from the notion of community.

Undocumented migrants and work

The context in which we carried out this research was one of a global economic downturn, on-going global inequality and segmented domestic labour markets. Part of the segmentation is based on a migrant division of labour, and even within the concept of migrant the divisions are further disaggregated by immigration status (Wills et al, 2010). It is undocumented migrants who are the most disadvantaged and the least able to secure either human rights or employment rights. In the UK the broader political and policy framing for migrants continues to be one of restrictive immigration controls, raids on businesses employing people without correct documentation and the deportation of 'illegal' entrants, refused asylum seekers and visa overstayers. Undocumented migrants and undocumented migration are portrayed as a risk to societal cohesion and integration, a threat to state sovereignty and as workers who take jobs and undercut wages. Within such a hostile environment it is not surprising that undocumented migrants approach work with caution and are forced into the informality of ethnic enclaves and ethnic enclave employers.

One of the characteristics of ethnic enclaves, particularly among new and recently arrived migrants, regardless of status, is that the informal family and community networks they offer can result in access to the labour market often within the specific co-ethnic economy (Nee and

Sanders, 2001). The extent of an individual's inter-ethnic ties and their social, economic and cultural capital will affect access to wider societal resources and opportunities outside of the ethnic enclave. Access to different forms of capital affect migration routes and destinations and post-migration experiences, and so class should be central to the analysis of migration scholars (Van Hear, 2014). Class is also a determinant of resistance and protest (Pero, 2014); although it is not only class that affects experiences, especially in relation to employment, where intersections of gender and ethnicity are also significant.

Migrant labour tends to be polarised at either the highly skilled, well-paid end or the low and unskilled end of the labour market. These divisions dictate not only access to labour markets but also modes of entry into nation states. While highly skilled migrants are actively recruited by developed countries, those with low levels of skills are seen as less desirable, regardless of the needs for low-skilled and flexible labour (Ewers, 2007; Portes, 2009). It is, in part, due to the needs of highly developed economies for low-paid and flexible workers that successive pieces of immigration legislation have failed. According to Castles (2004), undocumented migration has grown in response to neoliberal labour market deregulation and the increase in casual employment, sub-contracting and informal sectors. Undocumented migrants, in particular, find work in the informal parts of the economy, but this is likely to subject them to greater degrees of discriminatory treatment and abuse (Wright, 2007).

Previous research identifies some patterns in terms of labour market experiences. Undocumented migrants are potentially the most vulnerable to the poorest working conditions and most unscrupulous employers, with little or no power to contest their treatment, due to their 'deportability' (de Genova, 2002; Holmes, 2007; Rutherford and Addison, 2007; Vertovec, 2007; MacKenzie and Forde, 2009; Wills et al, 2010). Work is often found in restaurants, take-away shops, off-licences, small grocery stores/supermarkets, construction, factories, food processing and agriculture. Within these kinds of work, men are usually found in the more physical roles, reflecting Anderson and Ruhs' assertion that 'certain types of bodies (most obviously, gendered, racialised, and aged) are considered more suitable for certain types of work' (2010b: 20). Labour markets are complex and fragmented by gender, nationality and ethnicity, as well as through a migrant division of labour and co-ethnic hierarchies of power based on immigration status (Vertovec, 2007; Wills et al, 2010).

Undocumented migrants can, and do, use different forms of capital, in the same way as other migrants, to enhance opportunities in the labour market, though their need for invisibility often makes their experiences markedly different (McIlwaine, 2014). Moreover, the abjectivity, liminality and deportability associated with their undocumented status (Menjívar, 2006; Willen, 2007; Gonzales and Chavez, 2012) means that while different forms of capital are advantageous and essential, they still do not mitigate against the effects of status (Bloch, Sigona and Zetter, 2014). Status will affect the sectors of employment, types of employers and kinds of jobs that can be obtained, or it requires risk taking in the form of constructed or borrowed documents to ameliorate the effects of status (Vasta, 2011). However, the extent to which undocumented migrants will take risks is correlated with the circumstances of migration and their individual fear of return, so refused asylum seekers, who fear persecution, are more cautious than others and least likely to work or use fictive or other people's documents than are other undocumented migrants (Bloch, 2014).

Work is more often, though not exclusively, represented as being found in small businesses owned by co-ethnic entrepreneurs within the ethnic enclave or within ethnic-minority worker-dominated niches, in which an ethnic group dominates a sector or sub-sector (McGregor, 2007; Schrover, van der Leun and Quispel, 2007; Bloch, 2013; Bloch and McKay, 2013). However, within the often limited ranges of jobs and sectors, there is a body of research that also demonstrates the effectiveness of micro and localised individual and collective strategies to make incremental improvements to working lives, in terms of levels of pay or to ensure migrants' indispensability as workers and as conduits for jobs for others from the same country or community of origin (Cleaveland and Pierson, 2009; Gomberg-Muñoz, 2010; Bloch and McKay, 2013). Acquiring and using fictive or other people's documents as a mechanism for combating document-based exclusions is another strategy that can be used to enter the more regulated parts of the labour market (Vasta, 2011; Reeves, 2013). Significantly, as Gonzales and Chavez note, in spite of their lack of power, 'undocumented migrants are not powerless' (2012: 259).

However, the current policy climate, both within the UK and at European Union (EU) level, which is increasingly hostile, has been significant in shaping working lives and, to some extent, employer recruitment. The threat and the reality of raids on businesses, the possible arrest and deportation of workers and fines on entrepreneurs have consequences, even if they are not the stated aims of the policy (Bloch, Kumarappan and McKay, 2015). Engbersen and Broeders argue that labour market tactics are fluid and reactive to external events, such as the implementation of new policy, and so any change in policy will lead undocumented migrants to 'change tactics, look for ways of circumvention and move to other spheres and contexts' (2009: 874). The case of workplace raids, for example, has resulted in a retreat among undocumented migrants into less visible and more informal sectors of the economy (Engbersen and Broeders, 2009).

Ethnic enclave employers

Workplace raids and fines also affect employer recruitment, although they do not eradicate the hiring of undocumented migrants in ethnic enclave businesses because it makes greater economic sense as wages are low, kinship and social networks dictate obligations and employers can hold political positions that will deter compliance (Bloch and McKay, 2015). Drawing on the North American sociological literature, we use the term 'ethnic enclave entrepreneur' to describe those businesses which employ co-ethnic workers and that are more likely to be clustered within ethnic enclaves, which are areas consisting of migrant groups concentrated in a particular spatial area, serving predominantly, although not exclusively, their own ethnic market (Portes, 1981; Portes and Bach, 1985; Light et al, 1994). Limited data about this group make it difficult to provide a comprehensive analysis of the experiences and contributions of migrant entrepreneurs (Jones et al, 2014). However, the literature suggests that employers can and do hold stereotyped views of what constitutes a good worker and which workers are to be trusted. Social capital in the form of networks is used for recruitment, as it offers an informal reference due to the pre-existing link with the workers. This means that labour forces are produced and reproduced around particular social categories including ethnicity and gender (Waldinger and Lichter, 2003).

One of the areas that we explore in Chapter Five is the reasons why some migrants go into business while others do not. Knight (2015), in her recent research on Polish workers in the UK, suggests that the factors that differentiate migrant entrepreneurs from migrant co-ethnic workers are their acquisition of human capital in the destination country, along with their social networks. Hormiga and Bolivar-Cruz (2014), as a way of explaining the higher levels of migrant entrepreneurship, suggest that this is based on a higher tolerance of risk than is generally present in the home population. Both put forward a gendered account of entrepreneurship, as males may have wider access to more diverse forms of capital, while female entrepreneurs may be more located within their kinship networks.

Co-ethnic networks provide the often essential financial capital to enable a business start-up (Chaudhry and Crick, 2004; Kitching, Smallbone and Athayde, 2009) as well as the expertise and emotional support that enable new entrepreneurs to establish their businesses and to succeed. The propensity to set up a business is influenced by individual migration histories, labour market opportunities for work and vertical mobility in the workplace, experiences of discrimination and exclusion from the labour market and a 'natural' progression from employment to self-employment (Chaudhry and Crick, 2004, Wahlbeck, 2007; Kitching, Smallbone and Athayde, 2009; Bloch and McKay, 2015). It is also determined by access to forms of capital, both financial – the most important – and also social capital, as the ability to utilise advantageous networks is of key importance in the establishment of new businesses. So too is human capital, in the form of knowledge of the business (Valdez, 2008; Smallbone, Kitching and Athayde, 2010). What the literature suggests is that different forms of capital are vital for employers and migrants in different ways, and this is an area that we will explore throughout the book.

The research basis for the book: methods and methodology

The empirical chapters in this book (Chapters Three to Seven) are derived from data collected as part of an Economic and Social Research Council-funded project, 'Undocumented Migrants, Ethnic Enclaves and Networks: Opportunities, Traps or Class Based Constructs?'. The research field-work was carried out in 2012 and early 2013. We collected qualitative interview data with 55 undocumented migrants in 2012 and 2013 and 24 ethnic enclave employers in 2013, from Bangladesh, China and Turkey (including Kurds from Turkey and Northern Cypriots), all living in London at the time of the interviews. In addition we carried out an asynchronous internet focus group with seven ethnic enclave employers who had also participated in face-to-face interviews.

Undocumented migrants and employers from the three countries were selected because they offered variations in experiences in relation to migration patterns, migration drivers, and also in terms of sectors and profiles of workers. Previous research (Bloch, Sigona and Zetter, 2014) suggests that Chinese undocumented migrants come to the UK motivated largely by economic imperatives. Work is found mainly in Chinese restaurants, fast-food shops and supermarkets. A minority work in building and construction, in factories and in food processing, representing a mix of enclave and non-enclave employment. Access to wider networks and sites for employment are limited by language and status. There is a long history of migration to the UK by migrants from Turkey, including Kurds, a discriminated-against minority, with Turkish migrants arriving from the mid-1960s (Erel, 2010) and Kurds from the 1980s onwards (King et al, 2008). Motives depend on whether the migrants are Turkish or Kurdish, with the latter group comprising of some refused asylum seekers. Employment is mainly in restaurants, fast-food outlets, retail and textiles within ethnic enclave businesses. Undocumented migrants from Bangladesh appear to be located mainly within the food industry, both restaurants and fast-food outlets; they have had a long history of migration to the UK, with numbers increasing significantly from the 1970s onwards (Tackey et al, 2006). All three groups have established community networks and associations and comprise both long-term and more recent undocumented migrants, which was important for our research in order to try to explore a range of experiences.

There are no sampling frames available for either undocumented migrants or migrant entrepreneurs and so we used non-probability methods, combined with purposive sampling. The interviews with undocumented migrants were carried out in first languages by community interviewers, who were actively involved in identifying potential interviewees through community organisations, faith groups, personal contacts and snowballing. Snowball sampling is a strategy used to obtain respondents through referrals among people who share the same characteristic and is especially useful when the research is sensitive and/or the population is hidden, as it can alleviate the problems associated with a lack of visibility among some potential study populations. It does rely on members of the target populations being known to each other (Faugier and Sargeant, 1997; Atkinson and Flint, 2001) and is effective when this is the case.

To reach a more diverse sample we recruited interviewees through a number of different starting points including community organisations and community law centres, faith groups, the personal contacts of the interviewers, members of the project advisory group and cold calling in areas with clusters of people from the target groups. The larger the range of starting points for the sample, the greater the potential diversity (Bloch, 2007) and so this was a priority for the project. We also set quotas to try to achieve a mix of experiences by gender and length of time in the UK. The quotas were to act as a guide and we took a flexible approach, due to the difficulties of accessing undocumented migrants. The profile of the final sample is shown in Table 1.1 and

Table 1.1: Sample of undocumented migrants, by country of origin, gender and length of time in the UK

Base number = 55

	Bangladesh	China	Turkey	Total
Gender				
Male	11	14	15	40
Female	4	6	5	15
Length of time in the UK (years)				
Less than 2	2	0	2	4
2 but less than 5	2	10	4	16
5 but less than 10	8	8	7	23
10 or more	3	2	7	12

indicates a bias towards men. Among the Turkish group of interviewees 11 were Kurds from Turkey and one was a Kurd from Northern Cyprus. Throughout the research we were aware of the potential hierarchies of power, based on status and social class, that can be present in research interactions. However, potential research participants can and do protect themselves in terms of their social relations with researchers and have the power to make decisions over whether to participate (Lammers, 2005), so long as research adheres to ethical principles including informed consent, anonymity, confidentiality and sensitivity to the research situation. As part of interviewer training, prior to the start of the fieldwork we carried out detailed sessions on access, the study population, the research process and transcription. Ethics informed these areas and we added a dedicated session on ethics and the specific ethical issues that might arise in relation to the study population. Our research ethics were informed by the guidelines from the British Sociological Association and the Refugee Studies Centre at the University of Oxford.

We were aware from previous research that sensitivity and flexibility during the research interaction were particularly important, and so breaks during the interview and the possibility for the interviewer to use their judgement to suggest stopping before the end of the interview if it seemed that interviewee was distressed were options. Certainly in a few interviews breaks were taken, but in the end all interviewees were happy to complete the interview process. We also knew that interviewees might request information from the interviewers and so we produced a signposting document to give to those who were interviewed, with details of support organisations that could provide advice and information. We also produced a Rights Guide for both employers and undocumented migrant workers, setting out the rights to which workers are entitled, including those that applied regardless of status. This helped to ensure that interviewers were not put into a difficult situation of being expected to provide help and advice that they were not qualified to give.

Our ethical standpoint recognised the obligation to protect the physical safety and general welfare of interviewees and interviewers. Interviews were carried out in a place of safety – sometimes NGO offices, at the university in a private room, in workplaces, cafes, in parks and other public places. In line with ethical guidelines, the interviewer informed one other person, prior to each interview, when and where the interview was being carried out and the interviewer was to call before the start and at the end of the interview, to inform the contact that they were safe. Additionally, to safeguard the welfare of interviewers, who might have listened to traumatic narratives, we maintained regular, sometimes daily contact and held a number of debriefing sessions during the field-work and at the end of it to allow interviewers to talk about their experiences in the field and share details as they wished or needed to.

The interviews with undocumented migrants were recorded and transcribed by the interviewer, who also applied a pseudonym and anonymised the transcripts, taking out references to place names, names of businesses, people and any other possible identifiers. After the transcripts were submitted to the university research team every transcript was read to check that no markers remained that could potentially jeopardise the anonymity of individuals, workplaces or specific locations. We followed similar procedures in terms of anonymising the transcripts from the interviews with 24 ethnic enclave employers.

The 24 employers we interviewed varied in terms of the sector of their business or businesses, the length of time in the business and in the UK as well as their own reasons for migration. Only one interviewee was not a migrant – Ali, a woman from Bangladesh who jointly owned and managed an undertaker's business. Table 1.2 shows the main characteristics of employers and of the business or businesses that they owned.

Table 1.2 shows that the final sample of employers comprised seven Bangladeshi, eight Chinese and nine Turkish entrepreneurs of whom six were Kurdish and one was Northern Cypriot. Five interviewees were female and 19 were male. Length of time in Britain ranged from nine years to over 40 years, and four interviewees had been asylum

Table 1.2: Employers' characteristics and businesses

Base number = 24

Name	Country of origin	Whether employed undocumented migrant in the past	Whether employing undocumented migrants now	Business(es)
Ahmed (male)	Bangladesh	No	No	Restaurant
Ali (female)	Bangladesh	No	No	Undertaker
Amedi (male)	Kurd from Turkey	No	No	Garage (mechanic)
Chen (male)	China	Yes	No	Restaurant and supermarket
Demir (male)	Northern Cyprus	Not known	No	Hair salon
Hasan (male)	Bangladesh	Yes	Yes	Take-away
Jaf (female)	Kurd from Turkey	Yes	Yes	Restaurant
Mahmood (male)	Bangladesh	Yes	No	Clothing shop
Peng (male)	China	Yes	No	Restaurant
Rahman (male)	Bangladesh	Yes	Yes	Take-away
Rami (male)	Kurd from Turkey	Yes	No	Take-away and pound shop
Reza (male)	Bangladesh	Yes	No	Laundry
Sahin (male)	Turkey	No	No	Food import/ export business
Serhati (male)	Kurd from Turkey	Yes	Yes	Restaurant
Sindi (male)	Kurd from Turkey	Yes	No	Shop
Tan (male)	China	Yes	No	Restaurant
Tovi (female)	Kurd from Turkey	Yes	Yes	Two restaurants and one cafe
Uddin (male)	Bangladesh	Yes	No	Restaurant
Wang (male)	China	Yes	No	Restaurant and construction
Wu (male)	China	No	No	Gadget shop
Yildiz (male)	Turkey	Yes	Yes	Hair salon
Yin (female)	China	No	No	Chinese medicine
Zhou (female)	China	Yes	Yes	Restaurant and take-away
Zue (male)	China	Yes	Yes	Construction (shop interiors)

seekers in the past, so we had a mix of experiences that enabled us to explore the range of employers' strategies and their priorities.

The university-based research team carried out the interviews with 24 employers either as one-to-one interviews or in pairs. In three cases, in interviews with Kurdish entrepreneurs, one of the community researchers, who had acted as a gatekeeper, also attended the interview at the request of the interviewee. Similar to the interviews with undocumented migrants, we used a number of different access points for employers to ensure greater diversity. Employers were located through community organisations, cold calling at businesses in enclave areas and through the networks created by the community researchers while accessing undocumented migrants. Employers can be difficult to access, especially where they might be contravening employment regulations (Ram et al, 2000), and these problems can be compounded by the sensitive nature of the research. However, through networking and cold calling we were able to successfully complete interviews with employers.

Mapping the book

This section outlines the content of the remaining seven chapters of the book. Chapter Two provides the legal, policy and rights contexts in relation to undocumented migrants in the UK and also more widely in the EU and internationally. We discuss the reasons for the incremental tightening up of immigration controls and the increasing focus on undocumented migrants in an attempt to manage the migration of those who are seen to be challenging the sovereignty and security of the nation state. These controls relate to both borders and in-country regimes such as employer sanctions. This chapter also locates undocumented migrants within the broader human rights frameworks and shows that while rights based on personhood exist in theory, in reality accessing those rights without having a formal status is almost impossible.

Chapter Three is concerned with the migration drivers, the differences between and within country-of-origin groups and the extent to which coming to the UK was by choice or circumstantial, due to smuggling routes. We then explore the realities of the journey, which in some cases took several months and involved different modes of transport. The chapter then considers the ways in which people enter the country and, for some, status mobility, including decisions to try to regularise status or to remain undocumented.

In Chapters Four and Five we turn our attention to the work, working lives and work strategies of both undocumented migrants and ethnic enclave entrepreneurs. Chapter Four considers how people find work and how this alters over time as networks are developed; where people find jobs in terms of sectors of employment, within or outside of the ethnic enclave and the extent to which undocumented migrants are mobile by choice or necessity are explored. Terms and conditions of work and workplace relations are examined in relation to intersections, including with status, gender, country of origin and length of time in the UK. The focus of Chapter Five is on the employers' perspectives; we present their experiences of setting up businesses and their business practices, especially the recruitment of workers, preferred worker characteristics and practices in relation to the employment of undocumented migrants. We also explore employers' views on the impact of immigration controls and sanctions on their businesses and business practices. In Chapters Four and Five we note the importance of kinship and social networks in the economic lives of both undocumented migrants and minority-ethnic employers.

In Chapter Six we focus once again on undocumented migrants and explore their networks on arrival, how they build networks and how networks are experienced and used. We then consider participation in community organisations and other activities and pastimes outside of work. For most people networks were restricted to others from the same ethnic and linguistic group, although as people's lives changed so did their engagements in different kinds of networks and activities, including those that have a transnational element.

Chapter Seven considers the impact of being undocumented and the ways in which it interacts with access to public and other services. The different ways in which undocumented migrants navigated exclusions are considered as well as the role of kinship and social networks as safety nets and places to obtain support during the most difficult times in the absence of statutory provision. We find that status permeates almost all aspects of life and decision making, although the impact is not uniform and responses are variable.

The final chapter, Chapter Eight, is the conclusion, where we return to four central themes, looking at social networks and their value to undocumented migrants, the aims and impact of government policies on migration, risk and risk avoidance and, finally, the interaction of class, gender and ethnicity with legal status.

TWO

Policy, law and rights

In this chapter we focus on the creation and positioning of undocumented migrants within policy, law and human rights frameworks. We explore the European agreements, international rights frameworks and the role of citizenship as a mechanism for inclusion and exclusion and locate some recent developments in the UK within that general framework. 'Illegality' is, according to Chavez, 'socially, culturally and politically constructed', something that is produced as a consequence of 'political decisions' (2007: 192). However the state of 'illegality' is produced or constructed, it is nevertheless acutely felt and experienced in almost every facet of life, (see for example, Willen, 2007; Chavez, 2012; Holmes, 2013; Bloch, Sigona and Zetter, 2014). As de Genova argues:

> It is deportability, and not deportation per se, that has historically rendered undocumented migrant labor as a distinctly disposable commodity. (2002: 438)

Contextualising migration policy

Within nation states, undocumented migrants are conceptualised as being outside of the framework of laws and regulations, lone, independent and hidden individuals, whose assumed but unseen presence causes fear and anxiety, whose numbers are always unknown (Samers, 2008; Vollmer, 2011). There are continuous calls for tougher regimes of control, which are proposed as a method of dealing with – and removing – the problem, but which in reality have singularly failed to do so. This is primarily because the policy aim has never been to eliminate the presence of undocumented migrants. The reality is that states require migrant workers, and so what Chavez calls 'a legal fiction' occurs (2007: 192) where it is politically expedient to be seen to be controlling migration but, in reality, it is only 'legal' flows that states can have any real control over. Moreover, other forms of immigration control such as border police and the deportation of some migrants are used 'in order that most may ultimately remain (un-deported)' (de Genova, 2004: 161).

The presence of undocumented migrants provides governments with the justification for increased controls, not just on migrants themselves but on the whole population. Thus, particularly in periods of crisis, the undocumented migrant presence is both the scapegoat and the justification for policies which otherwise might be resisted, for example, biometric checks or the introduction of identity cards. Policies on undocumented migration can be contextualised around the following factors: an ambivalence by government as to the fate of persons in the territory (Vasta, 2011); both as a response to and as a product of labour market changes and as a method of controlling labour (Bloch and Chimienti, 2011; Triandafyllidou and Ambrosini, 2011); through the tightening of border controls (Menjívar, 2006) and in the construction of the 'good' and 'bad' migrant (Wright and McKay, 2007); through 'statelessness', a denial of the right to rights (Arendt, 2004; Blitz and Otero-Iglesias, 2011); and finally through the production of the 'undocumented' (Düvell, 2011b). Goldring, Berinstein and Bernard argue, in relation to Canada, that policies 'routinely generate pathways to multiple forms of precarious status' so that citizenship and illegality can be seen as 'historically produced and changeable' (2009: 239). Samers too makes the point that undocumented immigration is produced and that there would be 'no undocumented immigration without immigration policy'. He asserts:

> If undocumented immigration is produced by stricter regulations, then the state is not so much *controlling* it, the popular press not so much *reporting* it, as they are both *creating* it. That is, undocumented immigration is created through popular and governmental arguments such as 'we need to reduce the number of "bogus asylum-seekers"' (i.e. so-called 'economic migrants'), 'firm but fair' immigration policies; (conventional) conceptions of how labour markets operate (e.g. linear push–pull theories relating to the supply and demand for labour); the economic evaluation of immigration based on a cost versus benefit rationality (e.g. viewing 'illegal immigrants' and asylum-seekers as 'scroungers' burdening a restructured and cash-poor welfare system); and perhaps the most insidious, the construction of mythical percentage-based 'thresholds' (in France, the infamous *seuil de tolérance* – the threshold of tolerance) which supposedly dictates when 'white' citizens will revolt against the presence of immigrants and ethnic minorities, and when racial violence will erupt against the presence

of immigrants and ethnic minorities. These circulating discourses can be argued to mould immigration policy, rather than the other way around. (2008: 576)

By focusing on ambivalence we draw on the work of Vasta (2011), who argues that it is the state which both sets up the regulations and structures that cause individuals to be undocumented and then is ambivalent as to the impact that these have on the individuals concerned. Whereas states have responsibility for the welfare and protection of those on the territory, the assignment of the label of 'undocumented' removes individuals from access to such protections. The undocumented are non-persons for the purposes of state obligations, both to citizens and also to non-citizens resident or otherwise on the territory. Ambivalence means that the state can ignore the consequences of undocumented status. It can do even more; it can legislate to make people undocumented (for example, by tightening existing controls) and then can declare itself not liable for the consequences to the individual. As de Genova noted more than a decade ago:

'Illegality' is the product of immigration laws – not merely in the abstract sense that without the law, nothing could be constructed to be outside of the law; not simply in the generic sense that immigration law constructs, differentiates, and ranks various categories of 'aliens' – but in the more profound sense that the history of deliberate interventions that have revised and reformulated the law has entailed an active process of inclusion through 'illegalization'. (2002: 439)

The existence on the territory of undocumented migrants both responds to and produces labour market outcomes which advantage employers and not only disadvantage those without documents but also have the potential to introduce disadvantage within the wider labour market that includes those with documents as well as those who are citizens. The system of international labour migration is indeed:

a worldwide system of interrelations in which the underdeveloped countries underuse and fail to employ their labour force, and the developed countries find in the former an almost inexhaustible source of low-cost labour. (Alba, 1978: 510)

The segmentation of labour markets increases the demand for migrant workers and this occurs 'where sectors of the labour market are eschewed by native workers because they are low paying, have little security and are low status' (Koser, 2010: 188). If this is true for all migrant workers it is even more the case for those who are without documents and who are without the options of redress against poor treatment at work (Rutherford and Addison, 2007).

The growth in the informal economies of EU member states since the start of the 2007 economic crisis (Williams and Renooy, 2013) provides the context for the further informalisation of the relations of production and the precarisation of work. Member states have introduced measures to address informal work by taking either 'a deterrence approach', which sets out to obtain compliance by punitive measures against non-compliance, or an 'an enabling approach' to encourage compliance by stopping undeclared work ever taking place. Williams and Renooy (2013) suggest that punishing non-compliance has become more commonplace, in some cases by removing legal protections, so that compliant workers are equally attractive. Thus, informal work has become the norm rather than the exception after 2001 (Munck, Schierup and Delgado Wise, 2011: 249). It is the structure of the labour market that drives undeclared work and it is the growth in forms of temporary/flexible work that has required a labour force that is more compliant.

In every advanced industrial economy there has been a tightening of controls on immigration and a constant narrowing of the routes that migrants have to enter a territory legally. We demonstrate this later in this chapter, in an in-depth examination of recent immigration law in relation to the UK, where a constant stream of changes have been aimed at denying entry to wider groups, making legal avenues for migration increasingly limited to the most privileged minority (Bloch and Chimienti, 2011). It is also clear that since the start of the economic crisis in 2007, migrants, who were previously required during the phase of neoliberalism because they supplied the cheap and flexible labour needed, have become problematic and unwanted (Bloch and Chimienti, 2011; Munck, Schierup and Delgado Wise, 2011). Having labour at the margins allows states to both exclude and utilise when needed. This is not a new phenomenon; guest-worker schemes that are designed to invite migrants when needed but remove them when not are part of the fabric of state responses to migration. Writing in the 1970s about Mexicans in the US, Alba noted that the immigrant labour system 'makes it possible to import labour when necessary and export it when it is considered redundant' (1978: 510). This point needs to be emphasised, as particularly in periods of economic or, indeed, social crisis, the presence of a group that can be identified as both foreign and different and as without a right to be present on the territory absolves governments of the responsibility for the crisis and allows it to be pinned to the door of those without documents. This is one of the reasons why, it could be argued, in the run-up to the European elections in May 2014 and, in the UK, to the national elections in 2015, the focus of all of the main political parties has been on clamping down or addressing undocumented migration and the perceived lack of state control over migration.

Governments have responded to this perceived lack of control of migration in different ways (Oelgemoller, 2011). One strategy has been the incremental tightening of the conditions for entry, under policies aimed either at 'managing' migration or at limiting it in specific ways. Another method is to attempt to physically shore up borders, with the aim of keeping out those whose presence is not desired. Biometric technologies are increasingly used to regulate and control mobility, and in so doing contribute to the development of new inequalities (Scheel, 2013: 590). However, as Scheel (2013) also stresses, the existence and use of such technologies does not guarantee 'success' in terms of keeping out those whose presence is not desired. Government policies in relation to undocumented migration are littered with examples of failures, if successes were to be measured by the non-presence on the territory of those without documents (Engbersen, 2001). Numbers have not decreased, in fact more external and internal controls have resulted in the expansion of the migration industry, which works to facilitate journeys, although at a financial and human cost (Koser, 2005). These controls do not stop migration flows because migration drivers are too complex and too varied and global inequalities are too great to stop people from moving (Castles, 2013). Border controls, instead of acting as a deterrent, have the opposite effect and instead produce and facilitate greater numbers of undocumented migrants (Düvell, 2011b). In the next section we explore the protection that international treaties offer to everyone based on concepts of universality and personhood. In reality, however, protection is contingent on citizenship, as it is enforceable by the state and so leaves undocumented migrants unable to access human rights (Samers, 2002).

Protection through international law

At international level there are three key instruments that are most relevant to the protection of migrant workers. The first is the 1948 Universal Declaration of Human Rights, which, although a declaration and in itself not legally binding, since 1968 has been identified as constituting an obligation on members of the international community, that is, all sovereign states. The Declaration has provided the basis for a number of other legal instruments at international level, including the second key instrument, the 1990 International Convention for the Protection of the Rights of All Migrant Workers and Members of their Families (the Migrant Worker Convention[1]), which came into force in July 2003. The Preamble to the Convention states that it takes account of the principles 'embodied in the basic instruments of the United Nations concerning human rights' and makes particular reference to the Universal Declaration of Human Rights, the International Covenant on Economic, Social and Cultural Rights, the International Covenant on Civil and Political Rights, the International Convention on the Elimination of All Forms of Racial Discrimination, the Convention on the Elimination of All Forms of Discrimination against Women and the Convention on the Rights of the Child. Importantly, the Migrant Worker Convention specifically refers to the relevant instruments as adopted by the International Labour Organisation (ILO), and specifies these as including the Convention concerning Migration for Employment (No 97), the Convention concerning Migrations in Abusive Conditions and the Promotion of Equality of Opportunity and Treatment of Migrant Workers (No 143), the Recommendation concerning Migration for Employment (No 86), the Recommendation concerning Migrant Workers (No 151) and its supplementary provisions, the Convention concerning Forced or Compulsory Labour (No 29) and the Convention concerning Abolition of Forced Labour (No 105). The Preamble to the 1990 Convention specifically recognises the expertise and experience of the International Labour Organisation in matters related to migrant workers and their families and states:

> One of the objectives of the International Labour Organisation, as stated in its Constitution, is the protection of the interests of workers when employed in countries other than their own.

The 1990 Convention recognises the vulnerability of migrant workers and that this has to be addressed through specific protection. This is the only Convention that includes all migrant workers, regardless of status, and in so doing it represents a major shift in the position adopted at international level. Its first principle is that nation states should take action to prevent and eliminate clandestine movements and trafficking in migrant workers, but it also asserts that they should, at the same time, assure 'the protection of their fundamental human rights'. The Preamble further notes:

> Considering that workers who are non-documented or in an irregular situation are frequently employed under less favourable conditions of work than other workers and that certain employers find this an inducement to seek such labour in order to reap the benefits of unfair competition;
>
> Considering also that recourse to the employment of migrant workers who are in an irregular situation will be discouraged if the fundamental human rights of all migrant workers are more widely recognized and, moreover, that granting certain additional rights to migrant workers and members of their families in a regular situation will encourage all migrants and employers to respect and comply with the laws and procedures established by the States concerned.

For this reason the term 'migrant worker' is defined widely, in Article 2 of the Convention, as 'a person who is to be engaged, is engaged or has been engaged in a remunerated activity in a State of which he or she is not a national', with no indication as to a need for documented status. Thus, in theory, all migrant workers have the same level of protection. The protection extends to a right not to be discriminated against (Art 7), a right to leave the state (Art 8), a right to life (Art 9), a right not to be subjected to torture or to inhumane treatment (Art 10), the right not to be required to undertake forced or compulsory labour (Art 11). Other rights guaranteed under the Convention include the right to freedom of thought and opinions and the rights to privacy, property and liberty. Article 51 is particularly important, as it recognises that migration status can change in the course of the migrant's stay in the destination country and provides for a right to seek alternative work even where the work visa had been tied to a particular job. In this way it separates rights of residency from rights to work and provides for an extension to the latter, in cases where the former exists. It states:

> Migrant workers who in the State of employment are not permitted freely to choose their remunerated activity shall neither be regarded as in an irregular situation nor shall they lose their authorization of residence by the mere fact of the termination of their remunerated activity prior to the expiration of their work permit, except where the

authorization of residence is expressly dependent upon the specific remunerated activity for which they were admitted. Such migrant workers shall have the right to seek alternative employment, participation in public work schemes and retraining during the remaining period of their authorization to work, subject to such conditions and limitations as are specified in the authorization to work.

With such important established rights it might be thought that the protection of undocumented migrants was therefore guaranteed in their working, personal and civic lives. However, this is not the case, simply because, unlike most other international conventions, the Migrant Worker Convention has not been signed by the majority of nation states, indeed it is the sending states, that are seeking the protection of their citizens, who have signed, while receiving states that have the obligation to protect have to date not signed (Bloch, 2010). The only countries in Europe that have signed are Albania, Armenia, Bosnia and Herzegovina, Montenegro, Turkey and Serbia.

The final set of key instruments has already been referred to, and these are the Conventions of the ILO. The Convention concerning Migration for Employment (No 97) (as revised) obliges signatory countries to provide information to the ILO on national policies in relation to migrants (Art 1), to maintain an adequate and a free service to migrants for employment (Art 2), to take steps against misleading propaganda against migration (Art 3) and to facilitate entry and departure for migrants. The Recommendation concerning Migration for Employment (No 86) defines as a migrant for employment those who migrate for work, and states that it 'includes any person regularly admitted as a migrant for employment' (para 1). It thus appears (although not clearly stated) that Recommendation 86 is applicable only in respect of migrants with regular status. However, the Migrant Workers (Supplementary Provisions) Convention 1995, No 143, does apply to undocumented migrants. While it calls on states to eliminate clandestine migration, it specifically provides for employment rights to those who are on the territory without permission and without a right to work. The key provisions are in Art 9, which states that where a worker's position cannot be regularised, she/he should 'enjoy equality of treatment for himself and his family in respect of rights arising out of past employment as regards remuneration, social security and other benefits'. The Migrant Workers' Recommendation 1975, No 151, while generally covering the rights of documented migrants, also says that in the case of those without documents, decisions should be taken by the state as soon as possible as to whether their status can be regularised and, in the case of those who are not appropriate for regularisation, they should nevertheless 'enjoy equality of treatment for themselves and their families, in respect of rights arising out of present and past employment as regards remuneration, social security and other benefits as well as regards trade union membership and exercise of trade union rights'.

European policy and laws on undocumented migration

As the EU has expanded, so too has its competence in the area of migration and the harmonisation of policies around immigration and asylum. The EU has been active in trying to manage migration and to police the external borders, adding a supranational tier to the ways in which irregularity is produced (Bloch and Chimienti, 2011). The opening of borders within Europe has resulted in attempts to control external borders, increase security, reduce smuggling and trafficking and to 'burden share' in relation to asylum. National sovereignty and national particularities make it difficult to agree policies and not all countries are signatories to all agreements. Controlling external borders, tackling 'illegal' immigration, including smuggling and trafficking, and harmonising readmissions and removal measures are all aspects of the EU project.

One of the major criticisms of EU policy is that it restricts the opportunities for refugees to seek asylum. Schuster (2011) has been particularly critical of the Dublin Convention, which specifies which country is responsible for examining the claim of an asylum seeker who has travelled through a 'safe third country' before applying for asylum, arguing that EU policy has turned some refugees into undocumented migrants by preventing them from seeking asylum or entering in a regular way, while at the same time shielding member states from international legal obligations.

European policy in relation to migration is contradictory, with both a desire to encourage migration so as to respond to skill or job shortages, and at the same time a tightening of border controls to keep out those who have not been given permission to enter or stay (McKay, Markova and Paraskevopoulou, 2011). While immigration has normally been considered as a matter to be determined at the level of the nation state under the principle of subsidiarity, what we can observe, particularly over the last decade, and especially in relation to undocumented migration, is a convergence of state policies which in turn has led to the promotion of EU-level policies. EU policy is also strongly associated with its identification of 'illegality', and this concept of the 'illegal', the 'criminal' and the 'underworld' has permeated all aspects of EU policy in relation to undocumented migration. Where migration is conceived in this way, then, it not surprising to find that the main direction of such policy has been in the tightening of borders and a focus on what is referred to as 'return', but which is simply deportation. Between 2006 and December 2013 FRONTEX, the European Agency for the Management of Operational Cooperation at the External Borders of the Member States of the European Union, coordinated 209 Joint Return Operations, returning 10,855 people (European Commission, 2014).

While there has been discussion on the issue of undocumented migration at EU level at least from the mid-1970s (Triandafyllidou and Ilies, 2010; Vollmer, 2011), it was the adoption of the Schengen Implementation Agreement for the abolition of internal border controls among the signatory states (which included all of the then EU member states, although the UK and the Republic of Ireland were not signatories) and increased control of the common external borders in force from June 1990. Since the early 1990s the extent of legislative measures at EU level has grown exponentially, so that in 2006 the European Commission could note that 'addressing illegal migration has been a central part of the EU's common immigration policy since its inception in 1999'.[2] The legislation is, however, subject to the scrutiny of the courts at EU level and a number of recent judgments have indicated that member states have an obligation to protect human rights, even in the case of those without documents. The courts have held that the principle of proportionality is paramount in addressing the issue of irregular residence, so that 'various factors – e.g., duration of stay, integration into the labour market, social integration, links with country of origin (or of nationality), criminal record – are relevant for assessing the proportionality of forced return rather than regularisation' (International Centre for Migration Policy Development (ICMPD), 2009). Current policy priorities at the EU level include readmission agreements, returns and sanctions and we will explore these areas before considering the use of amnesties or regularisation in a number of EU states, although the current policy of the EU is to deter member states from mass regularisation or amnesty programmes (European Pact on Immigration and Asylum: Council of the European Union, 2008).

Readmission agreements

The concept of readmission agreements between countries of migration and EU member states was advanced in the Rabat Action Plan of 2006, when EU and African state representatives agreed to a partnership aimed at offering a response to the issue of controlling migration flows. Again, undocumented migration was linked with criminality and therefore measures aimed at reducing it were advanced as being in the interests of both the sending and receiving states. A Communication to the European Parliament in 2011[3] describes such agreements as 'a necessary tool for efficient management of migration flows' and states that 18 agreements had been reached by that year. The report suggests that, where 'used properly', the agreements do provide added value and are an important tool in tackling irregular migration; however, it also found that the agreements were rigid in some aspects and that there was 'scope for improvement' as regarded monitoring their effect and their impact on human rights.

These agreements apply to return not only to the county of origin but in some cases to the transit country. Thus there has been an agreement between the EU and Libya that involves the return of persons who have passed through Libya on their way to Europe. However, the focus on control and surveillance is unlikely to stop irregular migrants from travelling through Libya and into Italy or Malta (Hamood, 2008). The balance between the protection of human rights and the security of borders has shifted from the former to the latter, and EU policy does not take account of the lengths that individuals go to and the risks that they will take to reach Europe, even when they are aware of the risks entailed (Hamood, 2008; Schuster, 2011).

Return, or 'deportation by any other name'

Readmission agreements are linked to the EU policy on returns. In 2002 the EU Council of Ministers adopted an Action Plan to combat illegal migration and the trafficking of human beings in the EU. In the same year it adopted a Return action programme, which was eventually formalised into the Return Directive, aimed at establishing common EU-wide minimum standards in relation to the return of undocumented migrants. The Directive on Common Standards and Procedures for Returning Illegally Staying Third Country Nationals (2008/115/EC) represents a key plank in EU policy in relation to undocumented migrants. In principle, it favours the concept of 'voluntary' return, but this is only a preference; the Directive clearly assumes that forced returns are part of EU migration policy, and indeed in practice, and drawing on the limited data available, it seems that several member states have adopted the strategy of forced deportation.[4] Anderson, Gibney and Paoletti argue that deportation is:

> a particularly definitive and symbolically resonant way of dividing citizens from (putative) strangers, [it] is liable to generate conflicts amongst citizens and between citizens and the state. Although often used by governmental elites as a way to reaffirm the shared significance of citizenship, deportation, we suggest may serve to highlight just how divided and confused modern societies are in how they conceptualise both who is a member and who have the right to judge who belongs. (2011: 547)

The European Commission's 2014 report to the Parliament states that its aim is to ensure that third-country nationals are returned if they lack the legal grounds to stay in the EU and to do this fairly and transparently with respect for rights and dignity. It is recognised, though, that member states' policies and procedures are often both fragmented and unclear (European Commission, 2013). Additionally, the policy risks being in conflict with the positions taken by sending-country governments, as 'policies of migration control "directly and substantially" impinge upon the interests of foreign governments' where 'their cooperation is an "essential condition for policy implementation"' (Ellermann, 2008: 168). Deportation is not just a feature of European and European nation state policies, it has been also been a long-term feature of US migration policy (Hagan, Rodriguez and Mullis, 2011). In the US, however, there has been a fundamental shift from voluntary returns to formal removals and this reveals a deportation dilemma, which is that deportation has social costs to individuals, families and communities (Hagan, Rodriguez and Mullis, 2011; Rosenblum and Meissner, 2014). Moreover, it does not in fact stop would-be migrants attempting to return to the country from which they have been deported, and so what emerges is a cycle of mobility that is almost impossible for nation states to control (Schuster, 2011).

Sanctioning employers

In order to tackle 'illegal' employment at EU level, in May 2007 the Commission adopted a proposal for a Directive providing sanctions against employers of illegally staying third-country nationals. This proposal is concerned with immigration policy, not with labour or social policy. Its main objective is to sanction employers, not the illegally employed third-country nationals. Directive 2009/52/EC of 18 June 2009 sets out the standards that member states should apply in relation to sanctions. In the Preamble of the Directive it is argued that there is a correlation between 'illegal' immigration and the possibilities of employment in the EU for those without status. While the Directive applies to those who do not have a right to work and are undocumented, it does not apply to third-country nationals legally resident, regardless of whether they have a right to work. It applies to 'activities that are or ought to be remunerated, undertaken for or under the direction and/or supervision of an employer, irrespective of the legal relationship'. Article 6 sets out the obligation on employers to pay for outstanding work, including to make social security contributions. It also sets out the rights of workers to be informed about their rights to unpaid wages, with a presumption of entitlement to at least three months' wages. Critics of sanctions as a policy tool argue that it is a form of privatisation of immigration control, shifting the obligation from the state to the employer and in so doing extending the policing of immigration to civil society (de Lange, 2011).

Sanctions operate in a number of countries of destination and although they are portrayed, in part, as trying to safeguard workers against employer exploitation the reality is the opposite, with workers being more susceptible to exploitative working conditions and less able to participate in collective workplace action and trade union activities (Gordon, 2007; Dwyer et al, 2011). Commenting on these anomalies, Gordon noted that sanctions, have '*increased* the appeal of undocumented workers to unscrupulous employers and gave employers a way to derail organising campaigns in immigrant-heavy workplaces' (2007: 540). In taking this position Gordon (2007) follows the direction of de Genova, who in 2002 was already arguing, in relation to US employer sanctions, that the result has been 'tantamount to an extension of the "revolving door" to the internal labor market of each workplace where undocumented migrants were employed' and that all that sanctions have done has been to encourage a new industry in the production of false documents, imposing 'further expenses and greater legal liabilities upon the migrant workers themselves, while supplying protection for employers' (2002: 427), since employers receive a pre-warning of inspections and use that period to dismiss undocumented workers.

In the UK context, employer sanctions were first introduced as part of the 1996 Asylum and Immigration Act and implemented in

January 1997. Under the 1996 Act, employers are required to carry out checks to ensure that all new employees have the right to work in the UK. A failure to comply is a criminal offence, which initially carried a fine of up to £5,000 per worker, increased to £10,000 as part of the 2006 Immigration, Asylum and Nationality Act and to £20,000 under the 2014 Immigration Act. While the UK legislation is similar to the EC Directive it has one important element of difference. It does not provide for the right for undocumented migrants to be paid for the work that they have done, where they have no rights to work and where the employer has either not made payments or has paid below the statutory minimum, even if the reason for doing this is that the employer knows the individual is undocumented and thus vulnerable. Dewhurst, looking at the situation in Ireland – which, like the UK, also refused to implement the provisions of the EC Directive due to the provisions on upholding minimum labour standards in pay – suggests that the reasoning behind the Irish opt-out was based upon 'misinformed assumptions about the purpose of the provision of outstanding remuneration arising out of a "disconnect" between immigration and labour policy at a domestic level' (2011: 389). While more work is needed in order to assess the efficacy of sanctions as a method of deterring undocumented migration, bolstering laws that protect migrant worker rights may be more important so as to ensure fair wages, adherence to labour laws and fair recruitment policies for all workers (Levinson, 2005).

Where there are sanctions, then a likely consequence is that there will be raids on employers' premises. In the UK, raids focus on minority-ethnic employers, who are over-represented among those targeted. In contrast, non-minority-ethnic employers largely remain unsanctioned. A report by the Independent Chief Inspector of Border and Immigration, published in early 2014, found that there had been a large increase in raids without warrants and that in two-thirds of the cases examined there was no justification for the use of the power and that there were 'widespread non-compliance with guidance, ineffective performance reporting and extremely poor assurance processes' (Vine, 2014: 11). Furthermore, Vine suggests that immigration officers have targeted certain employers, identifying fast-food outlets as sites where raids have been carried out in the absence of the specific intelligence required to justify the use of the power. The consequence of sanctions can be a more fragile employment environment and an increase in workers' vulnerability, pushing them further onto the margins and into ever more precarious situations (Dwyer et al, 2011). As undocumented workers are less likely to complain than other workers, employers do not have to improve terms and conditions of work or provide benefits to these workers (Finch and Cherti, 2011). Sanctions, in addition to their impact on workers, can also put at risk the businesses of many small employers (Bloch, Kumarappan and McKay, 2015).

Is regularisation a solution?

In a number of EU member states the response to undocumented migration has been to regularise status. Mass regularisations have occurred in Italy, Spain and Greece in particular, and also in France and Belgium (Poelemans and de Sèze, 2000; Levinson, 2005; Kraler, 2011). Regularisations have generally been temporary measures and those regularised often quickly fall into an irregular status, for example, on loss of the employment upon which regularisation had been conferred. Goldring and Landolt (2011) found in their research in Canada that those whose legal status had at some point been precarious experienced a long-lasting, negative effect on job security. Even in those cases where they had been able to shift to a more secure status, they were more likely to remain in precarious work, as compared to respondents who entered with and remained in a secure status. Regularisation is an assertion of state sovereignty and is usually identified as a generous measure by the state that it can both bestow and remove.

We would question whether regularisation, on the basis on which it has occurred in most cases, is effective in responding to undocumented migration or that it can be viewed as a human rights response; rather, it has become a partial and inadequate measure to deal with the consequences of ever-tightening immigration controls. It gives even greater authority to the nation state by giving it the sole power to decide when regularisation can take place and who will be regularised and it permits the state to use regularisation as a way of collecting data on those who are undocumented. Furthermore, since most regularisations do not give a permanent right to reside and work they mainly mark migrants until the next period of undocumented status. Migrants who take the risk of requesting regularisation also place themselves at risk of deportation in cases where their application is rejected. It is not regularisation that migrants necessarily desire; what they want is a right to work under conditions that are equal to those of the documented, and regularisation of itself does not address this if migrants remain vulnerable in the labour market. Indeed in those countries where mass regularisations have occurred they have not resulted in a movement out of informal and vulnerable employment; indeed they lock migrants into vulnerability, where leaving or losing a job has a consequence for migration status (Levinson, 2005).

Papademetriou (2005) argues that it is the best way of dealing with undocumented migration but admits that it is at most a 'stopgap measure' and is evidence of the failure of other policies on migration. Kraler takes a different position, suggesting that regularisations are a response to the shift from more informal systems of migration governance to 'more systematic and rigid forms of migration management' (2009: 6) and, based on a comprehensive review of the regularisations which have taken place in the EU member states, argues that:

> The main conclusion that can be derived from these observations is that single, stand-alone measures cannot be an appropriate response to tackle migrant irregularity. Rather, any responses must consist of several measures in different areas that take account of this diversity. (2009: 13)

The European Commission opposes regularisation, arguing that it encourages the undocumented to migrate on the assumption that they will eventually be regularised. However, there is limited evidence for this and the ICMPD (2009) also found no evidence that regularisation was then used by migrants to move around Europe. Migrants appear to move towards those countries with labour markets that offer the best opportunities for work, and thus are more likely to wish to gain entry to countries like the UK, despite the fact that, of practically all the member states, it is the least likely to offer regularisation (ICMPD, 2009).

UK immigration rules and the construction of illegality

In this section we consider how immigration policies have changed over time and how the status of 'illegality' has been constructed, with the consequence of potentially driving larger numbers into undocumented status. As changes have been so rapid the law is continually in flux and there is no certainty as to its application. In such conditions those who have entered without authority, and the much greater number who have entered legally but who are outside their permitted residence or work conditions, have little option but to remain (Gordon, 2007). UK immigration policy in the post-1945 period has been in three separate phases. The first phase, 1945 to 1980, racialised immigration controls by curtailing the rights to entry for black and Asian migrants from former colonial and Commonwealth countries. The second phase, from the late 1980s onwards, was concerned with restricted asylum admission, and since the 2000s the aim has been to manage migration, including of clandestine entrants and undocumented migrants (Sales, 2007; Bloch, Neal and Solomos, 2013).

Racialised immigration controls

Until the 1960s immigration to the UK was seen as an entitlement to citizens of the former or existing UK colonies and Commonwealth. Its colonial past and its chosen method of rule within its colonies had created a model of citizenship which imposed rights and obligations on all those born and living within the territory of the British Empire. In this way British colonialism and Empire building differed from that in many of the other colonial powers. However, by the early 1960s the political arguments in favour of this continued relationship were under strain. The arrival of large numbers of peoples from former colonies, from the late 1940s onwards, the racist discourse that surrounded this migration and the independence movements in the colonies themselves were utilised as arguments for restricted immigration. The 1962 Commonwealth Immigrants Act changed the rights to British citizenship conferred under the 1948 British Nationality Act and instead distinguished between citizens of Britain and its colonies and those of independent Commonwealth countries, creating a racialised system that excluded those of black and Asian origin rather than those of white descent (Solomos, 2003; Sales, 2007). The 1971 Immigration Act further restricted the entry criteria to those who were either born or had a parent born in the UK, once again favouring those of white heritage and virtually excluding all others (Sales, 2007).

However, it is the period since 1980 that demonstrates the shift in political strategy and that led to the construction of illegality in the UK context. Notably, the pace of change with respect to immigration law increased significantly, particularly from the 1990s onwards, creating a continued uncertainty as to the extent of entitlement. This encouraged those who were already present in the territory to remain and not to risk a return, on the basis that any new immigration regime would be even more restrictive than the one that had preceded it. The 1981 British Nationality Act altered the basis on which citizenship could be claimed, establishing the criteria of 'close connection', a category that was dependent on the location of birth of the individual or relatives, going back two generations. This meant that those born in the Old Commonwealth countries such as Australia, New Zealand and South Africa who could trace their ancestral roots back to the UK could claim citizenship. For those, however, who had no such ancestral roots, other than in a New Commonwealth country such as India, Pakistan and the countries of the Caribbean, indeed the bulk of the British Empire, status became that of British Overseas Territories Citizenship, a status which did not recognise the full rights of citizenship.

In 1988 the government passed another Immigration Act that restricted family entry, with spouses no longer being granted settlement on arrival but only after a probationary period, putting women at risk of being forced to remain in abusive relationships in order to escape deportation (Raj and Silverstone, 2002; Adams and Campbell, 2012). Having established a more restrictive immigration regime, the government then moved to restrict rights to contest status entitlement. By the end of the 1980s, virtually all primary migration from the Commonwealth had ceased and asylum seekers became the main primary migrants, and this resulted in a new direction in immigration policy.

Focusing on asylum

During the 1990s there were three pieces of immigration legislation: the 1993 Asylum and Immigration Appeals Act, the 1996 Asylum and Immigration Act and the 1999 Immigration and Asylum Act. Each Act placed more restrictions on asylum seekers within the UK, limiting access to welfare, employment and mobility but arguing that Britain was an attractive destination for 'bogus' asylum seekers who were really economic migrants trying to use the asylum route to enter Britain rather than 'genuine' refugees who needed protection (Sales, 2007).

Under the 1993 Asylum and Immigration Appeals Act the rights to appeal against a decision on a right to enter the UK, either as a visitor or as a short-term resident or prospective student, were restricted. The 1996 Asylum and Immigration Act accelerated the appeals system for asylum and introduced a list of 'safe' countries from which generally any asylum claim would be refused. Two years later the four-year qualifying period for grants of settlement to those given asylum was abolished. A year later the 1999 Immigration and Asylum Act provided that there should be one only application for asylum, attracting only one asylum claim. Thus, where the claim was incorrectly presented applicants were no long able to submit a fresh application.

Throughout the 1990s internal measures were also introduced. Under the 1996 Asylum and Immigration Act, right to work checks were introduced and employers found to be hiring someone without correct documentation were fined £5,000. Access to welfare entitlements for those who did not seek asylum at the port of entry was stopped, as these asylum seekers were assumed to be 'bogus', although there were safety nets for those who were deemed to be destitute. The policy objective was to deter economic migration (Hynes and Sales, 2010), although it is clear that asylum seekers know little about possible destinations, are often dependent on smugglers and, if given a choice, would prefer to go to countries where they have existing family and/ or social networks (Gilbert and Koser, 2006). Finally, under the 1999 Act dispersal was introduced to 'spread the burden' of asylum seekers outside of London and other main urban centres, leaving asylum seekers isolated, vulnerable and excluded and often in localities with high levels of deprivation (Hynes and Sales, 2010). Throughout the 2000s changes were made to the asylum system. In 2002, for example, the employment concession was removed and asylum seekers who had been waiting for more than six months for a decision on their claim were no longer allowed to apply for permission to work. Mostly, however, legislation during the 2000s has been concerned with managing migration and clandestine entry, as well as cohesion, identity and integration.

Managing migration

Since the start of the 21st century there have been six new pieces of immigration legislation. The 2002 Nationality, Immigration and Asylum Act required that applicants for asylum should make their application as soon as reasonably practicable after arrival. Exceptional leave to remain (ELR) was replaced by humanitarian protection (HP) and discretionary leave (DL) so that only those who were deemed to be in genuine need of protection would be granted leave to stay.

The 2004 Asylum and Immigration (Treatment of Claimants, etc.) Act was aimed at deterring and preventing behaviour that was calculated to be designed to frustrate the UK asylum process. The Act introduced two new offences, one of being undocumented without reasonable explanation and the other of failing to comply with the re-documentation process. In 2006 the Immigration, Asylum and Nationality Act removed the right to indefinite leave to remain in most asylum cases, so that, for the future, those who had successfully claimed asylum would be granted five years of limited leave, with the right to apply for settlement at the end of the period, but no guarantee that the application would be accepted.

The 2007 UK Borders Act created the penalty of 'automatic deportation' for those third-country citizens sentenced to 12 months' imprisonment or more. In most cases, save in some where asylum was claimed, appeal against deportation is held after the individual has been removed, and the number of persons being deported has risen (Gibney, 2008). Under the Act, the power of immigration officers was increased in relation to entering and searching homes for documents and in relation to 'illegal' working, as well as more rights to detain. The same year also saw a complete reversal of previous immigration policy in relation to work, with an ending of work visa provisions and their replacement with a five-tier system which was to apply with respect to all third-country applicants, including students (who applied under the Tier 4 provisions). Although the system envisaged the entry of low-skilled migrants under the scheme, the provisions appertaining to this (Tier 3) were never introduced and the new work requirements limit entry in most cases to highly skilled or highly resourced migrants (Tiers 1 and 2). The consequences, we would suggest, have been to further the likelihood of irregular or undocumented migration.

The 2009 Borders, Citizenship and Immigration Act extended the residence period prior to naturalisation from five to eight years and refugees were required to meet the language-proficiency tests and the 'Life in the UK' test prior to obtaining citizenship. In 2010, in recognition of the fact that the large backlog of asylum applications had placed individuals in a situation where they either needed to have access to independent financial resources or to work without documents, those who had been waiting at least a year for a decision on their claim were given a right to work, although only in those occupations deemed as shortages.

One of the most contested changes in recent years is that related to private servants in diplomatic households and to overseas domestic workers. In 1998, following publicised cases of maltreatment of such workers and a campaign of unionisation supported by migrant activist groups, this mainly female workforce had obtained the right to change employer. In 2012 the right was withdrawn to allow for a stay only while they remain with the original employer, and furthermore they cannot gain the right to apply for settlement. However, it should be noted that in the case of *Siladin v France* [2005] ECHR 545, the European Court of Human Rights held that Ms Siladin, a domestic worker whose working conditions gave her no freedom of movement and no free time, was being held under a condition of servitude and that the state had obligations to regulate the private employment relationship and that consent could not legitimise slavery or servitude although the same was not the case in relation to forced or compulsory labour, so that only someone who has been trafficked has a route of redress (Mantouvalou, 2006).

And so the changes continue to occur. In 2012 the deportation rules were changed so as to allow for the deportation of anyone sentenced to at least four years in prison, despite the existence of family or private life in the UK. A rule which permitted an application for individual regularisation after a presence of more than 14 years in the territory was abolished in 2012 and at least 20 years' residence is required before an application to stay can be made. In 2013 the English-language test was made stricter, requiring applicants to hold a B1 level English speaking and listening qualification.

The 2014 Immigration Act has, as one of its provisions, an extension of the right of the Home Secretary to strip individuals of their citizenship if 'they are not conducive to the public good'. This goes beyond any provisions to deny continued citizenship to, for example, those convicted of serious criminal offences, and places the individual who has acquired documentation at some stage of migration always in fear of this being removed. The above also should be considered in the context of changes to the UK legal aid system, effective from April 2013. Previously there had been a right to financial support for individuals taking legal cases (including migration claims) where their own resources were insufficient to fund a claim. This entitlement drew on a core principle of law, that no one should be denied a right to legal redress simply because they had insufficient financial resources. However, the system of legal aid has increasingly been under attack, with growing restrictions to the right to obtain it. In relation to migration, these culminated in the 2013 changes, which completely remove the right to legal aid other than in cases involving an asylum claim. The outcome is that migrants attempting to assert a right to remain or a right to work lawfully must fund their own legal claims.

The exclusivity of citizenship

Nation states exercise a fundamental power in the confirmation of citizenship. Only the nation state, within the confines of its borders, can determine who is or is not accepted as a citizen. Thus, border controls and the definitions of citizenship by nation states are related to immigration policy (Bloch and Chimienti, 2011). Citizenship confers rights on individuals but its denial results in the denial of rights and is one of the ways in which nation states exclude. Indeed the absence of citizenship, even in a context where socio-legal status provides for a right of residence and of work, both compromises rights and may be relevant in promoting forced labour (Dwyer et al, 2011) or precarious work. Munck, Schierup and Delgado Wise offer a notion of 'precarious citizenship' for those migrants 'made increasingly vulnerable by the global economic crisis' (2011: 249). If nation states can award and refuse citizenship, then migrant workers are always vulnerable to the vagaries of immigration law and to the withdrawal of existing rights.

Earlier in this chapter we discussed human rights that are contingent on citizenship. The conferring of rights based on the hierarchy of status (Morris, 2002) leaves undocumented migrants unprotected (Nash, 2009). Gordon argues for the promotion of 'transnational labour citizenship', which, as in the case of national citizenship, would be acquired through the individual having demonstrated adherence to a set of laws and rules, in this case a commitment to worker solidarity and to the upholding of labour standards. Such a model would shift the locus of worker entitlement from the employer, to link immigration status with membership in organisations of transnational workers and 'in exchange for the authorisation to work they would receive as members, migrant workers would commit to the core value of labour citizenship: solidarity with other workers in the United States expressed as a commitment to refuse to work under conditions that violate the law or labour agreements' (2007: 509). It is thus 'the ways in which workers' organisations create membership regimes, set and enforce rules for those who belong, and approach their goal of improving wages and working conditions' (2007: 505). It also encompasses 'the normative expectation of solidarity among workers and active participation by them in the democratic governance of their own institutions' (2007: 505).

Gordon argues that trade union membership or other community activism, as also in the case of national citizenship, is based on adherence to a set of rules and that labour citizenship and national citizenship operate on the basis of similar ways of behaviour. Gordon's concept of transnational labour citizenship offers an alternative position to one that suggests that, for the migrant worker, the only route to rights is through the acquisition of citizenship. She argues instead that international labour citizens would have the right to enter and leave the country at will and that this would provide a route to permanent residence, where desired. Transnational labour citizenship recognises the value of a commitment by workers to the upholding of employment rights and identifies this with a commitment to citizenship in the way that it aims to promote solidarity between all workers, regardless of migration status. It requires of migrants that they demonstrate membership of a trade union organisation in their country of origin and a commitment to join a trade union in the destination country. A commitment to abide by labour standards and to report any undercutting of terms and conditions resulting from the worker's immigration status has the potential to foster genuine points of interest between migrants and non–migrants.

Barbero similarly has called for the recognition of 'acts of citizenship' that take account of 'actors not currently recognised as legal and political subjects' (2012: 529). In a study of the struggles of undocumented migrants in Barcelona and in other cities in Spain in 2001, Barbero argues that a number of the actions taken by them 'converted previously undocumented immigrants into subjects of legality, and to a certain extent, into citizens' (2012: 529). More recently Judge has also argued for a new definition of citizenship that recognises the contribution and struggles of migrant workers. She too questions the limitation of citizenship to the territory of a nation state and argues that there is a place for the assertion of rights' claims that:

> reinforce a conception of citizenship that, although different from national citizenship has the potential to address their distinctive social location. (2014: 29)

Conclusion

This chapter has explained the framework within which undocumented migration is operational and has asserted that it is states and not migrants that foster undocumented migration, as a product of tightening immigration controls. By focusing on the key instruments that governments have resorted to in destination countries, in response to migrants and undocumented migration, the chapter has demonstrated that none of the legislative measures introduced is positioned to answer the problems raised by undocumented migration. The measures that EU member states, in particular, have adopted represent crude responses to a much wider problem of uneven development, poverty in many areas of the world and the attraction to employers of labour that is not in a position to complain and that cannot assert its rights. In the next chapter we begin our analysis and presentation of the empirical findings. We explore, from the perspectives of undocumented migrants, their the reasons for migration, their experiences of the migration journey, their routes into becoming undocumented and their attempts to regularise or decisions not to try to regularise their situation.

Notes

[1] http://www2.ohchr.org/english/bodies/cmw/cmw.htm.

[2] Communication of July 2006 (COM, 2006: 402).

3   COM (2011) 76, dated 23 February 2011 final, http://ec.europa.eu/dgs/home-affairs/news/intro/docs/comm_pdf_com_2011_0076_f_en_communication.pdf.
4   Annual Report of the European Commission on the Return Directive. [

THREE

Migration: motives, journey and status mobility

"I travelled by all sorts of means. Sometimes we travelled by lorry; sometimes walked, we had to climb mountains … We actually didn't know where we were as we were on the move. You travel through different places along the way. There are different ways to go west … The snakeheads can get everything done for you. All you need to do is pay them the money … There were six of us inside the container. Three Chinese and three Asian guys. The lorry came to a stop in the middle of nowhere and someone opened the door; we jumped out of the container. None of us knew where we were. We didn't know that we were already in the UK." (Hai, male, from China)

Hai is one of 17 interviewees (Table 3.1) who entered the UK clandestinely. He came to the UK aged 23 and was looking to see something of the world. The UK had not been a planned destination for him but was simply where he had ended up. Destinations, he said, were a matter of 'fate'; in his experience it was the snakeheads that decided routes and destinations. In China he had worked on the land and described himself as a 'peasant', which meant he had no transferable skills. His experiences in the UK have been a succession of short-term jobs in and outside of London that started with cockle picking, but have included working in kitchens and selling DVDs. He has not attempted to regularise his status, fearing the formal registration and finger printing that occurs when seeking asylum.

The focus of this chapter is on migration journeys and routes into becoming undocumented. There is no one experience of these processes; instead they combine with structural barriers and immigration policies, personal circumstances, opportunities and resources, both economic and social (Geddes, 2005; Hagan, 2008; Koser, 2008; Bloch, Sigona and Zetter, 2011; Schuster, 2011). In Chapter Two we introduced some of the main structural barriers in place at the level both of the EU and of the nation state, noting how immigration controls can in fact be counterproductive, 'with new controls producing new evasions' (Geddes, 2005: 330). This includes the flourishing of the migration industry as a lucrative and sometimes necessary business that can and does offer returns for all parties involved (Koser, 2008). Beneficiaries, in addition to the migrant and the agent/smuggler, can include family members, who may contribute collectively to meeting the costs of the journey as part of a household or family survival strategy, with the expectation that the migrant will earn and remit money (Koser, 2008).

Clandestine entry or entry into the UK using forged documents or other people's documents is facilitated by agents or smugglers and is just one of the ways in which migrants are defined as undocumented. Overstaying a visa and/or having an asylum claim refused and remaining rather than returning to the country of origin are the two principal routes to becoming undocumented, as we noted in Chapter One. What is key is that status is not static; people move in and out of regular and irregular statuses, sometimes when it is expedient to do so as part of their migration strategy, and sometimes it just happens almost by default, due to bureaucratic systems (Jordan and Düvell, 2002; Bloch, Sigona and Zetter, 2011). This means that the route through which a migrant enters the UK may not in fact be their reason for migration. For example, an asylum seeker might enter clandestinely or on a visitor's visa, while someone who migrated for economic reasons might enter the country on a student or visitor's visa (Bloch, Sigona and Zetter, 2011). Being undocumented is relational and dependent on the categories used to label different migrants for bureaucratic and administrative purposes, rather than necessarily a true reflection of migration motives, which can be mixed but also fluid (Zetter, 2007; Bloch, 2008).

However, the hidden nature of these migration routes and pathways into 'undocumentedness' means that little is known, in reality, about the numbers involved. In Chapter One we presented an overview of existing data. In this chapter we focus on the actual experiences of migrants as they enter the UK using various routes and strategies, some of which are regular, some of which are not. We consider the pathways in and out of different statuses and the ways in which some have tried, albeit without success so far, to permanently regularise their status. While some undocumented migrants exercised a significant amount of choice in relation to their journeys and their status, others had been left vulnerable and disillusioned by their experiences, especially those who had been through the asylum system.

This chapter is in four parts. First we offer some background about our interviewees in relation to their motives for migration and reasons for coming to the UK. We then explore the journey itself and the different ways in which migrants initially entered the country. The third part of the chapter examines migrants' routes in and out of different statuses and how and why they found themselves undocumented at the time of the interview. Finally, we explore both attempts to regularise status and decisions for not attempting to do this.

Deciding to leave the country of origin and come to the UK

Reasons for migration

Migration motives are often complex. The prevailing situation in the country of origin alongside social networks, perceptions of economic opportunities, freedom from persecution as well as opportunities for a new experience, to learn a language, participate in education or as a rite of passage, can all act as migration drivers (Hagan, 2008; Castles, de Haas and Miller, 2013; Bloch, Sigona and Zetter, 2014). The circumstances in the sending country will affect the motives for migration as well as the routes used to enter the destination country. Among our interviewees, motives were most often economic, but family reasons, to escape persecution and to seek asylum, to study and for an adventure were all among the reasons for moving. The prevalence of different motives varied by country of origin, in the sense that Kurds from Turkey were in some instances driven by discrimination and persecution on the basis of ethnic group, while migrants from China and Bangladesh were most often migrating for economic reasons and these included supporting family members. Although, as we report in Chapter Four, wages are low and work insecure for undocumented migrants, wages are nevertheless high in comparison to wages in the countries of origin, so this makes the move economically viable and for some an imperative as a household survival strategy.

For those from China and Bangladesh the economic drivers were: not being able to make a living in China or Bangladesh, to make better money in the UK and/or, in the case of those from China, because the exchange rates in the past had been favourable, making the UK an attractive destination. Bling was not unusual when he stated that 'I came to the UK because I wanted to earn money'. The business in China that he had been involved in had not been good, so, he said, 'I thought I should go abroad to find work' – and given that he had two children and a wife in China whom he had to provide for financially, for him this was an imperative. In fact nine of the 20 undocumented migrants from China whom we interviewed had children in China, although not all were dependents, some now being adults. Among the 15 interviewees from Bangladesh, seven had children in Bangladesh, although it was not just children that needed to be supported but wider family networks. Arif, for example, who had been in the UK for seven years, was referring to the more extended family when he said that he came to the UK because 'I couldn't manage supporting my family on the work I did in Bangladesh'.

Cheung, a 48-year-old man from Jiangsu in China, who had been in the UK for 13 years, talked about why he had decided to move and why the UK was the chosen destination rather than other possibilities:

> "I wanted to come to the UK because I wanted to earn some money. I was thinking that the pound had a higher exchange value against the Chinese yuan. I came here almost by chance. An opportunity came rather unexpectedly for me to go abroad. Some of my friends suggested that I should come to the UK; before that I had no particular plan to come here. In fact, I didn't know much about the UK before I came." (Cheung, male, from China)

However, there were information exchanges between people in China and the UK and this created a migration flow although experiences did not always live up to expectations, something that has also been found in other research (see Bloch, Sigona and Zetter, 2014). At times interviewees expressed both a lack of knowledge about what to expect as well as disappointment with the reality of their circumstances in the UK. Chow had been in the UK for four years and had worked short term in different restaurants and take-away shops. She had obtained a student visa and so, on arrival, she could work part-time, which made things easier for her. However, during her time in the UK not only had her visa expired, but she had also had a young child and although she had a partner, another undocumented migrant, she was isolated and lonely and had few financial resources. In the following quote she reflects on her motives and experiences:

> "I decided to come to the UK because many of the people in our place were coming to the UK then. Everyone said UK was a good place to come, a place that might give you some hope. Everyone said that the pound was good money to earn because it had a high value against the Chinese yuan; that you'd get quite a bit of RMB [yuan] with one

pound. That was why I wanted to come to the UK. I had not realised that the situation here was rather different from what I had expected. I probably would not have come to the UK, had I known that I would end up like this." (Chow, female, from China)

Others too noted their shock and disappointment on arrival, where the reality was so different than the London, a global city, they had imagined. Piro, a Kurdish man from Turkey, explains his experiences on arrival:

"I was imagining a London full of lights, I would insert a coin into a machine, the lights would be on. I would play tennis with sparkling light around. I was thinking life was very comforting or fun here, like tennis courts everywhere. Even on my first day, I realised the impossibility of such life here because the first place I came to was Haringey [area of North London]. My whole dreams collapsed even on my first day."

Family networks also led to decisions to migrate, but not necessarily economic ones. Two of the female interviewees from China had left due to marriage breakdown and, in the case of one of these women, fear of persecution as a consequence of having more children than permitted was an additional factor, as she explained:

"I came to the UK because of the breakdown of my marriage in China. Also, in China you are only allowed to have two children [in the countryside] but I had given birth to three. Because I had one child more than permitted, the only way for me was to hide myself and evade the fine. During that time my relationship with my husband worsened. I left China in order to escape the penalties." (Chun, female, from China)

Having children in the UK had influenced both Isha from Bangladesh and An from China to come and to remain in the country, though for An, who had come on a visitor's visa in 2009, earning money became a factor in her decision to overstay her visa:

"I came here to visit my daughter. My daughter was a college student. She has gone back to China now. But I decided to stay on. Because my visitor's visa has expired, I am not legally allowed to stay here now. I wanted to stay because I wanted to earn some money." (An, female, from China)

Some undocumented migrants from Bangladesh came to the UK initially to study, others to fulfil a dream and some due to political problems. In some cases there was more than one reason for migration. Kadir, for example, came to the UK to study so that he could progress faster economically because his family, he said, were "so poor".

The reasons for migration among those from Turkey, including Kurds from Turkey and Northern Cyprus, were varied. Like others, they included some who were economically motivated, some who had family reasons and even a minority who were seeking an adventure through migration. However, this group also included asylum seekers. The Kurdish cases differ from those of others in our study as they form a discriminated-against minority group in Turkey and so a much larger proportion have been through the asylum system in the UK or were forced to leave due to persecution. Shivan, who was 28 and had been in the UK for four years, described his situation:

> "I came here to make my asylum claim; somehow I could not make it when I entered the country. I have not made my claim yet. In such conditions I cannot make it. My arrival was not expected, it was all of a sudden. I was not thinking of the life like now, I was very inexperienced. Due to political reasons, I had to get out of the country. I did not plan to be a kebabcı [in Turkish, the one who serves kebabs]. Before coming here I was involved in a clash involving 30–40 people due to political conflicts at university. I had to hide somewhere from the police and other political group immediately after. My father tried to find a way to send me abroad. There was no time or opportunity for me to arrange or plan my life here." (Shivan, male, Kurd from Turkey)

Shivan talks about the suddenness of his departure, and among the Kurds he was not alone, others too had left in acute circumstances and without the opportunity to properly plan and prepare.

The literature on migration has focused increasingly on the complexities of decision making and on mixed motives for migration as well as on the inadequacies of bureaucratic labels in representing lived realities (Zetter, 2007). We also found that decisions were complex: sometimes there was no one main reason but a number of factors contributing to the final decision to move countries. Rojda, for example, a Kurd from Turkey, said that although she was not particularly political, her father was in prison and had been subjected to torture due to his political activities. Often, simply by association, family members can be at risk; but in addition Rojda had opened a business and had gone bankrupt, and so she hoped to improve economically through migration. She described her reasons for migration as "both economic and political".

The UK as a destination

While some interviewees had wanted to come to the UK, actively employing strategies to reach their desired destination, for others the UK was simply where they ended up, often as a consequence of financial resources and smuggling routes. Those who had actively wanted to come to the UK were influenced by perceptions of economic opportunities, the immigration and asylum system and the presence of family and social networks. While among Chinese interviewees exchange rates were a factor, as noted above, among Kurds the perception of the immigration regime as compared to that of other countries in Europe was also influential, as the following quotes illustrate:

> "[We] were told England was more advantageous compared to other countries, for example in France they do not give status very easily." (Hasan, male, from Turkey)

> "My initial plan was to stay in Switzerland. I had some relatives. That's why I chose it, but then I did not want to stay there. The conditions for the asylum claim in Switzerland were very hard." (Zana, male, Kurd from Turkey)

Roni was Kurdish, but in his case he stated that he had not been motivated by political factors or perceptions of the immigration system. Roni came the UK because his wife's relatives were already in the country and she "forced" him to come. Others too had family in the UK, and that was advanced as their reason for selecting it as a destination. Economic factors played their part too – both as a driver for migration and as a reason to come to the UK. Mahir, who was

Turkish, explained how there was nothing to farm for villagers in his area who did not own land. Rural-to-urban migration was not uncommon in Turkey, but life in the city was not always good and economic survival was a struggle, and perceptions were of the UK as somewhere where there were greater opportunities.

Decisions to migrate and destination choices can be varied and complex, as we have shown. Linked to these are the capacity to move, which can be limited by structural barriers in the country of origin and the receiving country. In the next section we explore migration journeys and the ways in which they intersect with opportunities for regular migration between countries, transport routes and routes used by agents and smugglers.

Migration journeys

Migrants can exercise a degree of agency in the migration process, not just in terms of deciding to migrate, but of how and when, at what cost and with what assistance. Those using agents or smugglers to make their journeys are not passive actors, and the relationship between the migrant and the smuggler, in terms of the balance of power and choices, varies. At one end of the spectrum, migrants choose their destination and the role of the smuggler is one of a facilitator ensuring arrival at the destination. At the other end of the continuum, the smuggler decides the destination and this may not take account of the wishes of the migrant, but will instead be determined by profit margins, existing networks en route, border patrols and possible crossings. The middle position is a negotiation between the migrant and the smuggler, implying room for manoeuvre; trust is crucial to these exchanges (van Liempt and Doomernik, 2006).

Smuggling is of course a financial transaction, a business based on varying degrees of legality and illegality, due to the border controls that restrict movements and make mobility 'a privilege that is unevenly distributed among human beings' (Pécoud and de Guchteneire, 2006: 75). As pre-frontier measures and those relating to border management have become more restrictive, more punitive and more diverse, in part as a consequence of technological developments, an unwanted outcome has been growth in the migration business as the demand for people smugglers and agents has increased (Geddes, 2005; Koser, 2005).

In a study of the smuggling process from Afghanistan and Pakistan to the UK, carried out in 2004, Koser (2008) notes that different financial arrangements exist and not all money is paid in advance. Migration outcomes form part of the financial transaction, acting as an incentive for the outcome to be successful. Koser (2008) reported that the costs varied depending on the route taken, with direct flights being the most expensive ($13,000–$14,000), followed by indirect flights, where the prices depended on the transit country and were anywhere between $6,000 and $12,000. Overland routes were the cheapest but also most risky option, costing around $4,000.

Our research also found that agents, smugglers or snakeheads had been paid by some interviewees to help them make their journey. Those from China were most dependent on smugglers or 'snakeheads' to make their journey, including being smuggled clandestinely into the UK; around three-quarters had paid for their services. More than half of the Turkish and Kurdish interviewees had also used smugglers or *shebeke* and, like their Chinese counterparts, some had been clandestinely smuggled into the UK in the back of a lorry. A minority – just over a third – of Bangladeshis reported having used an agent to organise their journey, with most paying to have documents and visas arranged. The norm was to fly into the UK using the documents organised by agents. The assistance paid for and the method used to enter Britain depended in part on when the journey was made and the visa regulations at the time. What was noticeable, especially among interviewees from Turkey, was that the newer arrivals faced greater difficulties, and this was not surprising, given the fewer regular routes for entry.

Nearly all of the interviewees from China (16 out of 20) had paid large sums of money to make their journeys. Journeys could involve different modes of transport, periods of time in transit countries, as well as making parts of the journey on foot. Services provided to migrants varied, with some smugglers organising visas, documentation and flights, while other migrants were literally smuggled into the UK in the back of a lorry. Chueng, who came to the UK in 2009, had paid a travel agency 100,000 yuan (around £10,000) to arrange his tourist visa and journey and to find work on arrival. Others had paid more money to make their journey. Bobby had come to the UK in 1999 when he was 19 and paid £25,000 for a South Korean passport organised by the snakeheads:

> "All those arriving from China [undocumented] have their papers arranged by the snakeheads. All you need to do is pay the snakeheads if you wanted to go abroad." (Bobby, male, from China)

Bling also talked about the necessity of paying to make the journey and the negotiation with agents about possible destinations. He had used a six-month tourist visa to enter Britain, but stayed on after it expired:

Bling: "You have to pay them. Who would help you to go abroad if you don't pay any money? You see, I didn't know much about the UK; I had no idea what it was like. I wouldn't know how to get here. So I had to pay them to get me here. I needed their help for this. It was their business to arrange everything for me for the journey. I paid just over 100,000 yuan to come here. It's over £10,000. In China, a lot of people were trying to go abroad. It became trendy to go abroad. I was simply following the trend."

Interviewer: "You think it was a trendy to go abroad. Then why did you not go to, for example, Japan, the US or Canada instead? Why did you come to the UK?"

Bling: "The agent arranged the visa for me to come to the UK. Of course, you might also get it arranged for the US, or Japan and so on. But the visa for Japan was harder to get. You would have to have a Work Permit to go to Japan. That was a lot more difficult."

Interviewer: "You mean it was easier to get a visa to come to the UK?"

Bling: "That's it. It should be easier to come here. In any case I got everything arranged by the *zhongjie* [middleman or travel agent]. You tell them where you want to go and they tell you which country's visa they can get for you. In my case, everything was arranged by the *zhongjie*. They filled in the application form for you and got things done for you. The middleman just wants to make money from you." (Bling, male, from China)

Not everyone had the outcome they had expected in terms of destination or direct journey. Chun felt cheated by the snakeheads on arrival because she had been promised "a very good country", which to her mind had not included the UK. Fang had spent over a year getting from China to the UK, with one year in transit in Moscow. During the year in Russia the snakeheads had supported her. In the following quote she talks about aspects of her journey:

> "It took over a year for me to arrive here. We stayed in Moscow for a year ... The snakeheads gave us food. We ate just one or two potatoes a meal. It was a very hard time. It was very, very basic survival. We travelled into the UK from France. We had no passport or visa. We were inside the back of a lorry. We didn't come out until we were left some place in the [English] countryside." (Fang, female, from China)

Turkish and Kurdish interviewees had also relied on agents and smugglers, *shebeke*, to make their journey; more than half (11 out of 20), of whom seven described themselves as Kurdish, said that they had paid for assistance. Some of the journeys were difficult overland trips, then by boat to British port towns, while others had used *shebeke* for forged passports and airplane tickets. As with the Chinese undocumented migrants, there were varying degrees of individual agency in the process of migration and selection of the destination among Turkish and Kurdish interviewees. Cem spent seven days travelling from Istanbul to Dover in 1999 and paid £4,000 to *shebeke*. He reported knowing nothing about the route and, although he knew the destination was England, it was not his choice, as he recounts when he says:

> "To be honest *shebeke* decided about England. It was not my idea." (Cem, male, Kurd from Turkey)

Hevi, a 49-year-old Kurd from Turkey, would have preferred to go to Germany because of relatives, or to Greece because of the lifestyle there, but had no choice:

> "It was not my decision. *Shebeke* told me they were going to England so I had to come here." (Hevi, male, Kurd from Turkey)

The cost of the trips varied, but £10,000 from Turkey to the UK was a price mentioned by a few interviewees for the whole journey, although another pattern was to make the journey in stages, sometimes paying in separate parts. Hasan, for example, had paid £2,500 for the final leg from France to England in 2001:

"First I came to Bosnia on my own; you do not a need visa for that. Then through the *shebeke*, I came to Croatia, from there to Slovenia, from Slovenia to Italy, from Italy to France. Then from France, the *shebeke* brought me here. Up to France it took 24 days ... I have sisters living in France so I stayed 20 days in France ... I knew some people who went to Europe thanks to this *shebeke*, the one in France. My brother also came to London with them. I paid, it was not euros at that time, it was marks, I guess I paid seven or eight thousand marks, [that] was up to France. We paid £2,500 from France to London." (Hasan, male, from Turkey)

Travelling between Calais and Dover in the back of a lorry or the trunk of a car was the way that seven undocumented migrants from Turkey had first entered the UK. Hevi had experienced a particularly difficult journey, had been imprisoned for 12 days in Greece on the way and had also travelled from Italy to France by boat and then made his way to Paris. Once in Paris, he had received advice from a friend in London who had made the journey the year before and had then made his way to another city in France. In the following quote he describes his experiences:

"I asked [my friend] about how to come to London from France. He told me to go to a French city; he gave me the name. He said there would be some Iraqi Kurds doing such business ... My friend told me over the phone and described a location. I did not know it was a kind of tunnel, like a cave. I went there and I saw many blankets on the floor, but there was no one around. They keep the people who want to cross the border over there because you cannot cross on the same, on the day you want to, you might need to wait for a while. I went there but there was no one around. I saw the blankets, I took one of them and lay down. At dawn, one of them came, he was a bit drunk. I spoke in Kurdish. He asked who I was. I said I was one of them. He said let's sleep first of all. Some others came a few hours later. We went to a park. There was a tent in the middle of the park. A woman, a charitable person, delivers free food to homeless people, she helps the people sleeping on the street. Then I heard that the place where we stayed, the tunnel, is called Hilton. They said to the woman that I too was staying at Hilton. The friend of mine who was in London, he stayed with them for two months. I mentioned his name and they remembered [him].

I took my wallet out of my pocket. We looked [at] it together. I had 350 euros. Then they gave me back 50 euro and said 300 was the price for their help. I stayed two nights. They were watching the border every day. There were many lorries parked on the border. There were some other refugees waiting like me. There were even some families. One day they decided on one of the lorries. We started to run; they made me get on one of the lorries; they knew the lorry was coming to England. The driver was not aware of anything; we did that secretly. The journey took four hours. The lorry came to somewhere like harbour city. It was close to Portsmouth. The lorry stopped moving but I did not know for a while whether I should get out of it or not. The *shebeke* earlier told me to wait in the lorry until 11 pm. I could not, I could not breathe, I was hungry. I got out of the lorry. We were on the border. I followed the railway and saw some houses. I said to the woman in the train station "London ticket please". She gave me the ticket. This is how I came to London." (Hevi, male, Kurd from Turkey)

Others had relied on *shebeke* for false passports and/or visas that were used to travel by train and plane. What was evident, and similar to Koser's (2008) findings, was that not all of the money was paid up front; instead, full payment was dependent on safe arrival at a destination, as described by Agit and others:

"We paid £2,000 to come by a lorry. Of course you do not pay at the time, you wait until you come to your destination safe. I came in a comfortable way. I sat next to the drivers as if I was his assistant. Only when crossing the border in France [did] I have to go back side of the lorry and stay silent. When we were in the ferry he said you can leave whenever we get off the ferry." (Agit, male, Kurd from Turkey)

Those who had arrived in the UK earlier had been able to obtain visas. Zana, who was a Kurdish man aged 55, had been in the UK for 24 years:

"I came as a political refugee. You did not need a visa, you could get a visa at the airport. I came to the UK from Switzerland. When I first came, they kept me in interrogation for eight hours. They gave me a visa for a month. I did not say I intended to make an asylum claim, I said I came to London for a holiday for touristic reasons. I said this to the immigration officers of the airport; they gave me a one-month visa." (Zana, male, Kurd from Turkey)

Jiyan, a 44-year-old Kurdish male, and Roni, a 36-year-old Kurdish male, had both obtained Schengen visas, which had enabled them to travel visa-free from one Schengen country to another. Jiyan had travelled to the Netherlands in 1998 and Roni to France in 2000. In the following quote Roni, who had travelled with his wife, describes using *shebeke* to assist the process:

"We got a Schengen visa, which is not valid for here. We came to the border of France. [The visa] was original but we paid for it. The normal visa was £30–£40; but we paid 18,000 marks. The visa is original but *shebeke* got it." (Roni, male, Kurd from Turkey)

Although he could have organised it himself, Roni had felt it was easier to pay, and that had been the norm, as he explains:

"At those times, coming through *shebeke* was very common, one man out of three used to be involved in *shebeke* at those years. It was not difficult to contact *shebeke*. If you had money, there was no problem." (Roni, male, Kurd from Turkey)

Using *shebeke* meant not only that there would be some papers, but for some a clear explanation of what to do and when, as Mahir describes:

"before landing I tore my passport in the toilet of the plane and put it in the bin; *shebeke* had told me to do that. They [authorities] should not find any official documents on you. Mine was original so they would definitely send me back if they found me." (Mahir, male, from Turkey)

Six out of the 15 interviewees from Bangladesh also talked about agents or agencies to organise papers, visas and/or the journey. In comparison to undocumented migrants from Turkey and, to a lesser extent, China, their journeys were much more straightforward, involving a flight. Naser was not unusual among Bangladeshi interviewees who had paid an agent for help. He arrived in the UK at the end of 2008 on a visitor's visa that he had paid an agent to organise, as he describes in the following quote:

> "It is not easy for people to come. There are people who make duplicate papers and charge 5,000–6,000 lakhs Taka [roughly £5,000]. That is how I came, it was a visitor's visa. The agency [in Bangladesh] sorted everything out and I paid them 6,000 lakhs." (Naser, male, from Bangladesh)

Nafisa also used an agent to organise her journey. Her intention had been to come to the UK to earn some money and then to return to Bangladesh. The agent had promised that he would organise work for her in a restaurant on arrival, as part of the package, but the reality was different:

> "Before I came, the agent told me that his relatives had restaurants, that they could give me work, that they had good places to work and that they would need people. They told me that as soon as I arrived, I would get a job and earn a good wage … When I came here, I realised that the people that I was supposed to go and stay with [through the agent] had no work for me and they were in fact working for other people!" (Nafisa, female, from Bangladesh)

Using agents, agencies and smugglers to organise the journey was, as we have seen, a key mechanism for circumventing pre-frontier measures such as visas and those that relate to border management, including surveillance, biometric data and inspections (see Koser, 2005). The proliferation of the migration business is directly linked to border controls and our interviewees provide evidence of thriving businesses in sending and transit countries with linkages en route that offer a variety of different packages. Routes change in response to controls, as do destinations. More money provides more options and less-arduous and dangerous journeys. In the following section we focus on life once in the UK and, in particular, becoming undocumented, by exploring entry channels into the UK, status mobility and routes to becoming undocumented.

Entering the UK and pathways to becoming an undocumented migrant

Initial entry routes into the UK

The way interviewees had entered the UK most often was on a visa, either visitor (17), student (6) or business (5). Fourteen had entered the UK clandestinely, 11 using false documents and one as an asylum seeker. Table 3.1 shows the different entry routes by country of origin. People from Bangladesh and China used visas most often, while those from Turkey were more likely to enter clandestinely, reflecting what we already know about journeys.

Table 3.1: Initial entry route into the UK, by country of origin

Base number = 54; missing = 1

	Bangladesh	China	Turkey	Total
Visa	12	11	5	28
Clandestine	1	3	10	14
False documents	2	5	4	11
Asylum	-	-	1	1

Differences between men and women were evident; 13 of those entering clandestinely were men, only one was a woman. Most of the women interviewed (11 out of 15) had entered on visa: six on a visitor's visa, four on a student visa and one on a business visa. Among the men fewer than half (17 out of 40) had used a visa to enter the UK. However, the route of entry does not necessarily reflect migration motives but instead can simply be the most feasible or only mode of entry (Bloch, Sigona and Zetter, 2011). The argument that pre-frontier and border controls result in new ways of circumventing and navigating borders and an increase in irregular entry among asylum seekers, turning them into irregular migrants, that is presented elsewhere in the literature (Koser, 2005; Schuster, 2011) is certainly apparent in our study.

While only one interviewee had made an asylum claim at the border, a further 23 had made claims from within the UK, though what is striking that is the majority who had claimed asylum had initially entered the UK using either false documents (9) or clandestinely (10), while four had entered using a visa. This as an entry route for those who may then seek asylum demonstrates the difficulties in exiting and entering countries for asylum seekers wanting to make claims, as others have also found in relation to seeking asylum in Europe (see Schuster, 2011).

Not everyone who makes an asylum claim falls within the definitions set out in the 1951 Convention Relating to the Status of Refugees (the Geneva Convention) as a person with a 'well-founded fear of being persecuted' on the basis of 'race, religion, nationality, membership of a particular social group or political opinion' and who is outside of their country of habitual residence and who is unable to rely on the protection of that country. Moreover, among some, seeking asylum may be a used as strategy to provide a recognised status for the duration of the asylum process (Jordan and Düvell, 2002). Similarly, however, not all of those with a claim to refugee status will seek asylum, for fear of being exposed or having their claim refused, as they run the risk of deportation. In short, categories are bureaucratic and not always representative of the mixed and differing reasons for migration or the various possibilities for entering and existing in the destination country. Among our interviewees, 8 of the 24 asylum applicants were from China, 1 from Bangladesh and 15 from Turkey. Of the Turkish applicants, 12 described themselves as Kurdish and 3 as Turkish.

Kurds from Turkey are a discriminated minority, but this does not necessarily result in meeting the criteria for refugee status and may instead fall into the broader category of survival migrant (Betts, 2013). However, regardless of the asylum process and outcome of the claim, being a Kurd in Turkey will affect attitudes to deportation from the UK back to Turkey. The UK is seen as offering freedom to be Kurdish and to engage in cultural, linguistic and political activities, and fear of return is clearly articulated among undocumented migrants who have had their claims refused (Bloch, 2014).

Status mobility

Not surprisingly, issues of status mobility and routes to becoming undocumented vary between the three country-of-origin groups and reflect both entry routes and, to some extent, pre-migration experiences. Among the majority of interviewees from Bangladesh, the pattern was simple: arrive on a visa, overstay and as a consequence become undocumented. While some had arrived intending to overstay their visa, others had not intended to overstay but had made the decision once in the UK, as Hanif describes:

> "I came as a visitor. I got a [six months'] visitor's visa. Now
> I have been here 10 months. I had no intention of staying.

I stayed because I was enjoying life here." (Hanif, male, from Bangladesh)

Among those from China, routes could be more complex than among their undocumented counterparts from Bangladesh, although some had also simply overstayed their visa. Chao, for example, had entered on a six months' business visa and told how he had "stayed on after it had expired". Similarly, An had overstayed a tourist visa when she had come to the UK to visit her daughter more than three years ago. While her daughter had returned to China, An had "decided to stay on". Guang has also overstayed a visa. He arrived from China more than nine years before the interview on a business visa with his own passport and without paying snakeheads to make the journey, which was unusual. After his business visa expired he made an asylum claim but was refused and so remained instead as an undocumented migrant. Among some of those who had not claimed asylum there was a regret, as they had seen others granted leave to remain. In reality, though, as we have seen, claiming asylum does not in any way guarantee leave to remain; eight out of the 20 Chinese interviewees had claimed but been refused asylum. Being too scared to claim was something others talked about. Fang, for example, had also met people who had had to leave as a result of seeking asylum and had been too scared to apply, as she tells below.

> "Many of the people I met when I first came have all been given residential status or Leave to Remain; yet I'm still without anything. The reason I have no status is because when I first came, I didn't claim asylum. I didn't claim asylum because I was too scared to go ahead with making the application. I was afraid that if I went to claim asylum, I'd be detained and sent back to China. So I didn't claim. That's why I don't have residential status." (Fang, female, from China)

The end of the asylum process as the moment of becoming undocumented was most frequent among those from Turkey – particularly Kurds. The pattern was to enter the UK in an irregular way, attempt to regularise through an asylum claim and then become undocumented when the claim was refused. Hevi is an example of this. As we saw earlier in this chapter, he had entered clandestinely but had made an in-country asylum claim. When his asylum application was refused, he was given Home Office signing conditions, meaning that he had to report regularly to the local police, which he refers to as custody, and decided to stop signing:

> "I went to signature for a while. Then I quit. People said such custodies are like traps. When they find the opportunity, they catch you and deport you. I stopped going." (Hevi, male, Kurd from Turkey)

The Ankara Agreement was a route taken by a minority of migrants from Turkey as a mechanism for trying to regularise status. The agreement provides for the right of Turkish citizens to migrate on the basis of the submission and acceptance of a valid business plan. In the case of the UK, prior to April 2010 it was open to those already within the country, but since then the application cannot be made in-country. It is open only to Turkish nationals with a feasible business idea and enough money to support themselves initially. Arjin had been advised by her solicitor to apply under the Ankara Agreement after her student visa extension application had been rejected. However, she was rejected, appealed twice and was rejected both times, then elected to stay without documents. Pathways are not straightforward and avenues taken often depend on what is thought to be the best strategy, even if this is not a reflection of circumstances.

One of the most traumatic and complex trajectories we came across in our interviews was that of Rojda, who at the time of interview was 53 years old and had been in the UK for 25 years, although this had included one spell back in Turkey, after deportation. She described her initial migration motives as 'economic and political', although she had initially arrived, with her husband, on a tourist visa. Their children at the time were still in Turkey, being looked after by Rojda's mother and sister:

> "We came with a tourist visa; everything was official; there was a small [community] centre in London; when we came the people over there advised us to make an asylum claim. I was against it from the beginning. I said we should not, otherwise we could not go back to our country, but my husband did not listen to me; my husband made a claim; six months [after] our visa was expired and we [had] stayed as illegal for six months. After a year of claim, we brought our children from Turkey. There was a law in those years. Asylum seekers could bring their children at that time." (Rojda, female, Kurd from Turkey)

The asylum application made by Rojda's husband was refused, and because the children were at school only Rojda's husband was deported, although he returned after two years as she explains:

"due to our children, they could not send both of us; there was a law protecting the children at that time. My children were studying at that time, they could not deport me. My husband was in prison for a month and [they] deported him later on. Two years later he came back to London, he came through illegal ways, he came in the back of a lorry." (Rojda, female, Kurd from Turkey)

Rojda then made her own application, on the basis that if she obtained status her husband would also receive status as her dependent. However, unbeknown to her, the asylum case was rejected and a deportation order was served:

"I used to go to the Home Office once a month [to sign]. I was in touch with my solicitor, my case was still continuing, I did not have a refusal. [One day going to sign] they put me in a cell in the police station. They were forcing me to sign the deportation paper. I resisted, I was screaming, crying, asking them why they did not tell me in advance. I did not know that the court had given [the] deportation decision. How come my solicitor also not know about the decision? They deported me." (Rojda, female, Kurd from Turkey)

She remained in Turkey for around two years but then travelled from Turkey to the UK via Germany with the help of *shebeke*. This time she used a different strategy, the Ankara Agreement, to try to regularise her status:

"I applied for the Ankara Agreement. This time my application was again refused. Again on a weekly basis I started to go to the police station for signature. Oh my God! How nervous I was in each time, everybody knew that I could be arrested any time. Then I was again arrested. I went mad, I yelled at the officers. I said 'You are doing this to me because I am honest and coming here every week.' They were about to send me [to Turkey but] I had a psychological breakdown. Due to my health; they let me go because I screamed a lot. My solicitor talked to them.

They gave me three months' permission and then I should have gone. I promised them I would go back to Turkey in three months but I did not. How can I? My children are here. I have a life here." (Rojda, female, Kurd from Turkey)

Rojda has been living without papers for a number of years but her case shows the difficult pathways taken, some of which were clearly expedient and all of which show her determination to do what it takes to stay with her family and continue with her life in the UK. In the last 25 years, she has been detained, deported, been on a tourist visa, had both an asylum claim and an application for the Ankara Agreement refused and spent periods of time as an undocumented migrant. Trying to regularise status was something a number of our interviewees had attempted through the asylum system, visa extensions and the Ankara Agreement. Some had engaged solicitors to assist, though, not surprisingly, given the outcome of attempts to regularise, there was generally a negative appraisal of legal support as we explore in the next section.

Trying to regularise status: not trying to regularise

Being undocumented is not necessarily an end state but instead one stage in a fluid process between different types of status. In Table 3.1 we saw the different initial routes of entry, some regular and visible, others irregular or clandestine. For those who entered on visas, six months was the norm; different visas have different stipulations attached. Those on student visas, for example, have a minimum attendance requirement at an educational establishment and a maximum number of hours (20 a week during term time) that they can officially engage in paid work. We noted earlier that entry routes into the UK were often expedient rather than a reflection of the actual migration driver. In this part of the chapter we consider the ways in which some undocumented migrants have attempted to regularise their status and their experiences along the way. We also explore the choice not to try to obtain a regular status. What is significant of course is that whatever measures have been taken to date have all been unsuccessful. While some remain hopeful that things will change, others are resigned to their predicament.

Claiming asylum is the way in which most had tried to regularise their status although among our interviewees it had not been successful. In Table 3.1 we saw that 24 interviewees in the study had claimed asylum in the UK and that of these 24, 19 had entered in an irregular or clandestine way and four had used visas (three visitor's and one business visa), leaving only one who had claimed asylum on entry. While some had entered the asylum process almost immediately after arriving in the UK others had delayed claiming, until either their visas had expired or it seemed the right time for them. Bobby from China had arrived in the UK as a 19-year-old and had been in the UK for 12 years. He had arrived using false documents and had submitted an asylum claim, which had been refused, but had received permission to stay for 18 months with signing orders, followed by an additional 12 months' temporary leave to stay. His temporary stay has long since expired, though he has not given up trying to obtain status. His original solicitor has 'disappeared', as he describes it, so he employed a different firm to represent him.

> "My solicitor didn't follow up my [asylum] case. They disappeared. They are now nowhere to be found. I've now got another solicitor's firm to apply for a five-year leave to remain for me. I hope I get it; it will be much easier to make a living. So far there has been no news. It has been two years since I submitted it." (Bobby, male, from China)

Experiences of the legal system were not positive and the costs could escalate quickly. Of our 55 interviewees, half (23) had been in contact with legal services. For most, this was in relation to asylum cases, although some had sought advice on visa extensions and the Ankara Agreement. Among those from Turkey, and Kurds from Turkey, the Ankara Agreement was a way of trying to regularise status. Arjin, Ali and Bahar had arrived on visas and attempted to extend their stay through this route, although none of them had been successful and they all felt part of the reason was their legal representation. While some had gone to great lengths and expense to try to avoid becoming undocumented or to move back into a regular status after becoming undocumented, others had decided instead not to have a go at all, or to give up on their efforts. Getting to the end of the line with the asylum system or visas was the main reason for giving up, although some had consciously made the decision to opt out from the gaze of the state by not adhering to Home Office signing conditions or not attempting to regularise status at all.

One of the main reasons for not trying to regularise status was the costs involved, though another reason was fear, especially of the asylum system. Nasif, a 40-year-old woman from Bangladesh, describes the financial barriers, stating simply that "because I am poor I have no money, I am unable to get a solicitor", while Chao, from China said one of the reasons for not taking action at the end of his visa period was because "I was too scared to claim asylum". Fang was also scared; she had been in the UK for six years and had entered clandestinely. Although she knew other Chinese people who had been successful in making asylum claims, she said "I was afraid that if I went to claim asylum, I'd be detained and sent back to China. So I didn't claim."

Others thought that they had no case to make and so there was no point, or simply lacked the necessary knowledge to begin such a process. Cheung from China had entered the UK on a visitor's visa three years before he was interviewed and, in relation to residential status, said, "I don't think we would ever get it. I just don't see the possibility." As a consequence he had not tried to regularise his status and had been undocumented since his visa had expired. While some still hoped for changes in their status and planned to continue with their efforts, others were resigned to their situation and had no intention of trying to regularise.

Conclusion

This chapter has focused on the different initial migration drivers, experiences of migration and routes into becoming undocumented. We found that migration motives varied and that there were country-of-origin, ethnicity and gender dimensions to these variations. To make the journey to the UK, most relied on agents and smugglers to arrange documents and to organise the actual logistics of the journey, which for some were long and difficult and involved spells stuck in a transit country. The actual ways in which people entered the UK were not necessarily related to the reason or reasons for migration. Instead, immigration policies as well as immigration agents and smugglers dictate the routes people take and the options available to them. For instance, some people entered the UK on visas when the intention was to work and stay, while other entered on visas or clandestinely and then became asylum seekers. We found some movement in and out of statuses. Although everyone was undocumented at the time of their interview, for some this was seen as an end state, while others still had hopes or strategies to try to regularise their status.

In Chapter Four we turn our attention to living and working in London, which for many was the main reason for migration.

FOUR

Undocumented migrants living and working in London

"[It is] becoming harder for Chinese businesses to recruit workers ... It has become harder and harder to find suitable people; there are fewer people competing for jobs. Many people have gone home. You see, many bosses had to sell their businesses, just because they couldn't recruit the right people to work. It's more difficult to recruit workers. There are fewer people willing to work in take-away shops ... But it is also because of the [government] policy as a whole. You can't hire foreigners to work in take-aways and restaurants. They won't do such jobs. They won't want to do such jobs. You see, I think in the future it will become even harder to recruit workers for Chinese businesses ... If you are really committed to finding work, you'd be able to find something. Of course, whether pay is good or not is another question." (Jiang, male, from China)

Jiang was working in a take-away shop, doing deliveries in the late afternoons and evenings; at the time of his interview he had another part-time job working as a packer in a factory. He had arrived in the UK from China via Argentina, where he had spent time working for his uncle. Leaving Argentina because he found it unstable, he had decided to come to the UK using a passport and visa organised by the snakeheads. On arrival in the UK he had found work as a labourer in the building trade. He had worked nine hours a day, anything from five to seven days a week, depending on what was available and needed by his South Asian employers. Most of the other labourers were Chinese and the daily rate was £55 in cash. Work in construction was not stable for Jiang, which he attributed partly to the economic crisis, which had made homeowners reluctant or unable to spend money on their houses. In a search for a less precarious working life, Jiang had found a job, through friends, delivering food for a take-away shop. Quickly Jiang realised that the work was not secure because his labour was required inconsistently, sometimes daily and sometimes not for a week. Being proactive, he changed jobs and has been working in the same take-away doing deliveries for the last few years. Work in his current take-away is routine and consistent and the other employees are, like him, from Fuging, a Fujian town.

In the quote above Jiang raised issues that were mentioned by other undocumented migrants, notably that labour shortages could work to their advantage and that there was a lack of skilled workers in the restaurants and take-away shops as a consequence of immigration rules (see Chapter Two). The employers we interviewed of Bangladeshi and Chinese heritage noted that the lack of chefs specialising in Indian and Chinese cuisines, as a consequence of immigration rules, was putting a great deal of pressure on their businesses because they were constantly struggling to recruit chefs with both the correct documents and the skills they needed. They expressed their preferences for workers from the same ethnic group, and these workers could be hard to find (see Chapter Five). For undocumented migrants, however, immigration rules could in fact open opportunities for better-paid jobs than might otherwise be available, although not at the same rate of pay that would be given to someone officially eligible to work. The availability of work in the increasingly hostile climate of controls, raids and sanctions is essential to the survival of most undocumented migrants. Finding a job and staying in work was the main priority among the majority of those whom we interviewed. Their labour forms part of a larger picture that includes globalisation, inequality, immigration controls and changing occupational structures.

The shift from manufacturing to the financial and banking sectors and the expansion of the service sector have changed some economies, including that of the UK, and the jobs available within them. Importantly, within the context of this book, it is the need for and reliance on migrant labour for low-paid work in the service sector that can provide work opportunities. Indeed, as Castles (2004) argues, it is capitalism and its need for certain types of labour that ensures that immigration controls will never really work. Within the category of migrant there are clear cleavages and hierarchies based on immigration status, gender, length of time in the UK, access to resources and language skills, and this workplace ordering is found in employment clusters associated with migrant labour such as cleaning, the food and catering industries, hotel and hospitality, care work and construction (Cobb, King and Rodriguez, 2009; Wills et al, 2010). The 'ethnicity–citizenship labour hierarchy' used by Holmes (2007: 48) to describe the experiences of indigenous Mexican undocumented migrants workers in the context of North American farm work is apparent elsewhere. In particular, fear of deportation, costly journeys and debt can leave workers powerless and open to abuse (Rutherford and Addison, 2007; Bloch, 2013). The interviewees in our study, regardless of differences, were united by their undocumented status. Many expressed a sense of powerlessness to contest their situations – they were workers without rights living in a country with both employment and human rights.

Undocumented migrants experience exclusions that are both structural and self-imposed as a consequence of status, and these impact on working lives. Structurally, this group is not eligible to the rights associated with citizenship, including social and welfare rights. Without the safety net of social security benefits, work becomes essential for those who lack alternative forms of support such as family, friends or savings. Given that many of those we interviewed had economic drivers for their migration and some had accrued debts in making the journey, finding work and staying in work was a major concern and preoccupation. Framing the imperative of work is the threat of deportation or 'deportability', which maintains the vulnerability of undocumented migrants as workers (de Genova, 2002) and forms part of the concurrence of status with all aspects of working lives. Real and self-imposed restrictions are placed by individuals on their everyday lives and interactions (Willen, 2007; Bloch, Sigona and Zetter, 2014). However, this does not mean that undocumented migrants are without agency. Social networks and community organisations are used (Engbersen, van San, and Leerkes, 2006) and this group of migrants participates in the labour market in ways that enhance their situation and are considered and evaluated. This means that they are in fact not always hidden; within local communities they can be visible and participatory (Chauvin and Garcés-Mascareñas, 2014).

In this chapter we focus on the working lives of undocumented migrants and note throughout the constant juxtaposition of working lives with irregularity in five main areas: job search and routes into employment; jobs and sectors of employment; terms and conditions of work and the precarious nature of employment; experiences of work within and outside of the ethnic enclave; and workplace relations. While for the most part work is insecure, with poor terms and conditions, including long and unsocial hours without overtime payments, we also know that being undocumented does not mean a total absence of agency and that some undocumented migrants are able to make incremental improvements to their working lives by adopting particular tactics in terms of skills acquisition, job mobility and even geographical mobility (Bloch and McKay, 2013). This chapter will draw on the narratives of undocumented migrants with the objective of exploring generalities and individual experiences in order to reflect both patterns and diversity.

Searching for work

The ways in which people look for work reflect a combination of networks, language, access to technology and immigration status. What often distinguishes job search techniques among undocumented migrants from those of others is both their reliance on informal methods of job search and their lack of engagement with formal techniques and statutory job search agencies, where documents will be requested (Bloch, 2013). Given the importance of finding a job on arrival, our interviewees mobilised whatever resources were available to them, including their social networks. Table 4.1 shows that 32 people found their first job less than a month after arriving in the UK.

Table 4.1: Length of time taken to find first job, by country of origin

Base number = 52; missing = 3

	Less than 2 weeks	2 weeks but less than 1 month	1 month but less than 2 months	2 months but less than 4 months	4 months or more
Bangladesh	4	4	2	2	2
China	6	2	5	3	3
Turkey	13	1	0	5	0
Total	23	7	7	10	5

Most people found their first job through friends or relatives (30), although 13 had used job agencies and 12 by cold calling, newspapers or websites. There were differences in the ways in which the first job was found, by country of origin, which related to the absence or presence of pre-existing social networks. Half of those from China had found their first job through a friend from the same region in China, while eight of those from Turkey had used relatives, reflecting the networks and access to social capital that could be mobilised on arrival. While six from both China and Bangladesh had used agencies, only one person from Turkey had done this – possibly the others did not need to pay to find work, as they were able to use other methods. However, those who arrived on a visa – student, visitor's, business or transit – were most likely to use agencies for their first job (10 out of 13 who used agencies). Certain visas allow limited working hours, and so this enabled a more flexible approach to job seeking that was less dependent on informal networks, at least for the duration of the visa, although sometimes this initial access resulted in other work-related documents that could be used even when migrants moved into an undocumented status (Bloch, 2013; Chauvin and Garcés-Mascareñas, 2014).

Those with relatives or friends accessed the labour market more easily, frequently using those networks for actual jobs in cases where relatives owned businesses, and for information about vacancies. These contacts could also provide undocumented migrants with informal references. In Hasan's case, his uncle helped him, as he describes in relation to his first job in an off-licence, which is a shop with a licence to sell alcohol for consumption off the premises:

> "They were not relatives, but acquaintances from the same town. My uncle knew the employer, he became my reference. I worked there for two to three months in an off-licence." (Hasan, male, from Turkey)

Some expressed a preference for working for relatives as they felt safer and that they would be treated better:

> "I like working for people I know well. I think I'd rather work for my uncle than find another job. You never know what it's like out there if you work for some other people whom you don't know very well. You may even be bullied or treated badly, if you work for some others who are not so kind." (Huan, male, from China)

Relationships with relatives in the workplace could be varied and ambivalent. Those without relatives at work felt that those with relatives were afforded preferential treatment, while those with relatives felt that the ties of blood led to obligations that made them easily exploitable, like Welat, who expressed a bigger-picture view on business practices and family and migration:

> "In some cases the people in Europe order youngsters like me from Turkey, from their villages, they set up their businesses here. They need some young relatives to work for them; they do not trust everybody here." (Welat, male, from Turkey)

While employers want workers whom they can trust, it was not always the case that relatives could be trusted as employers. Mirza, for example, spoke of "not trusting" his relatives because when he had arrived in the UK and worked for them in their off-licence for three months they had not paid him but instead given him "pocket money". Mirza described himself as "naive" on arrival and it was this naivety that his relatives were able to exploit. A pattern emerged among those who worked for family members which was one of responsibility, where they might be taken advantage of, so helping new arrivals could be far from altruistic, as Ferhat, who worked in his cousin's garage, explained:

> "My cousin often goes on long holidays, up to six to eight weeks, and I manage the whole shop on my own. He wants me to get married and settle down so that I will permanently stay in London. He just thinks of his own interests. I do not think he cares about me ... he thinks I cannot leave him, as I cannot find a job without papers. I am also very sentimental about family relations. He also misuses this."
> (Ferhat, male, from Turkey)

Nearly half (24) said finding work was difficult, while 27 said that they found it easy. While being undocumented was seen as the major obstacle to finding work, language and skills were also identified as barriers. Skills initially depended on pre-migration experiences, and many of the jobs done prior to migration were not transferable to the context of a large city. The lack of transferable skills, coupled with limited or no English language among many of our interviewees, placed them in the least skilled parts of the migrant hierarchy. However, as noted earlier, there were jobs, and being willing to take the lowest paid and least desirable jobs meant that work could be found, as Guang explains in relation to delivery work:

> "not a lot of people would want to work as a delivery boy. So it was not too difficult on the whole ... Maybe because the pay is too low, not many people want to do that kind of job." (Guang, male, from China)

Most people had been in a number of jobs while in the UK. This was a combination of the precarious nature of some jobs and of the decision making of undocumented migrants who, in some cases, moved jobs if better or more secure jobs arose. Over time, finding jobs can become easier, due to networks (Anderson et al, 2006); also reputation, honesty, skills and a willingness to work hard for less pay – simply being 'hard workers' (McIlwaine et al, 2006; Gombert-Muñoz, 2010) – were important in facilitating mobility. Willingness to work hard was basic, as Deniz pointed out:

> "First of all, you need to be very hard working; you should not say 'I cannot work' or 'It is too much work'." (Deniz, male, Kurd from Turkey)

In fact, willingness to work hard trumped all other attributes, including family connections, as Roni (male, Kurd from Turkey) observed when he explained that his relatives had hired him, not out of kinship obligations, but because he was "a hard-working person".

There is a relationship between length of time in the country and number of jobs, but it is not automatic. Individuals could, over a relatively short period, have moved from job to job, but equally over a long period could have been in seemingly stable jobs. While job insecurity was of course a factor in mobility, individuals also made the choice to move jobs when new opportunities arose or when it was expedient to do so, or, in some cases, where the pull of the global city, with its greater access to networks and other means of support, directed them back to London. Important in job mobility were the networks that undocumented migrants developed, their acquisition of skills and their knowledge of the labour market. Over time, workers acquired information about jobs, employers and workplaces that were utilised in the search for subsequent jobs. However, while the networks offered some but limited progression opportunities, these rarely included movement outside of the ethnic enclave or ethnic-minority niches because the networks were comprised mainly of other migrants, and often those without status.

In Table 4.2 we compare the ways in which undocumented migrants found their first job and their current job. Most significant is the decrease in the use of agencies and the increase in friends and acquaintances as routes to work. Over time, people were able to build networks of work colleagues, social contacts based on friends and acquaintances and, through these, to share information about job vacancies and employers. Hevi, who had worked in numerous construction jobs, explains the work networks:

> "In each different job you also meet new people; you take their telephone numbers. You call them to ask for a job or to ask for suggestions about where to go to find a job." (Hevi, male, Kurd from Turkey)

Table 4.2: Ways of finding first and current job (%)

Base number first job = 55; base number current job = 42 (10 not working and 3 in original job)

	First job	Current job
Agencies	24	7
Employers	0	4
Friends/contact	38	53
Relatives	16	16
Self	22	20

Pros and cons of job-seeking methods

For many undocumented migrants, friends and acquaintances were seen as the best route to work and it was certainly the most successful, if measured simply by the way jobs were found. Friends can become a 'resource person' (Diminescu, 2008: 571), and this involved exchanges. People helped each other, as Jiang explains:

> "we offer help to each [other]. We don't charge a fee for giving each other help; you have to ask your friends for help; when you're far from home you need to rely more on friends for help. It can be difficult to find work if you do it on your own. Friends will keep an eye on businesses that they know of and inform you when they see some vacancy." (Jiang, male, from China)

In relation to work, friends undertook four key tasks: first, they provided access into certain jobs that would not have been openly available; second, they offered a minimum guarantee of reasonable treatment in the workplace; third, they were able to provide information about employers and the workplace environment; fourth, they offered the connection that some thought was necessary in order to be employed. In short, networks provided information about vacancies and employers, but also an informal reference that could influence the working environment. While facilitating work, the networks utilised were based on 'bonding capital' rather than the all-important 'bridging capital' that allows access to wider societal resources and opportunities (Lancee, 2012), and so the available networks were, as a consequence, limited.

For undocumented migrants the issue of trust is an important one, both the employer's ability to trust them and their ability to trust the employer, and this is something that evolves only from these networks and is part of the way in which this group protect themselves from potential exposure:

> "You need to have some contact, connection. They would never employ you out of the blue. You need to have a reference, like you know the cousin of the boss or you are a friend of one of their good employees; such things [are] necessary." (Cem, male, Kurd from Turkey)

However, a minority were cautious about networks, preferring instead to use agencies and middlemen, as that way they could be honest and open about their status and would not worry that, if caught, they might have created problems for friends or family. While some people from Bangladesh used agencies and some from China used middlemen or agents, it was very unusual for our Turkish and Kurdish interviewees to have used them because their family networks offered access to work, as noted earlier. Using agencies and agents had a cost implication, and prices varied. The agencies finding work for people from Bangladesh tended to charge between £20 and £50, with £30 or £40 being the norm. The agents or middlemen working with Chinese migrants advertised their services in newspapers and charged more – the range was £100 to £200, but the cost depended on the rate of pay given in the job. There was an element of caution in using middlemen, as some people had experienced scams, such as paying fees into a bank account and then being sent to places where there were no job vacancies, as Dai explains.

> "But not all the middlemen are reliable. They charge you a fee of £100 for recommending a job to you. Most of them charge £100. But in some cases, you go there to see the boss but they don't hire you, and you'll lose that £100 fee you've paid. Of course if you're lucky enough to be hired, then the £100 fee is worth paying." (Dai, male, from China)

Looking for work without relying on social networks or paying for agents and agencies was a route used by around a fifth of those we interviewed. This involved searching community-language newspapers, noticeboards, community websites, walking the streets and cold calling businesses. As with agencies, finding work this way removes the pressures and obligations that go with assistance from friends and relatives. Chow, a female from China, described how using the internet to find a job meant that it was easier to leave if it turned out not to be suitable. Jobs obtained through friends or family on the other hand created obligations of "loyalty".

One of the consequences of these methods of job seeking, and the reliance on work contacts and social networks as well as community papers and internet sites, was that it potentially limited the kinds of jobs and sectors that were open to undocumented migrant workers. Of course other factors played a part too, notably language and skills and, most of all, status, but the range of jobs and composition of workplaces were fairly homogeneous.

Jobs and sectors of employment

At the time of the interviews, 45 out of 55 interviewees were working. Of the 10 not working, half were men and half were women. Among the women, four had young children and were looking after the home and family. Work was, for the most part, clustered within the ethnic enclave, ethnic minority owned businesses and/or ethnic minority niches that are dominated by a particular ethnic group. The current or most recent workplaces of interviewees were almost exclusively small businesses operating within the informal and least regulated parts of the economy, due in part to the methods of job seeking and employers' recruitment practices, but most of all due to the migrants' undocumented status (see Chapter Five and Nee and Sanders, 2001; Ryan et al, 2008).

Sectoral clustering

Table 4.3 shows clustering within a small number of sectors, especially restaurants and take-away shops, where around half of those working were employed at the time of the interviews. Of the 10 not working, eight had been employed in restaurants or take-aways in their last paid job, showing the dominance of this sector as a workplace. A possible caveat, however, in our analysis of sectors and jobs, is the nature of the sampling, and in particular our reliance on networks and snowballing. This means that it is not possible to ascertain the extent to which the sectors of employment are representative of the wider population of undocumented migrants from China, Bangladesh and Turkey living in London. While other research suggests similar types of work, we are aware that the most hidden, such as those working in domestic servitude in forced labour situations or as sex workers, were not accessed in our study, although they have been interviewed in other research (see Lewis et al, 2014). We are also aware that assumptions as to where particular categories of workers are likely to work encourage a focus on those areas, possibly to the exclusion of others, and introduce bias within the selection methods.

Table 4.3: Sectors of employment (current or most recent main job), by country of origin

Base number = 55

	Bangladesh	China	Turkey	Total
Construction	2	4	1	7
Manufacturing	2	1	1	4
Restaurant/take-away	8	13	9	30
Retail and services	2	0	3	5
Other	1	2	6	9

Note: 'Other' includes hair and beauty, cleaner, computer repairs and child minder

Only Chinese migrants were working in take-away shops, the largest single workplace among this group. Bangladeshi and Turkish undocumented migrants were most likely to be working in restaurants. Within ethnic enclave businesses both economic factors and those based on stereotypes of what constitutes a 'good' worker come into play when employers recruit. Research by Lucas and Mansfield noted how employers explain the recruitment of migrant workers using terms that include 'motivated, reliable, committed, excellent attitude, hardworking, flexible, and superior work ethic' (2010: 171). However, there are further divisions such as those based on gendered notions of a good worker suitable for a particular job (Anderson and Ruhs, 2010b). In our research, workplaces were found to be fairly homogeneous in terms of the ethnicity of employees, especially restaurants and take-away shops, although divisions based on gender were apparent (see Bloch, Kumarappan and McKay, 2014). All the take-away employees were male, and restaurants were also male dominated. Only three restaurant employees were female – all from Turkey – and all three were involved in visible, front of the house work, either waitressing or cooking in front of customers. Significantly, they spoke English and were able to serve customers from different communities. In contrast, the male interviewees who were working in restaurants were almost exclusively located in kitchen jobs, as kitchen porters, cooks or chefs.

The reliance on informal social and community networks for recruitment and for job search serves to replicate the existing profile of workers in any given environment, in relation to skills and competencies. One employer, Uddin, a Bangladeshi man who owned two restaurants serving Indian cuisine, relied on his own community contacts to recruit workers and described his employees in the following way:

> "a hundred per cent permanently men. By and large, I would say ninety-nine per cent was Bangladeshi heritage."

It was more than just recruitment and status that influenced jobs. Lack of English is known to be a major barrier to social and economic participation (Nawyn et al, 2012). Among many of those we interviewed the lack of English meant that they were unable to work in any role that required English skills, as Fung explains in relation to her work in a kitchen before starting a family:

> "I didn't deliver meals, because I can't speak English. You need to be able to speak English with the customers for delivery duties." (Fung, female, from China)

In contrast, Chow, who could speak English, found herself in a much better position at work and with responsibilities in a small restaurant with five tables and a take-away business, She describes her situation, and the advantages her knowledge of English brought, as follows:

> "The couple didn't speak English. They relied on me a lot to run the shop. Because I could speak English, the couple often asked for my advice and help to deal with the problems they faced and I had a lot of freedom working there. I took charge of the counter and the tables. She had to rely on me for a lot of things. I had to take orders, take care of the telephone, and look after the sit-in customers who ordered dishes." (Chow, female, from China)

Current job and transferable skills

Table 4.4 shows the main jobs carried out, at the time of interview, by country of origin. Within the sectors, especially restaurants and take-away shops, there were a variety of jobs available with different skills sets. A minority of women had worked in kitchens in the past, but women worked mostly in jobs that were more overtly perceived as feminised, including waitressing, child minding and in hair and beauty.

Table 4.4: Current job, by country of origin

Base number = 55

	Bangladesh	China	Turkey	Total
Child minder	1	0	0	1
Cleaning	0	1	0	1
Computer repairs	0	0	1	1
Construction	2	4	0	6
Cook or chef	2	2	5	9
Factory (3 sewing machinists and 1 dry fruit packer)	2	1	1	4
Food delivery (take-away)	0	3	0	3
Garage mechanic	0	0	1	1
Hairdresser	0	0	2	2
Kitchen porter	3	3	0	6
Nail technician	0	1	0	1
Shop/off licence	2	0	3	5
Taxi driver	0	0	1	1
Waiting tables	0	1	3	4
Warehouse loading/unloading	0	1	0	1
Not working (including looking after home/family)	3	5	2	10

Note: Total number of jobs is 46, as one person had two jobs and 10 persons were not working

Within restaurants and take-away shops most people worked in the kitchen, either as a cook, a chef or a kitchen porter. Kitchen labourer/porter work was the least skilled and was often a starting point from which people were able to acquire food preparation and then cooking skills that enabled incremental pay increases, most often through moving jobs but occasionally from progression within the same business. Within Turkish restaurants the route was kitchen labourer to meze preparation to chef. In Chinese restaurants the progression route was daza (kitchen labourer) to handling the wok to chef, and in restaurants serving Indian food it was kitchen labourer to cook to chef. As Jiyan, who was a cook, noted, "You always start with washing dishes" (Jiyan, male, Kurd from Turkey).

Although not everyone progressed, certainly kitchen work in restaurants and take-away shops offered the chance for progression, although a glass ceiling was evident among those from China and

Bangladesh. Bobby, who had worked his way up from kitchen porter through to stir-frying rice and noodles, observed that without documents he could never become the chef. The glass ceiling meant that once you reached a certain level of job there was nowhere to go and no options for increasing money. Lok, like Bobby, had started as a daza worker in the kitchen of a Chinese restaurant. He had worked in a number of restaurants and take-away shops during his 12 years in England. Although some of the owners and managers were from Hong Kong, the workers were all from mainland China. In China Lok had been working in building construction and had no experience of restaurant work on arrival. He describes his experiences, skills acquisition, pay increases and promotions within his first job as follows:

> "When I first went to work there, the boss had to teach me
> how to do the job. I was new so I didn't know how to do
> it; he was rather impatient sometimes. I was cautious not to
> forget what he had instructed. I was careful not to make a
> mistake … I think to work as a kitchen labourer for £180
> a week was not too bad … My wage eventually increased
> to over £300 [per week]. (Lok, male, from China)

However, since this first job, Lok has simply moved from job to job, earning the same money and carrying out similar tasks, unable to progress or develop – in short, encountering a glass ceiling. In other types of work too there was a pattern of starting with the least skilled tasks and gradually gaining experience. Some people moved between sectors and jobs, carrying out a series of temporary or short-term roles.

While most people were unable to transfer their pre-migration skills and experiences into the UK labour market, a small minority with specific skills had been able to use them. In particular, tailors and hairdressers had found their skills to be transferable, although pay was still low. Two interviewees from Bangladesh had been tailors prior to migration and in the UK were sewing machinists, working 10- to 12-hour shifts and earning around £20 per day, regardless of the number of hours worked. However, Ali, from Turkey, had a very different experience in the textile factory where he worked. He highlights the better working conditions he achieved in the UK compared to Turkey, referring also to the financial rewards for his "mastership":

> "I get £6.50, £7.00 per hour. There are some people who
> get £5.50 to £6.00, but I get higher compared to them as
> my profession, [my] job is mastership. Last week I received

£364 from the factory. I work 50 hours a week; I have Sundays off. I also worked in a textile factory in Turkey [so] I can make the comparison. You start at 8am and you do not know when you will leave the job and go home. You wait months to get your money. Here every Friday at 5pm you get your money; some get cheques, illegals get cash; employers are reliable in this country." (Ali, male, from Turkey)

Two interviewees from Turkey were working as hairdressers in London and both noted the demand for their skills and their "profession". Bahar had worked as a hairdresser in Turkey for 19 years before coming to the UK and her regular telephone contact with a friend, prior to migration, revealed to her that her "profession is very valuable here because there are not many good hairdressers in Turkish neighbourhoods". Piro was also a hairdresser and talks about the creativity of his work, which he describes as "art":

"In this profession the main point is the talent. The hairdressers or barbers coming from Turkey are very popular in the UK. I have not had any issues in finding a job. It is also an enjoyable job." (Piro, male, from Turkey)

The reflection on art, craft and profession among this small minority with transferable skills was evident and enabled them to move away from, or avoid, the food sector or other largely manual-based work for men, or from unskilled and low-skilled work among women.

Employment terms and conditions

Almost uniformly the working lives of undocumented migrants were characterised by long hours and low pay. There was no sick pay, holiday pay or pay for unsocial or additional hours. Work was insecure and, in the absence of written contracts or any formal employment terms, there was often nothing that could be done about the situation. Our analysis identifies patterns in terms of pay, working hours and other terms and conditions in and between different sectors, and in some instances across country of origin groups. Given the importance of restaurant and take-away shop work among our interviewees, we will begin with this sector.

Working hours

Restaurant work entailed split shifts to cover the lunch time and then dinner service, with a break between the two shifts. Generally this meant working from around 10.30am until between about 2pm and 3pm and then starting again between 4.30pm and 5pm and working as late as was required, which could be between 11pm and 1am. Many restaurant workers lived above the shop, so the period between shifts meant going upstairs for a rest and then coming 'back down' for the second shift.

Chao worked in a take-away shop, doing deliveries, and he worked one, rather than two shifts, preferring the shorter hours this type of work permitted, to those worked in restaurants:

> "You normally start at 4.30pm in the afternoon; you work through the evening until roughly 12pm. You arrive to work at the shop at 4.30pm; then you would have your dinner there. You start work after the meal, and you work till 11.30pm or a bit later than that. On weekends, you'd normally have to work till 12pm or 12.30am." (Chao, male, from China)

Chao, like others, emphasises the lack of fixed hours, which provides employers with the flexibility to meet the needs of the business. Rojda, who was working in a cafe, explains both her situation and also those more generally in "Turkish workplaces" in relation to working hours:

> "My working hours are not fixed, I do not know what time I can go home. You start at 4pm and you stay until it is closed down; I do not know, it can be 2am or 1am, on Saturdays I was staying until 4am. In Turkish workplaces, restaurants, off-licence you are in the hands of the bosses, you have to stay. It is a fact that you work almost double, compared to the people who have status." (Rojda, female, Kurd from Turkey)

Most workers were paid a flat rate for their six days' work; there was no overtime or extra for the unsocial hours. This requirement of flexibility for no additional pay was not only in catering but in other areas of work too. Zana worked as a mini-cab driver and was supposed to work eight hours, although that was never the reality. However, as he explains:

"I get a weekly wage, not per hour. If I work more than eight hours, it does not change the amount of money." (Zana, male, Kurd from Turkey)

Pay structures

Pay structures were quite fixed and these were well known, so there was a similar going rate for a similar job between businesses (Bloch and McKay, 2013). However, there were variations between the three different groups. Bangladeshi workers in restaurants were paid less than others, with kitchen porters earning as little as £90 working in a Bangladeshi-owned restaurant, as compared to around £200 in Chinese-owned establishments. There is no simple explanation for these differences in pay. They may reflect the routes of entry into the workplace, the extent of labour shortages or indeed the nature of the obligations between the employer and worker, which may themselves be influenced by network type.

Many of the kitchen jobs included food and lodgings as part of the pay package, although the quality of the food provided was variable, with a minority complaining that they were allowed to eat only the cheapest ingredients and that the food excluded meat. Waiting staff generally earned more than kitchen labourers but there was variation in wages and tips. Reyan earned £240 and Mahir £220 per week for waiting tables in Turkish-owned restaurants, while Arjin worked six days a week also in a Turkish-owned restaurant waiting tables and earned a basic wage of £30 a day or £180 a week. Describing the variable nature of tips that allow employers to pay less, she said:

"I also get some tips, which also depend on the day, it is not regular. Turkish places always rely on the tips; that is why they keep the wage quite low. I know some restaurants in [north London borough], the men [employers] make you work 11–12 hours a day for six days a week and pay you £160 weekly, they say the customers leave too much tips." (Arjin, female, Kurd from Turkey)

Cooks were next best paid, although the rates of pay were once again the lowest in Bangladeshi restaurants. For example, and representative of earning across groups, Mujib was paid £200 a week by his Bangladeshi employer, while Bobby earned £280 as a wok chef and Shivan was earning £300 as a cook at a charcoal kebab restaurant. Chao describes the operation of pay hierarchies as an explanation for why he did not get a pay rise when he asked:

> "The wages are normally fixed for the different positions. For example, you can't pay the person washing the dishes more than the person taking care of the oil wok. If you increase the pay for the dishwasher, then you would have to increase wage for the person taking care of the oil wok as well; and you would even have to increase pay for the master chefs and other chefs. You can't increase pay for just one person. The wage levels are sort of similar for the types of work across the catering business." (Chao, male, from China)

The highest paid job was that of restaurant chef, and two interviewees from Turkey – both male – had achieved this status. What was interesting about their narratives, and in contrast to others working in restaurants, was that they both had a sense of value and felt as though they were in demand because of their skills. Agit had started as a kitchen porter and explained how "You start from the ground then gradually you move to a higher position". It had taken him two years to become a chef in his previous job, where he had started on £180 a week and finished five years later earning £370. He was earning £600 at the time of his interview and was satisfied with the money he earned, describing it as good money, though he was aware that this was in fact the average wage for a chef and that employers "cannot offer less than the average". Agit talked about creating a demand for his work, although within the limitations of being "weak" because of his status.

Like Agit, Deniz was also a kebab chef and had earned £300 per week, although he now worked three days a week, as his wife also worked and they arranged their work so he was able to look after their two children in the hours that she worked. He had been a meze cook in Turkey and was now a chef in a kebab restaurant, working behind the charcoal fire preparing kebabs and other special meals also cooked on an open fire. He described himself as having "a profession" and as a "good chef". Being well regarded as a chef certainly helped Deniz and the current employer did not ask about his status. According to Deniz, his employer does not know he is "illegal":

> "I guess he did not find it necessary to ask, he knew me earlier and he knew how good a chef I was. He almost

begged me to work in his restaurant. He wants me to work full-time." (Deniz, male, Kurd from Turkey)

As with kitchen and restaurant work, there was also a fairly standardised wage structure in other sectors. Welat had been in the UK for 14 years and had worked in London in many different businesses, including a bakery, supermarket and a grocery store, and observed that Turkish employers "all have same system, 12 hours a day, six days a week, £200 weekly roughly" (Welat, male, from Turkey).

Daily rates on building sites ranged from as little as £20 to £70 a day, although they were usually around £40 or £50. The lowest paid work on building sites was that done by a casual day labourer paid around £20 a day. Pay did depend on skills and experience and so it was possible to increase the daily rate, as Ron, who started on £30 a day, explained:

> "Wages were not very good. But then you'd work your way up, from when you didn't even know how to manage *daza* [labourer] work, to when you can manage it well, then gradually become proficient at it. You move your way up and become good at it, wages would go up along the way. It took me a year to have my wage increased to £40 [a day]. By the time I had acquired some carpentry skills, my wage had increased to £50 [a day]." (Ron, male, from China)

Even with increases, undocumented migrants were still paid significantly less than other workers and they were well aware of the disparities in both pay and working terms and conditions. In the next section we explore aspects of status and its impact on work and working conditions.

The intersection of status with terms and conditions of work

The impact of undocumented status on wages, especially in comparison to those of workers who did have documents and were working in similar jobs, was mentioned by many of our interviewees. It seemed that pay could be between half and a third of that given to other workers in restaurants and on building sites. Adam, originally from Bangladesh, was a cook earning £150 in a restaurant and stated that he earned "£50 to £60 less, roughly" than those with documents. Ron worked in construction and his earnings had increased from £30 a day to £70 a day, as he was now, he noted, "a skilled worker". He was one of the better-paid workers we interviewed but was well aware of the disparities. In the following interview extract, Ron talks about pay and conditions:

Ron: "There is no such legal welfare right. Maybe they know that we don't have legal status; they hire people like us because they know they don't have to give us such rights. They know it's cheaper to hire people like us. There is no contract, no job security."

Interviewer: "Would you say this £70 is the right amount for the job you are doing, or lower, or higher?"

Ron: "I'd say it's probably the minimum rate for the job. It's not particularly good at all. The foreigner [non-Chinese] may get £130 or £140 [for the same job]. But we Chinese will have to live with it, because we don't have residential status." (Ron, male, from China)

The lack of job security, sick pay, holiday pay and flexible, but unknown, maximum hours created a constant state of insecurity. Moreover, for those who lived above their place of work, there was the additional element of being tied in and having to accept the status quo because of the housing implications of leaving or losing a job. Afsal describes his life working and living above the restaurant:

"The illegals stay above the restaurant. They stay there, wake up in the morning, no breakfast or anything, just start work. If there is an opportunity, one may have a cup of tea but it seems work is greater than one's wellbeing." (Afsal, male, from Bangladesh)

In describing the dynamics of Chinese restaurants some people focused on their relationship with the master chef, length of time in the UK and skill levels, rather than status. This was because it is not unusual for some of those working in restaurants to be without status:

"[T]he working environment in a Chinese restaurant is like this: old workers would normally bully those who are new; skilled workers would lecture at the unskilled." (Chao, male, from China)

> Working in the kitchen, [the] relationship with the master chef is very important, because he is normally the guy making decisions there. If you can't get on with the master chef, you'll be asked to pack your things in one or two weeks." (Jian, male, from China)

The lack of paid sick days or paid holidays made it almost impossible to take a break from the structure of a six-day working week, 52 weeks a year, year in, year out. Taking time off meant losing pay, and for most was not an affordable option. Financial deductions or losing a day off were the norm for any holidays taken or days off sick, leaving people trapped in a relentless work cycle. If workers took a day off sick it would mean losing their regular day off to compensate.

The final aspect of terms and conditions to be explored relates to precarious work, which Lewis et al define as 'lived experiences that are characterised by uncertainty and instability' (2013: 4). Among our interviewees precariousness was expressed broadly in relation to insecurity, poor conditions of work and a lack of recourse to contest conditions. This powerlessness was understood as an inevitable part of the irregular migrant/workplace equation. Ron talks about dismissal from his labouring job at a building site:

> "They sacked me because they thought I was too slow. It's a ruthless world out there. They didn't give me any notice. When I was receiving my wage late one Friday afternoon, I was told not to come back to work in the coming week."
> (Ron, male, from China)

Being asked to leave when employers became anxious about workers' lack of documents or when they had been employed on a temporary basis to fill in when a business was short staffed was also not an uncommon experience and something that our interviews with employers corroborated (Bloch and McKay, 2015). Jiang from China had worked on construction sites and described this work as "casual work" where "nothing is fixed". Similarly Chun, also from China, who worked for cash in hand as a cleaner, explained her anxieties because the employers "may cancel it anytime. It's not a secure job." Restaurant work was equally insecure, as Fung from China observed about her previous work when she said, "when business is bad, the boss would ask you to leave".

Basic workers' rights are not accessible for this group. The common law doctrine of illegality of contract denies access to any employment rights to those who are undocumented (Inghammar, 2010; Dwyer et al, 2011; McKay, 2014). This means that undocumented workers have no rights to the national minimum wage, to protection against unlawful discrimination at work or to complain against unfair dismissal. The very detrimental effect has been highlighted in the case of *Onu v Akwiwi and another* [2014] EWCA Civ 279, which held that a domestic worker who had been mistreated by her employers could not, because she was undocumented, claim against that mistreatment on the basis of nationality. Without enforceable contracts there is no route available for recourse without visibility, and part of the condition of illegality is to try to minimise exposure (Willen, 2007). The idea that there can be no argument, no contestation and no recourse, as a consequence of status, comes through in relation to dismissal, and also in terms of pay, hours, working conditions and roles within the workplace.

> "They know we are weak. We are [treated] differently in all ways. Even with regard to hours worked. We do 14–15 hours every day with less pay; my position is weak and you can't really ask the owner. The legal ones work less hours. The illegal people have to do the work. It is exploitation. We are weak, [the boss] is getting cheap labour, [it] saves him taking another person on and saves him money." (Fadi, male, from Bangladesh)

In the above quote, Fadi, a restaurant worker who was responsible for packing take-away orders in the kitchen, talks about his situation. His reference to being "weak" is something echoed by a number of interviewees in relation to work experiences. Taking a relational approach to highlight differential treatment between those with documents and those without within enclave businesses, as Fadi does, was not unusual, as we have noted earlier. In the next section we explore experiences and views about working within the ethnic enclave.

Working within or outside of the ethnic enclave

Previous research suggests that undocumented migrants, for the most part, seek work within the ethnic enclave or within co-ethnic enterprises, and this pattern is replicated in our research (Schrover, van der Leun and Quispel, 2007; Bloch, 2013). The reasons for this are complex and varied. First, limited social networks alongside the mechanisms for expanding networks, due to homogenous workplaces and few opportunities to learn English, can leave workers trapped within the enclave; second, word-of-mouth methods of job seeking and job recruitment, through limited social networks based on trust, replicate the characteristics of workers within work settings; third, certain types of employers are thought to be more likely to recruit workers without documents, and so workers approach them for jobs (see Chapter Five); and fourth; working for family owned businesses and the obligations of family from both the worker's and the employer's perspectives also keeps workers within the enclave.

Only nine out of the 45 who were working at the time of interview were working outside of the ethnic enclave. Three were from Bangladesh, all women; one was working in a retail clothing chain, one as a child minder and one had a job as a sewing machinist. Five of those from China who were working had jobs outside of the enclave, of whom three were men in construction, which was an ethnic minority niche, one woman had a domestic cleaning job and one woman was a nail-care technician. Zana, a Kurd from Turkey who worked as a mini-cab driver, was the final non-enclave worker. Proportionally, women were more likely than men to be in non-enclave work, as fewer worked in restaurants and take-away shops, while more worked within the domestic sphere.

Even when undocumented migrants find work outside of the ethnic enclave they are more likely to be concentrated in particular sectors, working alongside their co-nationals, speaking the same shared language and often with other undocumented migrants. One of the main differences is the line of management. For those working in ethnic minority niches, there is often a foreman, from the same ethnic group as the other workers, who also speaks English. This pattern of employment is explained by Hai, who had worked as a cockle picker on arrival in the UK from China. He described the work in some detail; the hours depended on the tides, food was included and pay depended on the catch but was around £10 a day. The "boss" was English but they never saw or met him, as they dealt exclusively with a "foreman" who was also Chinese but spoke English:

> "Most of them [other workers] were my *lao-xiang* [country men]. It was easier for us to talk with your *lao-xiang*; it was easier for us to communicate and get along. They didn't have status. They were just like me. We didn't have residential status … A foreman is normally someone who can speak some English, someone who has been here longer and understands English. They can speak English with the

real boss. The real boss is normally a Brit. He is the real
boss. Only his words count." (Hai, male, from China)

Those working within the enclave had differing, and in some cases
mixed, views about their experiences. On the positive side, enclaves
were a route to employment and could be safe and comfortable places
to work, due to friendships, shared language and culture. The negative
aspects of enclaves were the low pay, poor terms and conditions and the
feeling of being exploited, without recourse as a consequence of status.

The fact that it is possible to find work in a business owned by a co-
ethnic employer is significant, especially given the difficulties of finding
work in other places. The common link with employers is seen as a
crucial element in job search for those without status, as Zana (male,
Kurd from Turkey) observes when he says, "you might be a relative, a
friend or a friend's friend". Finding work through these networks in
ethnic enclave businesses means that constructed documents do not
have to be bought and used or other risks taken in relation to papers.
However, as Bahar points out, those working in such businesses do so
because they have no choice:

> "If there is someone working in a Turkish place, they
> definitely have a reason for that. Either they do not know
> English, or they are illegal, or they are not qualified for a
> proper job." (Bahar, female, from Turkey)

Similar observations were made about Bangladeshi and Chinese owned
businesses, where undocumented migrants stressed that their only
option was to work in a co-ethnic business. However, the advantage
of the enclave, in addition to languages spoken and not being scared,
was also that workers could offer mutual assistance to each other. In
short, the enclave could provide workers with a feeling of safety and
solidarity, which, for those living in fear of raids and deportation, was
a very real and important aspect of their everyday existence. Having
co-workers from the same ethnic group and the solidarity of friendships
was very important on a day-to-day basis, making work a more social
place. These friendships could outweigh some of the other limitations
and injustices of some enclave businesses, leading some to stay in jobs
in spite of relatively unfavourable terms and conditions, as Chow, who
had worked in a restaurant before having her baby, explains:

> "The longest one was the job working in the restaurant
> owned by the Malaysian Chinese. I stayed there for about

15 months. Actually I had wanted to leave earlier because the pay was low. I stayed there for so long partly because my close friends were also working there. I was happy working alongside my friends." (Chow, female, from China)

There was also a sense of ambivalence about the enclave as an acceptable workplace. Hasan (male, from Turkey), for example, worked in an off-licence owned by his uncle, and on the one hand had said that he would like to work "with foreigners" so he could improve his English, but on the other hand was also happy working in "a Turkish environment" simply because "you share more". This idea of being paid more, having better terms and conditions, learning English and having access to wider networks was all seen as a positive aspect of work outside of the enclave, although being undocumented, and for some the lack of English language, kept people within these micro and localised co-ethnic environments and made them more vulnerable in the workplace.

Relations in the workplace

As noted above, most interviewees worked within ethnic enclave businesses and so were in environments where most of their co-workers were from the same country of origin and/or ethnic group. This was particularly the case in restaurants. Arjin worked as a waitress and said that in her workplace all the staff – waitresses, bakers, cooks and cleaners – were from Turkey and the customers were "usually Turkish" (Arjin, female, Kurd from Turkey). In the restaurant where Fadi worked in the kitchen, he described the workers as being "other illegals and also some who are legal" and "all Bengali", although some were British Bengali. While Fadi knew three or four workers were "illegal" others did not know the status of co-workers, saying that it was not something that was discussed. Not all workplaces, even within the enclave, were homogeneous. Roni, who worked in a large off-licence owned by his in-laws, explained through the use of stereotypes the reasons why the owners employed two workers from Pakistan while the other eight workers were from Turkey:

"They needed people immediately and these people came first. Plus they also do not mind about the money they get, they do not question how much wage they will get. Employers always prefer those who work a lot and accept

to get less. They do not care if they are Turkish or not."
(Roni, male, Kurd from Turkey)

In construction and in some other industries that were ethnic-minority niches, such as cockle picking as noted earlier, a foreman or line-manager system operated, and so the owners were rarely on site. Working relationships with co-workers and managers were extremely variable, although not surprisingly they had a big impact on the everyday lives of workers. Positive working relationships were those that were supportive and based on trust, respect and decency. These could often be based on shared backgrounds, culture and language.

Jiyan, a Kurd from Turkey, worked as a cook and felt that his boss treated him well and that there was trust. The fact that they were both Kurds "sharing the same political views" was significant, but less so than the value, to the employer, of the work that he did. In short, regardless of their shared politics and heritage, he noted that if his work had been poor "the employer does not keep you there". Being a good worker was the bottom line and the most valued attribute, hence the reason why undocumented migrants make themselves indispensable in the workplace (Gomberg-Muñoz, 2010).

Negative and difficult workplace relationships were based on bullying, unfair treatment and other types of conflict, including those based on differing political positions and regional and/or linguistic differences. Some Kurds talked about conflict between Alevi and Sunni, others mentioned the solidarity with other Kurds and some experienced political divisions with Turkish people, as Cem describes:

> "The main problem was political differences. The owner was Turkish; he was a true nationalist one. I was not free to speak about Kurds, there was even another Kurd working in the kitchen. We could not speak in Kurdish, it was very depressing. You are escaping from the oppressive atmosphere of Turkey and get into a similar atmosphere even in Central London; Turkish migrants in London hate people like me." (Cem, male, Kurd from Turkey)

When Cem was asked why Turkish employers would employ him when they do not like Kurds, a stereotype based on Kurdish rural backgrounds was offered as the explanation:

> "if you work like a donkey, everybody would like to employ you. The people from Istanbul or other metropolises cannot

work like us. We as villagers are very hard working, used to hard conditions. He [employer] even once told me that your people [that is, Kurds] work very hard, we have to work very hard so that such people will ignore our ethnicity or status." (Cem, male, Kurd from Turkey)

Among undocumented migrants from China regional differences came into play, causing conflict among those with different hometown origins, as well as those from the mainland and Hong Kong, where the latter were more likely to be business owners and managers. According to Lok, people from Hong Kong, "look down upon Chinese mainlanders", and he went on to reaffirm his regional connections by saying, "Fujian people are *our people*. We speak the same language" (Lok, male, from China).

Regardless of the impact of other differences and beliefs, being undocumented does put people in a disadvantaged position, one that affects relations in the workplace, and also individual behaviour. Although not everyone disclosed their status to their employers, most people had done so, or it was obvious that they did not have legal status because of the work they were seeking or doing. Status was seen by many as a major determinant of their relationships in the workplace. According to Kadir, "the legals were treated differently" (male, from Bangladesh). This differential treatment could be from co-workers, but also managers and employers. Nevertheless, in describing the dynamics of Chinese restaurants some people focused on the relationship with the master chef, length of time in the UK and skill levels, rather than status. This was because it is not unusual for some of those working in restaurants to be without status:

"Working in the kitchen, [the] relationship with the master chef is very important, because he is normally the guy making decisions there. If you can't get on with the master chef, you'll be asked to pack your things in one or two weeks." (Jiang, male, from China)

While undocumented migrants for the most part tried to just do their work and not cause any problems or draw attention to themselves, employers could also use their status as a mechanism to keep them under control and passive about their situation. It could be a weapon used by employers to suppress workers, including in relation to pay.

"I was working for 12 hours with the same amount of money that I started. I was working for £180, six days. My friend at that time started to work in a restaurant for £240. I asked for an increase. He was not approving. I was asking them to make my working hours less if they did not want to make an increase, still nothing. One day he came to close me, put his arm to my shoulder and said '… you want an increase but do not forget that you are an illegal in this country'. He talked in a way of warning me or reminding me of my position." (Arjin, female, Kurd from Turkey)

The advantages of good relationships with employers

Relationships with the owner or direct boss were important in decision making and, just as they caused people to leave jobs, they were also a reason to stay, as some people enjoyed good working relations. Li, for instance, worked for a building contractor on a daily rate that he knew was quite low. While others had left for more money, he had stayed with the same boss because he was "a *xiangqin*", a close fellow villager. This connection was advantageous for Li because the boss provided him with relatively stable work and he felt secure. While good co-workers were those who helped out, treated workers fairly and with whom it was possible to chat and occasionally share a joke, good managers were seen as those who were nice to their workers, paid on time, didn't shout, could be trusted – often due to shared heritage – and did their share of work.

Adam (male, from Bangladesh) found his current work in a restaurant to be very good compared to other places simply because the employer "is very nice"' Similarly Nasar said, "he is nice to us and the pay is correct. He isn't ripping us off. He knows that I am illegal" (male, from Bangladesh). This experience contrasts to that of most others, as noted earlier in the chapter, who felt underpaid as a consequence of their status. Mujib was happy because he was paid every Sunday as soon as the shift finished. Not all employers paid workers on time and some had even withheld wages, so being paid on time and the right amount provided an element of stability. Tanveer said his employer was nice but he did not pay on time, and so workers had to keep asking for money. The employer would say, "I'll give it today, tomorrow, ok the day after …" (Tanveer, male, from Bangladesh), and for those without status there was nothing that they could do but wait. Lack of action, or what Welat (male, from Turkey) described as "submissive behaviour", was because people were terrified of losing their jobs.

For Rojda, a shared background with her employers was crucial to her everyday life at work. She was well aware that her pay was low, her hours long and expectations to stay at work unreasonable, but nevertheless she described them "as good to us" because they were from the same country and she said they "speak the same language; same culture; religion" (female, Kurd from Turkey). Like Rojda, Roni also talked favourably about his employer, while at the same time pointing out that pay was low. Roni also referred to the fact that the working relationship transcended the workplace, and this was something that a small minority referred to in terms of help from their employers. Occasionally employers had helped their workers in others areas of their lives, such as immigration, lending money or sorting out bureaucratic problems. Bahar, from Turkey, who worked as a hairdresser and had a young daughter, had been helped by both her work colleagues and her former employer, who allowed her to bring her daughter to the shop. She said her employer supported her a lot, "like a relative", helping her to get a nursery place for her daughter. The support outside of work did not transfer into monetary increases but nevertheless she was happy at work and would not have moved if the employer had kept the business running. Her relationship with her current employer was very different; he treated her well, she felt, simply because she brought in a "good amount of money".

In this section we have demonstrated variable relations at work and different types of conflicts and connections. Ultimately, however, and regardless of connections, workers felt that employers were most concerned with their productivity and the economics of the business. In our interviews with employers, they presented a more caring, supportive and philanthropic picture of themselves, which we explore in the next chapter. Relations at work were variable, although this is not surprising, as all workplaces differ. However, what was apparent was that it was the very small aspects of work that made jobs better, such as being able to share a joke or talk about home, some job security, being paid on time and not being shouted at.

Conclusion

In this chapter our focus has been on everyday work and working lives among undocumented migrants in London. We have shown the importance of social networks for job search, the limited sectors of employment and the predominance of restaurant and take-away work, mostly kitchen based, among those we interviewed. There was a gendered dimension to work in this sector, with women more likely to be 'front of the house' waiting tables or on counters, especially if they had English language skills. Terms and conditions of work were largely standardised, although there were opportunities, albeit subject to a glass ceiling, to acquire skills and, in so doing, to move from the least skilled work, which was often manual labour, to more skilled work within both kitchens and construction. Hours were long, pay was low and there were no holiday or sick pay provisions. Work was precarious and people were asked to leave without notice, meaning that there was little or no security on a day-to-day basis.

Workplaces were often homogenous, although even within these seemingly homogenous workplaces within the ethnic enclave there were divisions and conflicts based on religion, politics, ethnicity and region. There were also allegiances based on commonalities, and these were valued. Hierarchies came into play around immigration status and the relational aspects of work, in terms of those with and those without status. However, there were more subtle divisions based on jobs, length of time in the UK and language. While this chapter has focused on undocumented migrants, in the next chapter we turn to migrant employers and consider their experiences and perspectives.

FIVE

Ethnic enclave entrepreneurs

"I've been raided before, a fine, what to do? ... They think we want to employ illegals, we don't want to but we cannot help it. If nobody works for you, you have to close down, lose all our money. That's the reason. You think people want to employ illegals? But we're not intending, [it's immigration rules] forced us to employ. That's the reason. The fine is ok, 'oh, one worker, you have a fine!' Whatever, you have a fine, they want money, that's all. They want money." (Tan, male employer, from China)

Tan was born in China and has been in the UK for 12 years, having arrived with the intention of setting up a small restaurant business. Above, he expresses the views of many of the employers we interviewed. They knew and feared immigration raids but felt that they had few alternatives – whether, like Tan, because they could not find workers or, as with many of the interviewees, because there were other imperatives that required them to employ those without documents. In this chapter we explore some of the dilemmas and experiences of what Zhou terms as 'enclave entrepreneurs' who are employers 'bounded by co-ethnicity, co-ethnic social structures and location' (2004: 1042).

Drawing on the North American sociological literature, we have used the term 'ethnic enclave entrepreneur' to describe those businesses that employ co-ethnic workers and that are more likely to be clustered within ethnic enclaves, which are areas consisting of migrant groups concentrated in a particular spatial area, serving predominantly, although not exclusively, their own ethnic market (Portes, 1981; Portes and Bach, 1985; Light et al, 1994; Logan et al, 2003; Zolin et al, 2014). Entrepreneurship may be an option for some migrants, where social networks facilitate the construction of small-scale enterprises (Waldinger et al, 1990; Chaudhry and Crick, 2004; Wahlbeck, 2007; Kitching, Smallbone and Athayde, 2009; Bloch and McKay, 2015), and those whom we interviewed had made use of those opportunities and, particularly in their first period of entrepreneurship, this could result in a focus on businesses that specialised in the provision of services to their network communities. However, for some this meant being trapped in an ever-narrowing market, increasingly crowded out by new entrants. Consequently, some of the interviewees were only just surviving financially, or indeed had already experienced business failures. In fact, among the 24 employers interviewed, six had either experienced business failure in the past or had started up their business as a result of the failure of the previous business owner.

This chapter provides insights into the experiences, businesses and business practices of minority-ethnic employers from migrant backgrounds. Although we review their routes into business, our main focus is on their employment practices, including the recruitment of workers; the impact of immigration controls, including sanctions on those practices, where relevant; the reasons for employing undocumented migrants; and the ways in which ethnicity and perceptions of workers based on stereotypes informed those practices. Motives for employing undocumented migrants are more complex than might apply to non-minority ethnic employers. Specifically, we discuss the obligations of family, kinship and geography; the sense of political solidarity and the need for trust within the employment relationship. The employers' emphasis on trust implies not just that they see co-ethnic workers as more 'trustworthy' but, equally, that some cannot ascribe trust to workers from other groups, perhaps because their own experiences of discrimination and poor treatment have made them cautious about entering into relationships with those who are not co-nationals or co-ethnic (Levie, Smallbone and Minnitti, 2009).

At the time of fieldwork interviews, eight of our 24 employers were open about employing undocumented migrants, and an additional nine no longer did so but had in the past. This means that, in total, 17 out of 24 were open about employing or having employed undocumented migrants. Some had established businesses relatively soon after arriving in the UK, while for others entrepreneurship had come at a much later stage in their careers. The relative success of some businesses had meant that entrepreneurs had established management structures that did not require them to be as present in the workplace as in the early days of their business, and some therefore clearly enjoyed a better work/life balance than in the past. Uddin, who was a male employer from Bangladesh, for example, described his two managers in the restaurant that he owned as running the business "and I float around".

The economic performance of migrant entrepreneurs, a heterogeneous group, needs to take account of key characteristics such as country of origin, age, cohort, first or second generation and education (Sahin, Nijkamp and Suzuki, 2014), and indeed we are conscious of the need to avoid ascribing characteristics to ethnicity or to the ethnic enclave, where they might arguably be a consequence of entrepreneurship itself (Barrett et al, 2012). Our interviews with employers confirm the diversity of circumstances and motivations that have led them to become entrepreneurs. There is indeed no one characteristic that predetermines whether someone adopts entrepreneurship as either a survival strategy or a route for advancement. However, there are a number of factors that combine to make the choice of entrepreneurship more likely or, indeed, inevitable. The chapter then moves on to look at how ethnic enclave employers manage their businesses, in the light of government policies on undocumented migration and in a context of skill shortages and low profit margins, and also how they justify their own entrepreneurial activities. While the enclave provides a measure of protection it may also have negative outcomes where it results in entrepreneurs being trapped within the enclave (Sequeira and Rasheed, 2006: 367; Clark, 2015). Moreover, as Jones et al (2015) note, minority-ethnic entrepreneurs experience 'skewed sectoral distribution … limited access to mainstream finance, and a lack of recognition of their role in the economy' (2015: 3).

While this chapter draws only on a small sample of 24 employers (see Table 1.2) and cannot therefore provide the quantitative data which Jones et al (2014) argue is lacking, we believe nevertheless that the qualitative nature of the data offers in-depth insights into the decisions among this diverse group to opt for entrepreneurship and about their business practices.

A choice of entrepreneurship or a survival choice

Levels of self-employment can, over time, vary between different ethnic groups and between men and women (Clark and Drinkwater, 2000; Levie, 2007; Levie, Smallbone and Minnitti, 2009). Place of birth is significant, with self-employment levels generally lower across the board among the UK-born than among migrants. The numbers that are self-employed have reduced among Indian and Chinese ethnic groups, due to greater access to paid employment opportunities (Clark and Drinkwater, 2007). Pakistani and Bangladeshi men are most likely to be self-employed and are concentrated in retail, restaurants and take-away shops and taxi driving (Clark and Drinkwater, 2007).

There are different reasons why people become self-employed or entrepreneurs, but for migrants there can be the additional factors of barriers to progression and exclusion from some parts of the labour market. According to Clark, high rates of self-employment among some groups 'cannot simply be taken as a sign of economic health and may, rather, be symptomatic of discrimination by the majority community' (2015: 8).

Knight (2015) has suggested that entrepreneurial migrants are differentiated from non-entrepreneurial migrants in relation to their acquisition, in the destination country, of both human and social capital. Moreover, migrant entrepreneurs have a higher tolerance of risk, although Hormiga and Bolivar-Cruz (2014) make this assessment by contrasting entrepreneurial migrants with their non-entrepreneurial co-ethnics. It could be that if a comparison was made between entrepreneurs generally and non-entrepreneurs, the former (regardless of ethnicity) would be more risk tolerant.

Limited opportunities in the labour market, or 'blocked mobility' (Valdez, 2008: 967), are one reason for choosing self-employment, but there are other reasons too. Where professional qualifications obtained prior to migration are not recognised in the country of residence, self-employment can offer an alternative to the less-skilled waged employment that might be available. Among those whom we interviewed, while routes into business were varied, for most it was a way of circumventing blocked mobility or the lack of opportunities. Aldrich and Waldinger have suggested that entrepreneurship is based on one or more of three components: 'opportunity structures, group characteristics, and ethnic strategies' (1990: 114). Reflecting on the first of these, in relation to the migrant employers in our study, four had not been able to find suitable work in the areas in which they had trained and qualified, and so business acquisition was not as a consequence of network utilisation, nor was it an aspiration, but rather a series of sometimes connected and sometimes unconnected events that made business acquisition the most effective option, something that others have noted too (Jones, Mascarenhas-Keyes and Ram, 2012).

Co-ethnic networks provide the often-essential financial capital to enable a business start-up (Chaudhry and Crick, 2004; Kitching, Smallbone and Athayde, 2009) as well as the expertise and emotional support that enable new entrepreneurs to establish their businesses and to succeed (Chaudhry and Crick, 2004; Wahlbeck, 2007; Kitching, Smallbone and Athayde, 2009; Bloch and McKay, 2015). Of the 24 employers we interviewed, eight could be described as coming from 'business-oriented' backgrounds and having always intended to set up a business, thus falling into Aldrich and Waldinger's second component, 'group characteristics'. Six had a family background in business, which included our one non-migrant employer, who had inherited the business, or were in partnership with another family member, and this provided a number of advantages, particularly at the beginning of their business career. Human capital, in the form of knowledge of the business (Valdez, 2008; Smallbone, Kitching and Athayde, 2010), may have provided specific opportunities that would enable them to acquire the skills needed to run a business, such as knowledge of how systems work, of how to manage staff and budgets and of how to deal with public institutions. In some cases interviewees had positively grasped the opportunities presented. Ali, who was our one UK-born interviewee and was a woman of Bangladeshi heritage, went into the business her grandfather had set up, as it offered her flexibility and also meant that for her, as a practising Muslim woman, it was easier to work in a mixed-gender environment, as she was working in the office with her relatives.

Last, falling into Aldrich and Waldinger's third component – 'ethnic strategy' – was Demir, a male employer originally from Northern Cyprus. Demir had been working in the hairdressing salon that he eventually bought for just six months when the owners wanted to sell and offered him the business. He scraped together money from family and other loans to buy the business. It had not been his goal but he was, in his own words, "young, determined, ambitious" and he took the chance when it presented itself.

It is clear from the narratives of the employers we interviewed that there were variable routes into entrepreneurship and no one experience. In the next section we explore employers' strategies towards the employment of workers and the impact among some, albeit often limited, of sanctions and raids.

Current and changing attitudes to employing workers

A number of the employers had acquired established businesses, along with the staff that had been working for the business at the time of acquisition. This meant that initially it was not they who had made decisions related either to the ethnicity or the immigration status of the workforce, but the previous owner or manager. Given the fairly rapid turnover in the ownership of many micro businesses, the acquisition of an existing staff pool is probably a constant feature of employment in sectors that consist of marginally financed businesses.

As individuals started to organise their businesses, they made changes in relation to the size of their workforce, based upon whether the business was growing or retrenching. However, the need to make such changes, in particular to take on workers where there were short-term seasonal peaks, led some to recruit undocumented migrants because they were the most flexible workers, as they did not have to be given the same rights as other workers. Ahmed, a male employer from Bangladesh, was currently employing eight people but stated that he sometimes had "to take some more people to help us" and it was this short-term or immediate need for staff that might affect the choices over whom to employ and whether or not to risk employing workers without documents. Some employers used agencies to find workers, and in most cases these job agencies were local and were focused on supplying workers from a particular ethnic group to a particular trade. However, this was not the preferred route to workers for most employers, as the informality of word of mouth referrals was both free and preferred.

Wahlbeck (2007) noted that flexibility, trust and perceptions of reliability were essential markers for employers in their choice of workers. We also found that employers expressed the need for certain worker characteristics. In the restaurant trade they needed workers who, in their view, could deliver consistent food and service, so as to meet customers' expectations. A particular work ethic was also important so that, as Hasan, who was a male employer from Bangladesh commented, if he did not like someone's work ethic he would simply "get rid of them", and this was said without any reference to the need for procedures for dismissal or to the requirements of employment law. But within this context of employer power, there was also a strongly advanced view that authenticity, knowledge and experience required that key staff at least, and the chef in particular in restaurant and take-away work, shared ethnicity with the employer and a heritage of the food being cooked.

In the hair and beauty sector, appearance was an essential requirement, according to all three employers. Demir stated that a requirement for good English was also essential, as was the ability to interact with clients, although this did not only mean interacting in English, since many clients spoke other languages. For Sindi, who was a Kurdish male employer who owned a supermarket, 'looks' or grooming were important, as he explained in the following way:

> "Looks are important for me. Some people are very messy, dirty. Even when you pass by them, they smell. I do not want such people in the shop. I also want respectable people. They have to be good; nice to the customers."

Other characteristics, which were highlighted as essential, included being a "good" worker, which for Uddin, a male employer from

Bangladesh, extended beyond work, to being a "good person", however that might be defined – and that was even more important than finding someone who had particular skills. His attitude was as follows:

> "find people firstly, who fit that role and if they have a little less expertise I would train them myself, I would bring them up to scratch."

For Wang, a male employer from China, it was the worker's "character", which he felt he could assess simply by observing, that for him was important. Whether individuals were "honest" was also a characteristic that was expressed as essential. Honesty could, in the view of Wu, also from China, be assessed through "just a feeling", which he would then test through a probationary period and if the feeling was not confirmed the individual would be summarily dismissed. Even just knowing that it was the "right person" was enough, even though there was no clear definition as to what such an attribute might consist of. Often, of course, these rather nebulous characteristics were coded terms for familiarity or shared ethnic identity.

Employment decision making

For employers, there were a number of factors that influenced their employment decisions, including in relation to employing undocumented migrants. They can be grouped as follows:

- skill shortages or general worker shortages that meant that employers saw their options as either closure or as hiring those without documents;
- obligations – mainly to family but also to close friends – that required them to offer work, regardless of the individual's status, as well as human or political obligations that overrode any concerns about risks to them or the business;
- the importance of trust in the employment relationship and the expression of this through national identities.

In response to one or more of these factors and in the context of immigration rules, employers had revised their employment practices, taking account of other factors outside of their immediate control, such as the economic crisis and the unwillingness of the next generation to go into the business. As they expressed it, the situation they faced at the time of the interviews in late 2012 and early 2013 was very different from that of a decade earlier, when finding staff had been relatively easy. Changes in immigration law had had the effect of making those without documents more needed than before, particularly for those operating in a business that would be at risk if there were staff shortages. The next sections will explore each of the factors affecting employment decisions in more detail.

Responding to worker shortages

Changes in immigration law had resulted in major staff shortages, particularly in the restaurant sector, which until 2006 had been able to recruit directly, at least to key jobs like chefs, under a sector-based scheme. A number of employers made reference to the problems they faced in finding staff and related these difficulties directly to the abolition of the scheme, which had previously enabled them to source workers from their countries of origin.

Of course the reasons why some jobs are more difficult to fill are also linked to the terms and conditions that apply, and in the sectors where these employers operated these were generally poor. Amedi, a male Kurd from Turkey who owned a small repair garage stated that it was not easy to find people, especially skilled people, because his company could pay only the minimum wage. Alternatively, and particularly in relation to the Chinese community, the view was expressed that the growth of the economy in China, together with the tightening of immigration controls here, had meant that it simply was "not attractive to come and work in this country any more" (Peng, male employer, from China).

Employers could not rely on the next generation to replace them in the business and this was seen as a problem for the future. While teenage and adult children helped out while living at home and during the holiday periods, it was clear that there was no or little interest in the businesses. Some of the employers we interviewed referred to this as a problem for the future because their businesses were not viewed as the types of business that their children aspired to enter, and indeed their own aspirant disposition, which had led them into business, had in turn infected their children with an ambition to aim higher, as Hasan explains:

> "They'll encourage their sons to get themselves a degree or whatever and once he's got that he doesn't want to come back to the restaurant." (Hasan, male employer, from Bangladesh)

Earlier in the chapter we referred to the importance of place of birth in determining the propensity for self-employment (Clark and Drinkwater, 2007). In particular we noted that those born in the UK were less likely to be self-employed than the migrant cohort. The impact of place of birth and education on choices was something that our interviewees were also aware of and they noted how it distinguished their children's ambitions from their own. Zhou, a woman from China, provides an example of these inter-generational differences and also of the gendered patterns of business enterprise among smaller Chinese restaurants (Chaudhry and Crick, 2004). Zhou first set up a take-away business with her husband as a means of securing their future and that of their children. While her husband took care of the kitchen, Zhou was responsible for the counter work, taking orders and dealing with customers, and as her children got older they too helped in the shop. In the following quote Zhou explains how the experiences and ambitions of her UK born daughters differ from her own, given their greater options and connections outside of the co-ethnic community:

> "I try to get, like, my daughters to help me some, a few hours over the weekend, but they are not really enjoying this kind of work, you know in the catering … this generation is different than my generation because my children are growing up here, they've got a bit of English influence in everything and they've got more – more choice to go outside and find a job, any job if they can. But when we came in here … we're so small, always we would stay inside the Chinese community. So that's why I don't think they'd like to do this." (Zhou, female employer from China)

Obligations and expressions of solidarity

The recruitment of workers could be complex and employers did not simply hire undocumented workers because they had experienced staff shortages; in a few cases they also made the point that their obligations to family would trump any concern about breaching immigration law and being fined. Thus, while Mahmood, a male employer from Bangladesh, stated that he would not employ those without documents, he tempered this with a comment that if it was to help a member of his family, he would do so. He described it as being very difficult for business people when family arrived, as the obligation to find work for them was paramount. For many, there were always going to be circumstances where risks had to be taken, especially where they involved employing members of the family who were undocumented. Mahmood explained that two of his relatives had needed work and that it was his obligation as a family member to help by giving them work, even though they had no documents.

What employers would do would be to adapt and consider how they could reduce risks, as Peng stated: "you don't want to take any chances, unless you are so desperate that you are willing to take the risk with the law". Here he reflects on the changes in practice in relation to undocumented migrants:

> "in the old days ... it was quite common to employ [undocumented migrants]; since the enforcement of the law, and let's make this clear, it's always been illegal anyway not to comply with – so as soon as everyone realised that that was being enforced more stringently than in the past, and yeah so we just have to adapt to the situation really. I mean, these days if you turn up to a restaurant and you have no documents people just don't want to know, certainly our ones anyway, that's the number one thing we ask for."
> (Peng, male employer, from China)

Almost as important, and depending on the individual's own political perspective and experiences of migration, was the expression of solidarity towards those without documents. Some employers empathised for political or humane reasons and were able to justify their employment decisions on the basis of one or the other. In some cases this also allowed them to avoid consideration of the terms of employment that they were offering but, although a minority did make it clear that they did not seek to exploit those without documents by paying them less, this was not necessarily expressed by all interviewees.

Serhati, a male employer who was a Kurd from Turkey and had been an asylum seeker in the past, was one of the most politically expressive of those whom we interviewed. For him it was clear that, politically, it was the right thing to do, to offer work to those who were in difficulties, particularly if they shared a political ideology. In answer to the question as to whether the sanctions regime had changed his employment practices, he responded as follows:

> "No, it won't change because you know [...] you can't just say 'you are illegal, I'm not going to give you a job', I can't say that. I would rather pay £5,000 fine if it comes to it, but you cannot sack the person because he's illegal,

because I've been there, I just can't say it." (Serhati, male employer, Kurd from Turkey)

His position was not unique, particularly among the more politically aware Kurdish employers, whose belief in solidarity was evident. Sindi, for instance, another Kurdish male employer, who owned a supermarket, provided a number of examples of where his political or indeed humanitarian position left him with no alternative but to offer work to someone without documents. For him, importantly, this sense of solidarity did not apply only to undocumented workers of Kurdish origin but to anyone who was oppressed. Jaf, a female employer and a Kurd from Turkey, operated similarly, but also displayed a humane response that caused her to hire those without documents and she spoke of a woman whom she had hired because she had children and needed to find work to support them.

Most of the employers expressed a preference for co-ethnic workers. In the case of the Kurdish employers, this was informed by an obligation to demonstrate solidarity: "I know how it feels being one of the others and now I'm given a chance to support my people, why not?" (Jaf, female employer, Kurd from Turkey). Her philosophy and that of Yildiz are summed up as follows:

> "Being a good citizen is not as important as being myself; that is what I am. Government is not going to lose so much money if I say little things, little lies, you know, but someone is going to change their lifestyle, that's more important to me than actually me being a good citizen. Because I pay already so much tax anyway." (Jaf, female employer, Kurd from Turkey)

> "But you think sometimes, what they gonna do? If I told them just go, you can't work with me and other places destroyed. What they do? They can't take any benefits." (Yildiz, male employer, from Turkey)

Particularly for those who had themselves experienced life on the margins as asylum seekers and/or held political ideals that were opposed to tough immigration controls, there remained a need to demonstrate solidarity with the most oppressed. But there were also other, more practical concerns, such as the fear that if individuals did not have access to work they could become dangerous.

"Yes I employed some illegal people. I just want to give you one example. One guy has been living in this country for 11 years; he still does not have documents. Not any organisations can help him. He had a daughter here, she was born ... after she is six or seven, they [authorities] also did not register her to the school. That guy [undocumented one] has to pay her to the school. That guy [undocumented], if you see the house, you will be shocked; one-bedroom flat above a restaurant. All the mess, dirt or the smoke of the restaurant is coming to the flat. No one can live there due to the bad smell ... and he does not have documents. Not any organisations can help him. He had a daughter here, she was born ... after she is six or seven? I know [if] somebody catches me, I have to pay. What is going to happen to him? There are lots of people like that. They start to do something bad, drug. If you keep him like this, he will steal something. He will start to do something very bad. I also know him. He is very strong guy. He can beat up two, three people at the same time. If you do not give him a job he at night catches me or somebody else and takes their money; he does not want to do such things, he wants to work like a human, like anybody." (Sindi, male employer, Kurd from Turkey)

In this situation family, political and personal obligations also came as a consequence of the economic crisis that was restricting the options available. Although the economy was rarely given as the reason, it was apparent that in most of the businesses staffing was the main outlay, so that reducing labour costs was the obvious route to business survival.

Balancing immigration rules, business needs and sanctions

Decisions about whom to employ and when were influenced by the interactions of the considerations highlighted above and the immigration rules and sanctions regime. While, as noted earlier, eight said that they were employing undocumented migrants at the time of their interview, which was fewer than had been doing so in the past, there was an awareness of the risks of raids and fines, but there were also views on how to minimise the risk. Chen, the owner of a restaurant and a supermarket business, stated that the fear of having a visit from the UK Border Agency (UKBA) meant that he did not employ anyone without papers – although at the same time he indicated that it was possible to get away with employing the undocumented, provided the numbers were small:

> "You see on our pay-roll we have to declare them, every single person. If you are a dodgy person they will tell you, if one or two. If too many, they will raid you." (Chen, male employer, from China)

Employers were mindful of the consequences of being caught in breach of regulations and most had informal procedures in place for document checks. In some cases these procedures had been introduced in response to the imposition of employer sanctions. Ahmed described the procedures he had in place in his restaurant as follows:

> "I normally take [a] passport copy, along with visa proof and all this. And, you know, I have to file, I keep it on file for Inland Revenue, so I will do that. So I keep these two documents on our file. So, normally I don't want to take a risk because if you take a risk now they – they charge you. For each employee that's not allowed to work in this country they will charge you up to £10,000. I have friend next to [a mosque in London], he was fined £30,000, three employees." (Ahmed, male employer, from Bangladesh)

Rahman, also a male employer from Bangladesh, who owned a take-away shop, explained how he would check prospective workers' documents, but this was difficult to do in cases when workers were needed urgently. Employers also expressed concern that they simply did not know enough to assess the documents they were presented with; but, as Rami (male employer, Kurd from Turkey) noted, provided that a worker presented him with a national insurance number he had no need to make any further enquiries.

According to Uddin (male employer, from Bangladesh), sanctions have "changed our attitude towards employing people". For others, the sheer size of the fine was a deterrent. This did not mean that they did not employ undocumented workers; there were other imperatives, as already discussed, that meant that they would take certain risks, but they would try to minimise these where possible, explaining that "we just have to take risks, and that's it" (Yildiz, male employer, Kurd from Turkey). Similarly Sindi, also Kurdish, openly stated that half of his relatives, who also were employers, took risks and employed undocumented migrants and that in his own case, while he could not completely avoid the risk, he had adopted a strategy to reduce it by employing fewer undocumented migrants than in the past. In fact he was not employing any undocumented migrants at the time of the interview.

At one simple level, being raided was "bad for business", as Wu (male employer, from China) who owned a gadget and computer-repair shop, put it. Some employers either had been raided by the police and UKBA or knew of other employers who had been. A Chinese healthcare company had employed two doctors who had been refused permission to work by the Home Office and claimed that it had "learnt lessons, so lots of admin work, paper work, money, everything involved" (Yin, female employer, from China).

Hasan's Indian take-away business had been raided in the past. He was angry and frustrated that someone had reported him to the authorities and that he had had no recourse and had been unable even to find out who had reported him. His view was that restaurants and take-away shops were more likely to be raided at weekends and this was a period to avoid having undocumented workers on the premises. Another way was to balance the risk in relation to the type of business or in relation to the skill shortages that the employer was experiencing. They might pay undocumented workers less, making employment of the undocumented more attractive to them. Alternatively, they might evaluate the sector they operated in based on their knowledge of businesses that had been targeted and conclude that is was unlikely that they would be raided.

Excluding undocumented workers from the registers of employees and thus treating these workers as if they did not exist was another strategy, as was paying workers in cash so that there was no record of their employment. While in theory this could be a strategy that helped to mask certain employment practices, in reality, when businesses are raided their documents, rotas and the individuals on the premises are carefully scrutinised, so such strategies may well not be effective. However, paying in cash did make it easier for those workers without a bank account and could also make it easier for the employer. For some employers, the raid was not just an attack on them and their business but they were also genuinely concerned as to the fate of their undocumented workers:

> "We once been raided by the Home Office so I felt that if I had somebody I would have been very sad if somebody been arrested in my workplace, not only work, I mean, of course I would have been upset if I'd paid £5,000 fine,

but also for those people who had to work because if they are illegal here somehow they have to make their living." (Serhati, male employer, Kurd from Turkey)

Awareness and an understanding of the rules was evident among those whom we interviewed, but equally there were conflicting imperatives faced by employers that affected their positions as well as their recruitment strategies. In the next section we focus on recruitment and the ways in which informal networks, based on trust, are preferred.

Looking for workers, relying on trust

Most of the employers we interviewed relied on personal networks when looking for staff and so there was often no need for formal recruitment practices because employees were just there and available. According to Peng (male employer, from China), "there is no recruitment as such, there's no mechanism for it, you just go along with it". Employers within the ethnic enclave were part of a wider community network and could operationalise those networks quickly and effectively if and when workers were needed. Rahman, from Bangladesh, who owned a take-away shop, explained that when he needed a worker he just called relatives or friends and asked, "do you know anybody to work here?" Using these informal approaches of community networks and existing workers to find new recruits had the effect of replicating the characteristics of workers and the homogeneity of the workplace environment.

Some had used other methods of recruiting workers, such as advertising in co-ethnic newspapers, using local employment agencies and taking on people who cold called at their businesses. However, on the whole, recruitment involved reliance on prior knowledge of workers, on having worked with them in the past or on finding them through word of mouth. In a few cases employers made reference to contacting government run Job Centres or private employment agencies when they had immediate staff needs. Most often when employers used agencies they went to ethnic specific agencies, similar to the ones that undocumented migrants had signposted as their route into employment (see Chapter Four). Mahmood, the owner of a clothing shop, had used agencies to find workers because it was difficult to locate female Bengali workers and these were the preferred workers for his type of business, given his clientele. Rahman, while stating a preference for workers who were recommended by friends and family to staff his take-away shop, indicated that if necessary he would use an agency. Likewise, Ahmed (male employer, from Bangladesh) said in relation to staffing his restaurant that he would "rather call these agencies, they will come, they will [send] somebody who is willing to work. Obviously they will check the documents". There are two points to highlight here. First, that Ahmed did not have confidence in state Job Centres to find workers for him. Second, that the advantage to him in using a job agency was that it would have to take responsibility for document checks which he thought would absolve him of any need to act. Peng was critical of routes that were not informal because of the quality of the workers:

> "I know the normal channels like Job Centres, adverts etcetera, you get all sorts turning up and it's just a waste of time most of it. So we mostly rely on personal references." (Peng, male employer, from China)

Newspaper adverts were referred to by 10 employers, but only one of these was Bangladeshi, whereas four were Chinese and five were Turkish/Kurdish/Cypriot. For Yildiz, who needed hairdressers, advertising in specific newspapers guaranteed that he would find workers who spoke Turkish, which reflected the language needs of his customers. Zhou, a female employer from China, found that Chinese newspapers were the right route for finding students to work in her restaurant, which, given that it was not located in a London borough with a significant Chinese population, was a way of reaching out to find Chinese workers; Wu, from China, owned a computer shop and found workers through adverts in his shop window. Conversely, Ali, a female employer of Bangladeshi heritage, the owner of a undertaking business, made it clear that adverts were not a suitable way of recruiting to that business – "it's never been like that, we don't recruit like that" – implying that knowing potential recruits in advance was essential. In fact all the workers in her business were either family members or workers whom she described as being "like family". Employers generally wanted assurances as to whom they were employing, and so employing someone they knew or someone who was known and trusted by someone they knew was seen as the safest approach. Uddin speaks of the process of staffing his business:

> "Because I worked in the restaurant a few years I made some impression, and made some friends and made some colleagues, made a mark. So I was able to rely on people to get me staff, in fact when I did open in fact it was one

of my colleagues who was a chef, was a good chef from London, so I invited him and he joined me because – not because it was a restaurant in [place], but genuinely because it was my restaurant. So that's how it was. And then he would look for other one, and I would get another waiter, he would find another one. That's how – there wasn't any agencies or anything, we could go and look for staff, it was just pure word of mouth, phoning around your friends and colleagues that you know ... I was a good employer, not just paying good money but being respectable, being caring, however you put it ... this feedback helped me to encourage people to join me." (Uddin, male employer, from Bangladesh)

Some did make reference to individuals cold calling at their business premises looking for work. Generally they indicated that this was not a route to hiring that they were comfortable with, mainly because there was a concern that individuals might not have documents or they had insufficient knowledge of them to permit trust, and from those who were undocumented, employers required an even higher level of trust. There were some exceptions, such as Sindi, who is Turkish and had offered work to a Pakistani man simply because he had come into his business so many times looking for work and he felt he should be given the chance.

Ethnicity, nationality and gender as core characteristics

For the Chinese and Bangladeshi employers, their selections were not expressed as actions of solidarity as much as the need to work with people with whom they shared elements of ethnic identity, although within this there was also a racialised notion about what constituted a good worker and who had the necessary skills and training for the work. For example, in Zhou's businesses – a restaurant and take-away shop – she preferred to employ Chinese workers who spoke Cantonese, her first language. Juxtaposed with these choices were sometimes negative stereotypes of other workers who were not co-nationals, co-ethnic or co-linguistic. According to Zue (male employer, from China), for example, who owned a construction firm, "English people are so lazy ... having tea every day and thus losing [us] money". Tan, who is referring to non-Chinese, explained that they did not possess the necessary skills for restaurant work:

"they [non-Chinese people] cannot work Chinese restaurant, not saying we don't employ the local, the local they cannot do it. They cannot write Chinese." (Tan, male employer, from China)

The language needs of businesses reflect either the client base or the languages used by staff to communicate, as Peng explained:

"It is true that for our, the Chinese restaurants, there's only so many jobs that you can give to non-Chinese-speaking people … the communication can be a problem in the kitchen; I mean you're talking about mostly East Europeans who are allowed to work in this country. But I mean, it just so happens, so we don't actually employ a lot of non-Chinese, not because we don't want to but because in reality once you start employing them they don't achieve the same performance as a Chinese person. And it certainly would create a bit of difficulty in communication in the workplace. That's not their fault but it's just reality. So, in terms of waiting staff, we do employ other nationalities. It's just a job." (Peng, male employer, from China)

Other employers also made a distinction between waiting staff and kitchen staff in terms of their skills and ethnicity. Chen (male employer, from China) was unusual because he employed non-Chinese workers. He referred to employing Central and East European workers, stating, "I can rely on Hungarian and Polish, they have got muscle", but again this selection evidenced stereotyping. Bangladeshi employers relied almost entirely on Bangladeshi workers. Mahmood needed his workers to be from the Sylheti region to allow them to interact with his customers, 95% of whom, according to him, came from that region. For Uddin there was logic in all of his staff being co-ethnic, as he explained:

"It's not a preference, it's just as it happens that way. Not just me, every restaurant is like that, and it makes sense as well because, although I always think you don't really need language, body language and eye expressions can get you out of most of the things, but knowing the same language and everything, it does work, does help each other." (Uddin, male employer, from Bangladesh)

For Hasan it was a shared knowledge of food, mainly acquired from a shared Bangladeshi national identity, that dictated his employment needs:

> "If I wanted a creative chef, I can't have an Englishman as a creative chef. The reason being, it's not that I'm saying he won't be able to do the job, it's like I could turn round to my chef and say 'oh chef, do you remember when we was a kid we used to have something from this fruit back home? Why don't we try making that?' I don't have to explain to him what the fruit is, what the – how it was done back home." (Hasan, male employer, from Bangladesh)

Nearly all of the employers identified their own workforce through the descriptors of nationality, whether referring to their own national origin or that of others. Thus, not only did they identify co-ethnic workers by nationality, but also other nationals. They might refer to employing a "Polish" person or an "Italian". Thus ethnicity and nationality were constant features in their employment discourse. When Serhati first opened his restaurant all of the staff were Kurdish, but today he describes his restaurant kitchen as follows:

> "In the kitchen he speaks Russian, he speaks Bulgarian, he speaks some Turkish, his English is ok, and we have a Bangladeshi boy, his English is fine. And we had a Turkish man, he didn't speak any English. We had another Bulgarian, he was speaking very good English. It changed. But in the last year we had a Greek girl, she was friend of mine, and we had a Romanian girl, she speaks about eight languages, she studies here and she's – it's brilliant, you know, she's 25 and speaks eight languages." (Serhati, male employer, Kurd from Turkey)

Demir (male employer, from Northern Cyprus) employed an Italian who also spoke Spanish, while another employee spoke Russian and Czech, enabling him deal with a multilingual clientele in his hairdressing salon. Knowledge of the clients' languages was obviously more essential in hairdressing than in restaurant kitchens, and in his interview Demir talked about how the London locality where his business was situated had changed ethnically, resulting in different languages among his staff. When he had first taken over the business, Turkish had been a language requirement, as the area was rapidly changing from an Orthodox Jewish area into an area of new migrants from Turkey and Cyprus. Now other languages were required and this was reflected among his staff.

However, for most of the employers, particularly those with restaurants, an ability to converse in their first language was more important, especially where the employer was not confident in English and preferred to use their first language when talking with staff. Language was indeed often as great a barrier for employers as for workers; for example, Rami, who was Kurdish, expressed his frustration at his limited English vocabulary, which meant that he could not give the names of all of the items he was selling in his shop. Some employers required that some staff also spoke English. Waitresses, for example, were normally expected to do so, and we saw in Chapter Four how this resulted in worker hierarchies. And, as noted above, many workplaces were changing; in relation to the Turkish interviewees, the non-availability of Turkish/Kurdish staff meant that they had to recruit from other migrant groups, so that gradually the common language was moving to English.

Most of the businesses were also gender segregated, some having clear gender divisions for particular jobs, and employers spoke of their workforce in gendered terms, ascribing particular abilities by gender. According to Reza (male employer, from Bangladesh), who owned a laundry, the "presser should be a man, this is good for the business".

Working conditions – the employer's perspective

In Chapter Four we focused on the terms and conditions of work from the perspectives of undocumented migrants. It is not our aim to explore the contradictions between what employers were saying and what undocumented migrants told us. Here we limit ourselves to presenting the workplace through the eyes of the employer. Employers generally described the work environment in a favourable light and identified themselves as good employers, sometimes expressing their actions as benevolent or paternalistic. Sahin (male employer, from Turkey), for example, described himself as "a good employer", while Zhou (female employer, from China) stated that she liked to "try to keep the staff as happy as possible". According to Demir, in relation to his hairdressing business:

> "I always run my business like a family business. I'm very attached with my staff. And before I employ them anyway I talk to them and I tell them like, 'I am like their

father, brother, everything'." (Demir, male employer, from Northern Cyprus)

The businesses that the employers owned varied in size from one employing just four persons to another employing 450. Where we were provided with the number of staff, and omitting the one very large employer, the average was around 15–20. Many of the businesses were open six or seven days a week, from early morning until late at night, and workers had long shifts, of between 10 and 14 hours. The long working hours meant that hourly pay was almost always very low. Some employers were open in speaking about the pay that they offered, while others were more reticent. Tovi, of Kurdish background, stated that although everyone got paid in cash she did not pay less than the national minimum wage, although there were differentials depending on the jobs they did, with kitchen assistants on the lowest rate and the head chef on the highest. Uddin, from Bangladesh, described a pay system in his restaurant where the highest-paid was the chef (£300–£400) and the lowest-paid were the kitchen staff (£150–£250), with the waiters getting £180–£250. However, these weekly rates were for six days' work a week, with a minimum day length of around 10 hours, meaning that average hourly pay, even for the best-paid chefs, was only very slightly over the national minimum wage. However, when considering wages it is important to factor in that some, including Uddin, gave their lowest-paid kitchen workers food and lodging above the shop. Nevertheless, for those on the lowest rate, pay amounted to £3 an hour, half the national minimum wage.

Others, such as Zue, were open in revealing that they paid below the going rate, stating that "we pay 30% less than the English pay a worker". Zue also set out the rates paid to specific grades in the construction business he owned. Labourers were paid £60 a day, more skilled workers such as carpenters would be paid £100 or £110, which was significantly lower than the £160 that "the English chippy[s] get". In spite of the low wages, employers almost always described their businesses as good places to work, with little staff turnover. Employers also talked about offering support to their employees outside of work, should they have any problems, and saw themselves on occasions as more than employers but also as friends, advocates and advisors.

Conclusion

This chapter has presented the workplace through the lens of the employer. It has revealed that for many employers the workplace was changing, and that while, on an individual level, entrepreneurship may have given them access to a more acceptable lifestyle, it was not completely unproblematic. The labour shortages that many of them faced had caused them to revise their business practices. There was evidence that some were more open to employing more diverse workforces, where diversity was identified purely through ethnicity or nationality; but in many other ways they showed a resistance to change, particularly with regard to the gendered nature of the workplace. Employers operated within a context of constrained choice, given, in many cases, their limited finances and their own attributes and characteristics, including their own linguistic limitations that made it difficult for them to interact with more diverse workforces. Some were also constrained by their obligations, accepting that they were bound by family, friends and the wider community, although in the current economic and policy climate it was clear that the extent of obligation to wider community networks was not unlimited.

We have shown that employers held stereotyped views of what constitutes a good worker and which workers were to be trusted. In recruitment, a reliance on their social capital in the form of networks replicated and cemented existing social relationships, so that labour forces were produced and reproduced around particular social categories, including ethnicity and gender (Waldinger and Lichter, 2003). Employers from all three groups conceptualised 'good' and 'trustworthy' workers though the identifier of shared ethnicity, and this generally excluded people from other ethnicities or origins from these positive conceptualisations. We have to reflect on why this position was consistently expressed throughout the three groups and it could be that their own experiences of discriminatory treatment and exclusion, which had directed them into enclave businesses, encouraged them to see the enclave as a space of safety and trust, in much the same way as the undocumented migrants did. Alternatively, these could be expressions of stereotypes that, while expressed through the lens of national group, actually referenced the status that pushed workers to work hard and to be 'good' and trusted workers.

The final issue that we reflect on is in relation to their appraisal of working relationships as positive, paternalistic and caring and, in some cases, even based on 'friendships'. However, in the context of relationships that in reality were extremely unequal, where power was firmly located with the employer, it is difficult to interpret them in the same way. While work relationships were sometimes affirmed by the employers as positive, and while we know that in some cases undocumented migrants also described aspects of their relationships in the same way, it is important to separate the circumstances that combine to bring these parties together from the realities of work, power and inequality.

SIX

Social networks and social lives

"I guess after quitting the job I became very demoralised; I also realised that all my networks were based on my work. After losing my job I also lost my friends. I guess I have met all my friends at the Kurdish centre. I did not need to meet people outside of work as there were many people – clients or just community members. OK we are physically in England, but mentally not. We are very dependent on community centres. We do not need to get out of the circle and meet new people. We imagine community centres as our homeland, Kurdistan." (Zilan, female, Kurd from Cyprus)

Zilan arrived in the UK in 2000, at the age of 22, using what she described as "forged documents" supplied by the *shebeke*. She applied for asylum at the border but her case was refused after appeal and so she is now living as an undocumented migrant. She has two sisters in London and was living with them at the time of her interview. Both sisters, like Zilan, had been active in Kurdish nationalist politics but, unlike Zilan, had been granted leave to remain in the UK. In the 11 years since her arrival, Zilan had worked both as a community advisor and also in the restaurant sector. At the time of her interview she was unemployed and, as a consequence, dependent on her sisters for housing and subsistence. In the above quote Zilan expresses the feelings of many whom we interviewed in relation to their networks which acknowledge the crucial role that networks play, while at the same time pointing to the restrictions they impose. These restrictions relate to the ways in which she has submerged herself within the micro social networks of other Kurds, making it almost impossible to move away and create links with people from outside the immediate community.

Previous research suggests that undocumented migrants, due to their status, are more reliant on social networks than are other migrants (van Meeteren, 2010). The extent to which these networks of family, friends and acquaintances offer help and/or are based on self-interest will vary, but they are nevertheless central in the lives of many without status (Ambrosini, 2012). Networks are fluid, taking on different forms and functions in different ways at different levels for different people. According to Hagan:

> social networks can both strengthen and weaken over time, can change differentially for different segments of the immigrant community, and therefore can have disparate effects on incorporation. (1998: 55)

Research exploring co-ethnic social networks interrogates not only the layers and mobility of these networks but also the extent to which they might be altruistic or exploitative. Erdemir and Vasta (2007) identify three modes of social relations: primary, that are the micro, face-to-face domain of family, friends and acquaintances; secondary, that are formal and include associations and organisations; and tertiary, that are distant and impersonal, such as newspapers and the internet. Different groups use social relations in different ways. Turkish migrants, for example, find solidarity within primary and secondary networks and are infrequent users of tertiary networks (Erdemir and Vasta, 2007). However, these social relations are not always without tensions and difficulties and can be modelled on altruistic kinship ties, solidarity and reciprocity and/ or economic rationality between employers and suppliers of housing and services and the irregular migrants who need them (Engbersen, van San and Leerkes, 2006).

Pre-existing social networks in a country can act as catalyst for migration, as we observed in Chapter Three. Half of the migrants we interviewed had well-formed networks of family and/or friends in the UK prior to arrival. Pre-existing social networks were particularly important on arrival because members of these networks offered newcomers information and advice, places to stay and either jobs or information about job seeking and job vacancies (see Chapter Four). These relationships could be complex and sometimes problematic. While Chapter Four focused on social networks as a route to employment, here we explore the wider functions of social and community networks in the everyday lives of undocumented migrants. We consider social networks on arrival, how networks expanded but also shrank, as well as their positive and negative aspects, from the perspectives of undocumented migrants. We also look more widely at networks and examine engagement with and the role of neighbourhoods, community groups, faith groups, political activities, sports and transnational connections in the lives of undocumented migrants. The geography of the study is significant because, by living in

London, our interviewees either lived in enclave areas or had access to such areas, although this did not necessarily mean that these areas were always visited or explored; in some cases they were actively avoided. Nevertheless, ethnic clusters facilitated community organisation, neighbourhood encounters and sometimes conviviality, access to faith groups and cultural activities, as well as jobs and social lives both for those with relatives here and for almost everyone who had friends and acquaintances from the same ethnic and/or linguistic group.

Family networks and obligations

In Chapter One we explored the ways in which networks can be presented as providing opportunities to individuals who without them would have fewer and less valuable resources (Nee and Sanders, 2001). It is certainly the case that family members can provide invaluable resources, but equally they can restrict opportunities, be a source of resentment and disillusionment and become something to be avoided and moved away from if possible. More than half of those interviewed had family members in the UK. 'Family' was usually quite widely defined, to include those who were distant relatives and sometimes simply those from the same town or village and who were, through this geographical tie, identified as part of a wider 'family'. Of the 28 who had relatives in the UK, 12 had a brother or sister; 5 an uncle or aunt; 6 had cousins; and 5 had other relatives. How individuals conceptualised 'family' derived from the support they had experienced. Zilan had a cousin but did not get on well with him, stating that "I do not consider him a relative". Given that she had two sisters in London who supported her, she certainly did not need an extended family. Bahar, who was without family members in the UK, spoke of friends as her substitute family, although she acknowledged the parameters of these relationships:

> "I do not have any family members here. I replace them with friends, but of course, they have their limits." (Bahar, female, from Turkey)

Thus, 'family' could exclude relatives where the relationship was deemed to be negative, and could include others described as 'like family' with the assumption that they would display solidarities attributed to family, even when they were employers, as Mahir explains in relation to his current employer:

"his father likes me a lot. Our families know each other, because of his father he let me work here. My brother had the contact with them before I came. They are also from my home town. His father likes my family so that's why I can work there." (Mahir, male, from Turkey)

Having family can be both positive and negative. On the positive side, on arrival the support offered can provide an important safety net while the new migrant gradually becomes accustomed to life in the UK and starts to find her or his own way. Moreover, for some this may even help to mitigate, at least in part, the consequences of their undocumented status if they arrived using clandestine routes and/or constructed documents. Some spoke of relatives having been helpful, providing accommodation or, in some cases, work. Fung, from China, described herself as "lucky" because she had relatives already in the UK who could help. For her, "as long as you have somebody already here in the country, it would help you a lot".

Family relationships also maintained a bond with home, mirroring relationships the migrants had known prior to migration and creating a sense of being part of a community, albeit co-ethnic:

"We are a very closed community. We visit each other here. We go to each other ... introduce other people who are from our village. Like the relationship we have in the village, we have the same sort of communication or contact here. It is not much different here." (Welat, male, from Turkey)

However, not all family relationships were viewed positively, and negative perceptions arose through feelings of exclusion, exploitation or simply because, in taking the decision to migrate, some individuals had been actively seeking to distance themselves from their families. We found that for some the reality of family connections was that they trapped undocumented migrants into exploitative working arrangements, reflecting what Vasta and Erdemir describe as an 'exploitative solidarity' in a context where:

ostensibly altruistic acts are undertaken in expectation of employing the labour of the recipient for personal benefit, profit, or gain without adequate compensation. (2010: 2)

For those who arrived young, the accepted obligation towards their relatives included respect and submission to their authority, even if they were unhappy in the relationship. Ferhat was 23 when he arrived in the UK and worked as a car mechanic for a cousin with whom he had a difficult relationship; nevertheless, as he stated, "despite everything he is still my relative" – indicating that even where relatives behaved badly it was difficult to challenge that behaviour.

Family obligations also meant that individuals would feel more excluded when expected favours were not granted or when the family relationships they had anticipated or had experienced prior to migration were absent, in the different family structures that operated in the UK. For Roni, who worked in a supermarket owned by a relative, the refusal to lend him money when needed was considered a particular betrayal in circumstances where no one in the family had been willing or able to help resolve his status problem:

> "Almost all of them have let me down. In our first year, they were good, then they forgot about us. Maybe they were fed up with us, I do not know, maybe they think we have a very complicated life." (Roni, male, Kurd from Turkey)

Not everyone had maintained contact with relatives and some did distance themselves over time, in part where they had found that family relationships had generated obligations on both sides that were sometimes onerous, did not meet expectations or were experienced as unequal, burdensome or complicated. Relatives might welcome individuals when they first arrived but subsequently distance themselves when required to give support, for example in immigration claims. In the following quote Chow talks about feeling let down by her cousin once she was in the UK:

> "Earlier when I was still in China, he had boasted to me that he could help with all sorts of things; 'just come to see me, would you?' he would say to me on the phone. But after my arrival, when I was at [the] time needing his help, he had already forgotten what he had boasted. So you see, he's a cousin but cannot even offer half of the help that I have received from just an ordinary friend." (Chow, female, from China)

Obligations were seen as going in two directions, both towards and from the undocumented migrant, and it was this desire not to have to comply with the expectations of relatives that prompted some to avoid their family. Piro explains why he chose to come to the UK, where he had no relatives, rather than to Germany, where he had many:

> "When you are with relatives, an expectation naturally arises. I did not want anyone to expect something from me. I wanted to be alone. When you are alone, you can fight more easily. I also do not want anyone to see my bad life conditions." (Piro, male, Kurd from Turkey)

Family relationships could also be perceived as restricting the development of other friendships, keeping undocumented migrants cocooned but at the same time trapped in relationships that were unequal, due to status. In the next section we explore relationships with friends and partners, and the support they offered, sometimes as substitute families but without the obligations and expectations of families.

Friends and partners

In a study of undocumented Polish migrants in Brussels, Grzymała-Kazłowska (2005) found that as migrants became more embedded, family networks were replaced by broad ethnic cooperation. In our study friendship networks also developed as substitutes or as replacements for family networks. Friends become a 'resource person' (Diminescu, 2008: 571) whose help provides work, accommodation or even assistance in setting up a business. Just as with family, the boundaries of friendship are affected by status, which both encourages and limits networks of friendship. Friendship carried with it obligations that reflected those of family, but were described as more reciprocal:

> "Now I have known a lot more friends than before. We help each other to find work. Say if I know a vacancy somewhere, I will let my friends know. I will ask them if they have a job or not, or if they are interested in this job and so on and so forth. I would recommend them to work there if any of them wants to have a go. I will telephone the place to help contact the boss and things like that." (Dai, male, from China)

In the exploration of friendships and partnerships we highlight the juxtaposition between caution and necessity, as well as the ways in which decision-making around social contacts and networks is seen through the lens of status, which dictates strategies and parameters.

Being undocumented: impact on personal and private lives

Networks were selectively and cautiously developed. The undocumented migrants we interviewed were, for the most part, careful about whom they associated with, and experienced added difficulties in meeting people beyond their immediate networks, due to the long hours worked, a lack of English language among some and the underlying anxiety and fear about disclosing too much to the wrong people – and these could include co-ethnic workers and employers and, in some cases, even family members.

Status also affected friendships or the desire to make new friends, as any new interactions result in questions that one may not want to answer, as Bobby explains:

> "Yes, it does affect the way we make friends. When you go out to meet people, they will eventually ask you things like: How long have you been in the UK? Or how do you get on with life? So on and so forth. Some of them may offer to take you to visit places of interest … But then, when you actually want to go out with them, you'd realise that there are places you can't get in, because there they demand visitors to have ID card and so on. So you'd be stuck if you haven't got the right ID stuff." (Bobby, male, from China)

Chao makes similar points to Bobby and also reflects on language as a barrier to friendships, but it is clear that the major issue is status:

> "If I could speak English well, it would help a little; but then it's still a problem for me to get to know more people from other ethnic backgrounds. I'd still be worried. I'd still be reluctant to go out to meet people I don't know, say if you go shopping and you can speak English, then you won't have much problem doing shopping, but the people you meet there may want to know more about you; and after a while you may become involved with each other more and more; you may want to join their activities; you may play football with the boys; as you become closer to each other, they may even ask for your telephone numbers, or your addresses and things like that. But do you want to let

them know these? I think I'd rather stay home instead. I think as long as I don't have proper residential status, I'd rather keep a low profile." (Chao, male, from China)

Isolation could also be self-imposed and operate as a defence mechanism. According to Chao, "I don't really want to go out". If you go out there is always the risk of being stopped by the police and arrested, so staying in and remaining isolated offers a safer, though lonely and constricted, alternative.

Work also made it more difficult to socialise. One of the consequences of status was long and unsocial working hours, making it hard to actually meet people outside of work. In addition to long hours, low pay limited activities, and either debts and remittances or efforts to save money ensured that socialising was kept to a minimum. As we showed in Chapter Four, most of those whom we interviewed worked within the ethnic enclave and so those whom they met through work were usually from the same country of origin and this made wider networks almost impossible, as Cheung explained:

> "We have no contact with the British. We work in the kitchen; that is where we belong. All you meet each day are just the few *lao-xiang* from China." (Cheung, male, from China)

The narratives of undocumented migrants showed that almost everyone felt the restrictions of their status and these were seen as barriers, whether structural or self-imposed, as a mechanism for self-preservation and risk management. Nevertheless, networks were crucial, as we saw in Chapter Four, as a route to work, but they also had a wider function of providing security, trust and a sense of belonging.

The importance of friendships

Friendships offered people the chance to meet up for chats, watch television together, go to the park or occasionally have a meal. Friends were the way of avoiding the alienation and isolation that was so much a part of being an undocumented migrant. Two different types of friends, "close", "good" or "best" friends and "ordinary friends", who were sometimes referred to as "acquaintances", were identified and it was only the former who could be relied upon. This way of assessing friendships had a gender dimension, as women more often differentiated between "ordinary" and "real" friends.

"They are only ordinary friends; we are not that close. They will not be willing to help if they are just ordinary sort of friends." (Chun, female, from China)

"I do not consider anyone of them as my best friends. I still think of my friends in Turkey as my good friends. I talk to them on MSN or Facebook. When I write to them about my problems, they reply in detail, long emails. They write to me long advices, or long counselling. I do not have many friends in London." (Arjin, female, Kurd from Turkey)

One consequence of differentiating the quality of friendships was that women were more likely to state that their friendship networks were narrowing, and of the five who spoke of having fewer friends than in the past, four were female. This narrowing network of friends was sometimes due to changing work circumstances, for example where the decline in factory employment meant that individuals were working in more isolated workplaces, as Rojda explains:

"In comparison to the past, I have fewer friends. I used to have more, in these [summer] months of the years, we used to go to the picnics with friends through the factory. I made many friends but as I stopped working there I lost my connection with the majority of them … When I see my friends from the factories, I become very happy. Sometimes I see them on the street, I become very happy. I can talk to them about everything." (Rojda, female, Kurd from Turkey)

However, just as with families, friendships could also convey rejection when relationships went wrong, and some of those interviewed believed that living in the UK had changed people's attitudes to friendships, making them less trusting and more likely to be exploitative. Hasan articulates the magnitude of this type of rejection for those experiencing it, referring to the changing behaviour of people once in the UK, towards money and away from community, which is something that others also reflected on:

"First of all, people here are changed, they are thinking of their own interests, always thinking of economic conditions. If I stayed with someone in Turkey for a year, they would not make it a problem, but people do make such things as problems here." (Hasan, male, from Turkey)

Friends might offer assistance freely, but they might also ask for money (if they were not close friends) in return; for example, when helping to find work, which was an important role of friends (see Chapter Four). Thus, while friends were trusted persons and trust was crucial for those without documents, friendships were carefully weighed up in relation to what to disclose and to whom; friendships were not always enduring. This meant that it was even more important to make new friends and develop new social networks.

Developing new friendships

Individuals did not rely only on their existing social networks; many looked to extend them and to build new networks, although these were still generally established around a shared country of origin, cultural heritage and language and, in many cases, a shared status as an undocumented migrant; in only a minority of cases did they go beyond these. Friends were made in different places, and among those from China it was mainly through work, as Jiang explains:

> "Say you have work mates, when your work mates' friends come to see them, you'd get to know the new faces. You meet more and more people through this and slowly, you'd have more and more friends. They are all from China." (Jiang, male, from China)

Huan had made his friends through the church he attended, which was unusual among undocumented migrants from China, who rarely participated in any activities outside of work. Huan is mindful of the relationship between friends and personal wellbeing :

> "Yes, I have got more friends now than in the past. I feel happier than before because I have made friends. The more friends you have, the happier you are. Slowly, you'd have more and more friends." (Huan, male, from China)

Among Kurds from Turkey, the group of interviewees most likely to have family connections in the UK, new friends, especially among men, were made through community centres, although as we explore later in this chapter this engagement changed over time. For some, these friendships were driven by a shared political ideology, and sometimes by pre-migration links, as Deniz explains:

"My friends are usually from the organisations, those who share the same political views with me. I know some of them from Turkey; I met some of them during the activities of these organisations." (Deniz, male, Kurd from Turkey)

Regardless of networks existing on arrival, new friendships could either displace family networks or operate to fill the gap where there was no family. Thus, the boundaries between family and friends became increasingly blurred.

Additional to the family or friendship networks which they had on arrival, almost everyone had formed friendships during their period in the UK. Imagining life without friends was almost impossible:

"They [friends] are important, I like spending time with them, you don't get to feel lonely, you get to be someone's friend, you go, you mix; if you are alone, I can't live alone like this. It will affect me psychologically, my head will go crazy, I can't live without mixing with people." (Isha, female, from Bangladesh)

Friendships formed post-migration were developed in a variety of situations, as we noted above, through work, church or community organisations and, regardless of the strength of the relationships, they were instrumental in finding jobs, as Jian explains:

"I have met a lot more people, particularly through my work ... the more friends you have, the more information you can pass to or receive from them; and therefore the better chance you would have in finding a job." (Jian, male, from China)

For others, friends were found on the streets of the neighbourhood or even, in Ai's case, in a detention centre. Ai had known no one in the UK before her arrival and was detained at the port of entry. She describes the building of friendships and also observes the different quality of these friendships:

"I got to know quite a few people who were also being detained there like me ... They treated me well and we became good friends. So when I got out I went to find them for help. Through them I got to know even more people later. They are the friends of my friends. Some of these people have since become my good friends. They introduced even more people … I have now got quite a few friends. But talking of good friends, I have just a few." (Ai, female, from China)

Occasionally friendships with people from outside the same ethnic or linguistic group were made through chance meetings or workplace contacts. Nabeel had a non-Bengali friend who had been a customer in the repair shop where he worked, whom he now met at least once a week, but, as Deniz explains, for such a friendship to develop there had to be a commitment from both sides, and he had found that a barrier to this was greatly differing notions of how leisure time should be spent:

"I also have a friend whose husband [John] is English; we get along well; … He came to our house last night, for all night. He tried to learn Turkish, I tried to learn English … sometimes we go to play football on Sundays. I am still not good at communicating with him but he is a good guy … But I also went out with John for a couple of nights and saw that the system is different, I could not get used to it. I do not know, they either talk too fast or I do not like their conversation topics, but I do not really enjoy that sort of night with John's friends. So he usually comes to our house with his wife and we all have a chat together. He also likes Turkish culture." (Deniz, male, Kurd from Turkey)

For those who had been documented at some point in the past, for example as students or with visitor's visas, friendships formed in that period were not always maintained once they had become undocumented, either through shame, lack of trust or again simply because working hours made social interchange more difficult. Reyan speaks of the friends that she had when she was a student but with whom she no longer has contact:

"I had friends; we were studying together, having chat, drinking coffee. It was like a social activity. But after quitting I started to work harder, I do not have time for anything else." (Reyan, female, from Turkey)

Among those who had no friendships beyond their co-ethnic group, the reasons given included being undocumented – "you need documents to be able to really talk to English people" (Tanveer, male, from Bangladesh); being too busy at work and working long and unsocial hours; or the lack of English, as Jian explains:

> "My English is limited. There are still a lot of problems for us to communicate with Westerners. Say if a Chinese friend calls to say that there is a job somewhere, you understand. But if it is a Westerner friend who calls to say that there is a job vacancy somewhere, they'd tell you to wait at a certain place so that they can come to pick you up, because you don't understand them so clearly." (Jian, male, from China)

What was apparent, regardless of how the friendships were formed, was that many of those whom we interviewed believed that it was important to constantly extend their networks, and this was approached systematically, our interviewees using terms that envisaged construction, such as "I built up my connections" (Soumen, male, from Bangladesh). At the same time there were differences by gender, age and, to some extent, occupation. Social capital in the form of networks therefore displays a gendered dimension that impacts on its role and meaning, and among those whom we interviewed females generally described a more careful building of friendships around shared ideas or values, whereas males more often described their friendships as more instrumental, aimed at furthering a particular objective, with the aim of gaining an advantage from the friendship.

Narrowing friendship networks

Some people were cautious and reduced their networks or, due to changing circumstances, like changing jobs, found that their circles had shrunk. For Rojda, friends were all "from my first years in London", from a time when she had worked in a textile factory and when she still felt positive about her migration and believed that she would resolve her undocumented status. Twenty-five years on, and with no resolution to her status, her desire to make new friends had lessened. For women, having children often led to the narrowing of social circles, due to their absence from the workplace and the barriers they experienced in interacting with people from other ethnic groups who also had children. Geographical mobility also affected networks, and those who moved regularly for work and lived above their workplace faced difficulties in maintaining meaningful friendships. However, some also elected to retreat from their existing networks, as they had become disillusioned with them:

> "I do not want to have any sort of friendship any longer, I prefer to be alone. I have had some bad experiences with my friends, backstabbing; I do not really want to talk about these, but my views about friendships have changed in this country. I try not to rely on others." (Shivan, male, from Turkey)

Networks were also carefully managed because they entailed risks. Fear of being caught and deported leaves undocumented migrants on the margins in terms of work, and also frequently in relation to decision-making about networks, where marginalisation and isolation are part of a strategy to remain as hidden as possible and, in so doing, to reduce the risks of being caught. Social networks involve the constant evaluation and re-evaluation of whom to trust and what to disclose to whom and when (Sigona, 2012). For some this can mean opting out of social interactions, as Shivan (male, from Turkey) explains when he says in relation to social interactions that "being illegal ... makes one paranoid".

Establishing and maintaining intimate relationships

The networks that individuals possessed did not depend only on friendships and family already present in the UK; a period of migration might also lead to the establishment of more enduring intimate relationships, through either living together or starting a family. Among the 55 interviewees, 25 had been or were currently in intimate relationships that were based in the UK. Four of these were already married prior to migration and had either migrated together or joined/been joined by their spouse. Twelve described themselves as married or cohabiting since arriving in the UK and, of these, seven had children with their partners.

Some of our interviewees – notably women from China – had formed relationships with male partners also from China and talked about them as husbands, although they were not legally married as their status did not permit this, while others found their status an impediment to intimacy. In the following quote Hevi talks about not disclosing his status, and also about how a potential partner might struggle to trust him:

> "Of course you feel bad; if you love someone [but] you do not tell her for not losing her, or you feel embarrassed to tell. I mean, for example, let's say a girl really loves me too

much, but still my status might scare her off because she has heard too many bad stories; for example a man is already married in Turkey but here he can say to the people that he is single; again some people just go out with other girls to get status, so what I mean is that a girl cannot trust me easily." (Hevi, male, Kurd from Turkey)

Many saw their undocumented status as a bar to forming or maintaining intimate relationships, either because they did not wish to reveal their status or because they worried that their intentions toward potential partners would be misinterpreted as wanting papers or that the precarity of their situation made forming intimate relationships impossible, due the uncertainties under which they lived. Being undocumented contributed to an inability, among some, to form relationships and to difficulties in maintaining them:

"I used to date with a girl. It was five years ago, very serious with her. She broke up with me all of a sudden. She did not tell me the reason. Then, one day she phoned me and said 'go and get residence from someone else'. I did not hide my status from her. We were together for four to five months." (Ferhat, male, from Turkey)

For those without status, relationships could be difficult to form, hard to maintain and, in some cases, unequal, and this could result in insecurity and dependency. Of course, this was influenced by migration projects: for some the priority was to earn money and not be distracted from that objective by relationships and children, while for others it was something that was out of reach due to their working lives and lack of status.

For women migrants, where choices are frequently more constrained (Martin, 2014), marriage could result in being trapped in relationships that were problematic but from which there did not seem to be any way out. Chun had actively sought out a boyfriend on arrival, as she had no family in the UK and no other networks of support. Although the relationship had broken down she nevertheless found herself confined within what had become an abusive relationship, and attributed this, in part, to the restrictions imposed by status:

"But my boyfriend and I quarrel all the time. We quarrel all the time for this and that, sometimes even over trivial things. He tells me to move out. I said to him 'where should

I move to?' He said: 'you must move.' But I can't move. I have nowhere to move to … I don't have the money to move out or to find another place to live." (Chun, female, from China)

Intimate relationships could be difficult in the context of status, but some of our interviewees aspired to having their own family life. As Mirza (male, Kurd from Turkey) said, "I would like to have a girlfriend, get married to have children". Those with families elsewhere dreamt of having their status regularised and of bringing partners and children to the UK or of being able to return home for visits. For those without family life, these were major aspirations and something that they felt that their status removed from them.

Community involvement and engagement

While everyone had primary social relations that could include family, friends and acquaintances, when it came to secondary relations with organisations and associations, there were variations that intersected with country of origin, gender, length of time in the UK, family commitments and working lives. Just as primary social relations strengthen and weaken, so too do secondary ones, although some of those whom we interviewed had never had any involvement with organisations and associations. As the fieldwork for this study was carried out in London, a global city characterised by a long history of migration, diversity and community formation, there were established Turkish, Kurdish, Chinese and Bangladeshi enclaves and a large number of community-based organisations that provide services and activities for migrants, refugees and asylum seekers and their children.

The work carried out by organisations can be funding-led, and resource depletion in a time of austerity can impact on the work that these organisations are able to carry out. Moreover, there can be tensions between the ways in which organisations need to present themselves in order to gain funding, often in relation to the commonalities of ethnicity, nationality and/or language, and the actual reality (Zetter and Pearl, 2000). Class, gender and political activism will all affect access to the services and provisions of community organisations (MacKenzie, Forde and Ciupijus, 2012), but so too will immigration status (Bloch, Sigona and Zetter, 2014). While those who had been through the asylum system – mostly Kurds from Turkey – tended to have used or to still use community organisations, at the time of the interviews undocumented migrants from China and Bangladesh were less likely to be involved with more formal organisations.

The positioning of Kurds from Turkey in relation to community organisations can change over time, reflecting differing modes of solidarity and different political positions (Wahlbeck, 1998; Erdemir and Vasta, 2007). Ties can weaken or individuals can be marginalised as situations and ideologies change (Griffiths, 2000). In our research we found that some people accessed community groups on arrival because they offered support and there was shared politics and mutual solidarity, as Hevi and Deniz explain:

> "I came to [X community centre] as soon as I came. I met the people here … patriotic people. I told the people that I was looking for a job in the construction business. There was a patriotic guy that I met here. The people at the centre gave me his contact details, he helped me a lot; he gave one of his rooms to me. He did not accept money from me, I guess he got sorry for me." (Hevi, male, Kurd from Turkey)

> "First of all, I am a member of [X organisations] … I participated in their activities as much as I can before getting close to my friends or finding some other friends through work. At the beginning, I found almost all my friends from these two organisations. In the first week of my arrival, I was always in [X] Centre due to my political views. Also I knew there were some guys from the same party who came to London before me – this was the place where I managed to contact them." (Deniz, male, Kurd from Turkey)

In time, though, working lives and family life could affect participation, as Hasan (male, from Turkey) noted when he said, "people usually go to the centres very often or regularly in the beginning, then in time they stop going". Similarly, Roni describes his changing circumstances and changing involvement:

> "When we first came, I used to go to [a Kurdish community centre] a lot. I met many friends, they were very active, involved in politics. I cannot go as I work almost every day. Even if I work for six days, I want to spend my off day with my daughter. I have one day off once a month." (Roni, male, Kurd from Turkey)

Others hinted at community fragmentation and problematic gender relations for women as reasons not to go. Nevertheless, community organisations were clearly strong and had an important role for some, although for others they were to be avoided.

The undocumented migrants whom we interviewed from China were the group least likely to be involved in community activities because long and unsocial working hours meant they had very little free time, because of childcare, their lack of knowledge about the existence of community centres, fear of using them and a perception that organisations were not for undocumented migrants. Chinese community organisations, formed in periods of earlier migration and organised around Cantonese Chinese, may have had little in common with the groups of more recently arrived migrants, mainly Fujian in origin. Sometimes this separation was expressed through differences in linguistic groups, or as a consequence of being undocumented. Jian (male, from China), for example, felt that because he didn't have residential status community activities, "are not for people like us". Jiang describes the multiple barriers to participation among Chinese undocumented migrants:

> "Most of us are busy with work … We don't have time to involve ourselves in any activity. We are busy working. We don't know where to find the Chinese organisations that could help us, or what they can help us with." (Jiang, male, from China)

The undocumented migrants from Bangladesh whom we interviewed were for the most part living in geographical clusters, with other people of Bangladeshi heritage. Nasifa acted as a volunteer, which was a way of improving her general wellbeing through social activities.

> "I like this as it involves interaction with other people and I don't feel tortured. I volunteer for various organisations during my day off. I go for my wellbeing and happiness … I am mainly involved in cultural organisations." (Nasifa, female, from Bangladesh)

However, as with all of those who were working, the long hours could get in the way of participating in events and activities. Time outside of work could be so limited that some, such as Qasim from Bangladesh, felt that when he was not working the preference was "to sleep". Engagement with and the role of community organisations in people's lives were clearly community specific, but also related to knowledge and perceptions of organisations, and time.

Activities beyond work and community centres

Outside of community centre activities and work, undocumented migrants are engaged in some organised and some more informal pastimes with other people. There is more variety in the social activities of undocumented migrants than is sometimes suggested (van Meeteren, 2012a). A small minority were involved in faith communities, political activities, sports or culture. However, for the most part, activities outside of work were informal and ad hoc and, because of the demands of work in terms of the hours and the lack of money, activities were almost always with people from the same ethnic group, with language being part of the reason, but fear due to status and experiences of racism were also mentioned.

For many, lives revolved around either work or childcare. Time outside of work was largely spent doing chores – such as clothes washing – catching up on sleep, but also watching films, TV in first languages and low key socialising with friends and family or in cafes to break the loneliness of life. A minority went window shopping or walking around the local neighbourhood or to central London, but travelling into the centre of London could be steeped with anxiety, due to status.

In relation to politics, as we noted earlier in this chapter, for some Kurdish interviewees, this was central to their community based activities and ideological positioning. For Bangladeshi and Chinese undocumented migrants, a few engaged in political activities, and these were more personal in their orientation. Huan, for example, who received British Overseas Citizenship (BOC) rather than British citizenship, campaigns for BOCs to be allowed to stay in the UK, which currently is not the case. Afsal describes himself as "the son of a freedom fighter" and is involved in meetings and gatherings to mark occasions related to the creation of Bangladesh in 1971.

Organised religion was participated in and central to a small minority. For Tanveer, his life outside of work consisted of going to the mosque and praying. Among a minority of Chinese undocumented migrants, churches played a role and these churches were often frequented by other ethnically Chinese people, as Chow explains:

> "I attend activities held in the church. That's the only place where I take part in activities. Most of the participants of church activities I go are ethnic Chinese people. We get

together regularly, attending Sunday services; sometimes we have meetings, like tea parties, where we discuss things like the difficulties we meet and how to deal with such difficulties." (Chow, female, from China)

Religious bodies can provide a social life and companionship, and this was important in an often work orientated and sometimes lonely existence. These can also been seen as safe places, where status does not matter, where advice and help can be found and where people can be equal (Bloch, Sigona and Zetter, 2014).

There was virtually no engagement with people from different ethnic groups, due to the barriers of language and status. However, racism could also be an issue, as Meher, who spoke English, explains:

"some British are really racist; if they are British they are racist. Bengali British are OK, they don't have any problem with the Bengali. It is the white British, they have the problem, racism problem." (Meher, female, from Bangladesh)

Having children certainly affected activities, both for women who were looking after their children and for men who were not the primary care giver but had some caring responsibilities for their children while nevertheless working long hours. Roni worked in a restaurant and had a daughter, and wanted to spend his limited time with her rather than socialising in other ways, as he explains in relation to his need to work and only the occasional day off:

"I go to park with daughter but I could not have a day off in the last month. She says 'Daddy we used to go the park, why we do not go any more?' I say 'I have to work on behalf of someone who has gone to holiday'. I do not say we need money and I need to work. They pay me £40 for the extra day. Maybe not much but it is important for us." (Roni, male, Kurd from Turkey)

Every now and then undocumented migrants from China went to Chinatown for dim-sum – in the case of Ron, two or three times a year. His life consisted of working, and then, he said:

> "I'd be very tired by Saturday, after a week's work. So for Sunday I'd stay at home to rest, to have some sleep and things like that." (Ron, male, from China)

Others rarely leave their local neighbourhood. Arjin, a young Kurdish woman from Turkey, rarely left her north London enclave because she was "too scared to go to central London". She had gone to the Westfield shopping centre, near the Olympic Park in east London, and had found the experience terrifying as there was a police presence.

Among Kurds and Turkish interviewees a minority went to *kahvehanes* – Turkish and Kurdish tea shops – though this was sometimes due to necessity to have some social interactions rather than a positive choice. Ferhat, for example, as noted earlier, worked in his cousin's garage and lived in a room attached to the business. Most evenings he watched Turkish satellite TV and had a lonely existence because the people he knew were mostly working when he had time off, so he forced himself to go out to meet people:

> "I go to *kahve* to watch football match. I really do not like going to *kahve*. I do not like paying card games. But I have to go to get socialised." (Ferhat, male, from Turkey)

These were gendered spaces, though, as men went to socialise while the women in our research frequented them only as workers.

Others did not socialise, either because of work or because of fear or a preference for solitude, like Shivan, a 28-year-old man from Turkey, whose life consisted of work and sleep, partly because he worked long hours in a kebab shop and partly because of his preference to be alone. Being alone, although for many a choice made out of the need to remain hidden, was not without difficulties. Reference was made to isolation, loneliness and incarceration by many of those whom we interviewed:

> "I stay at home most of the time … I don't see anyone or meet many friends here … I don't even go out except going to work. I stay home like being locked up in a prison." (Chun, female, from China)

However, life was not limited to the UK, and some undocumented migrants were actively engaged in transnational networks and activities, an area we explore in the next section.

Maintaining transnational activities

Undocumented migrants, like other migrants, are transnational actors who may engage in economic, political, social and cultural activities across borders. The nature and extent of transnational activities will be determined by motives for migration, the family networks in the country of origin and elsewhere and the transnational capabilities of individual migrants, which are determined by their experiences and resources within the migrant–receiving country (Al-Ali, Black and Koser, 2001a; 2001b). Among undocumented migrants, low income, economic insecurity and immigration insecurity can affect engagement in transnational activities (Portes, 2001; Bloch, 2008).

Van Meeteren (2012b) distinguishes between three types of transnational aspiration among undocumented migrants: investment aspirations, which are about working, saving and returning; settlement aspirations, held by those who want to stay; and legalisation aspirations, held by those who want to regularise their status because they associate legal status with a better life and who often are those who have escaped persecution. These different migration motives and aspirations also result in different types of transnational activities, with investment migrants remitting or saving the largest amounts of money and maintaining closer and more regular social contacts with family members in the sending country. Those who are concerned with legalisation and who have been through the asylum system and/or fear persecution are often more engaged with political activities than others (Bloch, 2008; van Meeteren, 2012b).

Economic factors had motivated migration in some cases, as we explored in Chapter Three, and so remittances could form part of the migration project alongside the obligations of kinship, as Soumen and Naser explain, although Naser suggests that this is not always an easy situation:

> "I sent money to my family, educated my brothers and help my sister get married and bring her here. We Asian families have an obligation to look after our families, our parents, our siblings and that is what I did. This is my responsibility." (Soumen, male, from Bangladesh)

> "We Asian families have an obligation on who is abroad. You see the four brothers remaining out there do not want to work but will pressure the brother who is abroad to send them money; they do not know how the brother in

England is paying and under what circumstances they are working to get that money." (Naser, male, from Bangladesh)

Having close family members remaining in the country of origin, particularly dependent children and partners, will, unsurprisingly, result in a greater propensity to remit money. Among those whom we interviewed, 14 had a partner and children in the sending country and a further six had children and no partner. Reyhan has two children in Turkey aged 14 and 8 who lived with her mother, and so she sends almost all her wages home to support them. This is possible because she lives with her boyfriend, who pays for the room they rent, and she eats at the restaurant where she works. Ron had been in the UK for four years and had paid off the debts he incurred making his journey. At the time of his interview he was sending home £1,000 a month to his wife and children in China, leaving him "a few hundred quid for my own expenses, for food, rent, travel, mobile phone and so on". Ron's aim was to earn and return, but he had not yet earned enough, saying that houses were expensive in China and so he had "not yet enough to buy a house".

Sometimes transnationalism works in the other direction, with families in the country of origin sending money or clothes to the UK, as Bahar explains:

> "Our families have sent us some money. My mum even sent some clothes for me and for my daughter so that we would not spend money for clothes. She even sent some food in boxes through people." (Bahar, female, from Turkey)

Those with close family in the country of origin tried to keep in touch through regular phone calls. Hanif had his parents, wife and 9 year old daughter in the village in Bangladesh and called them daily. For others, though, regular contact was not possible, due to their lack of financial resources. Nafisa, for example, had two older children in Bangladesh who lived with her younger brother, and a young son in the UK. Her contact with her daughters was limited, as she explains:

> "I cannot keep in regular contact as I do not have the means. I may buy a phone card for £5 but I have to think twice as I need to find a way of affording it. I have to be very careful about spending and need to keep account of what I have as I spend. It could be that I make contact with them every 15 days or so. I would buy a phone card for

£1. Sometimes the contact may be monthly. This is how it is." (Nafisa, female, from Bangladesh)

For others, contact with family in the country of origin changed as their lives in the UK changed. Chow describes how her orientation has shifted from China to the UK as she has established her own family:

"I used to call them a lot. Now that I have a family of my own with a baby to take care of, I don't call them as often as I used to. Of course when there's something that I need to talk with them about, or when there's some special occasion, I'd give them a call … Before I got married I used to miss home a lot, but since I had a family of my own, since I had my son, I don't have time to think about such things as often as before. Everyday I'd be busy with the things about baby caring. I don't really miss home as I used to. I am more concerned about the family here." (Chow, female, from China)

Others talked about missing their families, especially where there were children involved. Reyhan describes the absence of her two children saying that, "after talking to my children, I cry". Transnational relations were complex and could be difficult emotionally and psychologically, although most maintained them with varying degrees of regularity and emotional intensity. While some led active transnational lives, others were more orientated towards their everyday lives in the UK, which was not surprising, given their varying circumstances and the immediacy of trying to survive.

Conclusion

In this chapter we have focused on social networks, community engagement, activities outside of work and transnational relations. Most people had effectively and strategically built networks of friends while in the UK, and this was instrumental to everyday lives, especially when looking for work. Family relations were often more complex than those with friends, and difficulties could be accentuated between family members when working relationships were involved. While a minority participated in activities outside of work, either community based or some limited social activities, most led quiet lives that were often quite hidden, and this could result in loneliness and feelings of isolation.

Social networks were comprised almost exclusively of people from the same ethnic and linguistic group, although these networks were fluid. As people's lives changed, so too did their engagements in different kinds of networks and activities, including those with a transnational element. Having children and partners either in the UK or in the country of origin affected orientations and aspirations, although again these changed over time and could be limited by the demands of work and the effects of low income.

In Chapter Seven we turn to the consequences of being undocumented in relation to access to services as well as within public domains. These themes have been alluded to throughout the book, but in Chapter Seven we draw together the ways in which people experience and manage their lives without status.

SEVEN

The consequences of being undocumented

"Seriously, it is really very hard to be undocumented. Even when you run into [the] police on the street, you panic." (Cem, male, Kurd from Turkey)

Cem had already been in the UK for 13 years when interviewed. He had been politically active in Turkey and continues his political activities in London, although this had caused him some difficulties when working in Turkish-owned restaurants where other staff members were hostile to Kurds. Due to a serious back problem, he was now able to work only part-time and this made life even more difficult, as he had a young family to support.

Being undocumented has consequences in every sphere of life. In this chapter we focus on the ways in which undocumented migrants experience the exclusions of their status and develop strategies for managing these status-based exclusions. The context is of course crucial; status matters more in places where documents are checked or required, which means, argues Khosravi (2010), that illegality is produced and is, as a consequence, situational. As internal controls, such as raids and sanctions on business and document checks for renting housing, are increasingly rolled out into civil society, so too do the sites increase in which the effects of being undocumented are experienced. However, it is not only policy than impacts on the ways in which being undocumented is lived and experienced. Personal biographies are also crucial in understanding variable experiences (Anderson and Ruhs, 2010a). The variation in experiences in terms of personal characteristics and biographies – which can include the reason for migration, persecution and/or fear of persecution in the countryof origin if returned, age at the time of migration, education, gender, social capital – all determine the variable experiences of undocumented migrants. Moreover, differences will determine visibility, claims-making and access to certain public provisions.

In Chapter Four we explored the impact of being an undocumented migrant on employment experiences, and demonstrated the centrality of status to these experiences, as well as the exclusion of most undocumented migrants from the more formal parts of the economy simply because these are sites where documents will be requested. We are not suggesting that undocumented migrants do not use constructed documents to access parts of the labour market that might otherwise be closed (see Vasta, 2011; Reeves, 2013). Instead, we have observed that the additional risk of using fake or other people's documents was seen as a last resort, given that it was deemed to be a criminal activity and therefore increased risk. Indeed, desire not to be engaged in criminal activities was the background to many of the accounts that interviewees gave. For them, while being undocumented might not in itself (in their eyes) be 'illegal', using forged documents was.

In earlier chapters we explored the impact of status on employment and social lives and activities. In this chapter we first focus on the impact of being undocumented in relation to access to and use of public services, looking in particular at health, welfare benefits and police services. We then examine the ways in which status intersects with other spheres where documents are always or often required, notably housing, participation in educational opportunities, travel, opening a bank account and even obtaining a driving licence. What this chapter will show is that although the impact of status varies it is multi-levelled, affecting people in different ways within different settings, and it results in a range of responses to contexts and individual circumstances, and to a diversity of lived experiences, including levels of fear, anxiety, trust and disclosure.

Status in relation to health, benefits and civil justice

In this part of the chapter we focus on formal service provision – health, welfare benefits and access to police protection and justice – which are associated with social and civil citizenship (Castles and Davidson, 2000). Differential access to social and civil rights is one of the mechanisms through which states exclude non-citizens and has been part of the immigration regime since the 1905 Aliens Act. Entitlements are stratified along a continuum, with citizens at one end and undocumented migrants and refused asylum seekers at the other (Morris, 2007). However, exclusion from welfare increases the likelihood of irregular work, and preventing access to GP services potentially has wider and adverse health impacts and is costly if people resort to presenting at hospital accident and emergency departments. The economic and societal rationales for exclusion seem far from clear, nor do they seem to deter migrants, as has been posited as the rationale for successive Immigration Acts (Bloch, Neal and Solomos, 2013).

Health services

Health is one of the main sites of exclusion for undocumented migrants and we begin by considering access to health services and the strategies of undocumented migrants in relation to health and healthcare. Healthcare is significant because, on the one hand, it is often attached to national membership, so undocumented migrants, who are in breach of immigration regulations, can find themselves outside of healthcare provision; on the other hand, access to healthcare is a human rights' issue, and under human rights' treaties it is attached to the person, not to the state (da Lomba, 2011). While undocumented migrants are physically present in a country they may nevertheless be excluded from gaining access to the rights associated with citizenship, or be too fearful of accessing any entitlements, due to the risks of being caught and exposed (Bloch, 2010). However, binding treaties include the International Covenant on Economic, Social and Cultural Rights (ICESCR), which states, in Article 12, the right of everyone to enjoy the highest attainable standard of both physical and mental health. Cuadra emphasises the human rights' aspects of health, noting that

> The Committee on Economic, Social and Cultural Rights, which monitors and interprets ICESCR, advised that states are 'under the obligation to respect the right to health by, inter alia, refraining from denying or limiting equal access for all persons, including [...] asylum seekers and illegal immigrants, to preventive, curative and palliative health services; abstaining from enforcing discriminatory practices as a State policy; [...]' (para. 34). (2011: 267)

Healthcare provision and access to provision will depend on the welfare state within the migrant-receiving country, so there is no one standard of provision, although, as Cuadra (2011) points out, under the Council of Europe Resolution 1509 (2006) on the Human Rights of Irregular Migrants (Article 13.2), emergency care is a minimum right for everyone, including undocumented migrants. In the UK, under the 2014 Immigration Act, charges have been introduced for healthcare provision, including primary care (such as General Practitioner [GP] services) as well as some emergency provision. This is all new, and so to date it is unclear how the system will operate, although concerns include: implementation, the discriminatory aspects of provision and the impact on vulnerable groups, including pregnant women (Grove-White, 2014). In relation to health, therefore, the terrain is changing and although the fieldwork for this study preceded the 2014 Immigration Act, some interviewees expressed concern over their access to healthcare.

At the time of the fieldwork, while National Health (NHS) services continued to be free at the point of delivery for those 'ordinarily resident' in the UK, undocumented migrants, along with foreign visitors, were not considered ordinarily resident but were instead treated as 'overseas visitors' liable to a charge for most NHS treatment, including hospital treatment, although exempt from some charges, including for accident and emergency services and family planning (da Lomba, 2011). GPs have had a duty of care to provide urgent treatment for all; however, there seems to be an uneven approach to this, with some GPs insisting on identification and proof of residence before registering people as NHS patients (Kilner, 2014). Da Lomba notes that 'health-care provision for irregular migrants is nested within national debates on immigration and the welfare state' (2011: 368), and increasingly these intersections have become entangled within civil society, with those offering services, including healthcare providers, being expected to become part of the in-country immigration regime, which excludes people from necessary healthcare and creates confusion among healthcare professionals.

Uncertainties and disparities were a feature of access to healthcare among our interviewees. In particular, there was a degree of uncertainty about what was available, what were entitlements, regardless of status, as well as what was risky in the sense that it would bring them into contact with the authorities. Chimienti and Solomos (2015) conclude that the two main barriers to accessing public healthcare provision among undocumented migrants in the UK are finance and the fear of being reported to immigration. The consequence of these uncertainties was uneven access and variable use of NHS services. We found a number of different approaches to health and healthcare among undocumented migrants. Some had opted out of all contact with the NHS, while others paid for alternative medical treatments when necessary, notably by private doctors or healthcare practitioners from the same country of origin, as Dai explains:

> "The reason I am here today [in central London] was because I wanted to have a check-up but without status it is difficult even to have a check-up. I can only see medicine shops run by Chinese people. But these shops are not so comprehensive and the medicines there are very expensive. Sometimes you may feel a little better after some

medication; but the problem can come back to haunt you. I have no status so I can't see a GP, a Western doctor. I have been seeing Chinese health shops for help but these shops are not so well equipped or specialised. I don't mind my wage being too low, but the biggest problem is that I can't see a Western doctor, because I don't have UK status." (Dai, male, from China)

While using private doctors, usually from the same country of origin, avoided the NHS and language difficulties, it did incur costs. In the case of Chinese medicine not everyone was happy with the outcome, as the above quote from Dai shows. Dai went on to say that he had not been to a hospital because hospital doctors "won't see you if you don't have UK status". An acquaintance of his had been to the hospital and had been asked for identification papers and, being unable to produce these, had been given a pain-killing injection and nothing else.

However, others did use hospitals and some had even registered with GP practices, or tried to register, although experiences of these services and of practices in relation to access had been variable, leading to different perceptions and understandings among interviewees. While Cheung, from China, had gone to accident and emergency for treatment when he had hurt his leg, Asafal, who had been in the UK for more than six years, had forgone medical treatment for a work injury, based on the assumption that he was not entitled to treatment, as he describes:

> "I cut my hand at one restaurant. I was out of action for three days, nobody bothered to take me to a hospital. This is because I had no papers. What I found out very recently is that if I had been taken to hospital, I would have been treated. It has taken me six to seven years to realise that the threat is nothing." (Asafal, male, from Bangladesh)

Others had tried to register with a GP but had not been able to. Hasan talks about his experiences of trying to register with a GP:

> "I told them clearly that I did not have a status. They said they could not register me because they needed to inform details to the Home Office. They said it would cause a problem for me so I could not get registered." (Hasan, male, from Turkey)

Access to services is stratified by immigration status and that means that when migrants move in and out of different statuses their rights to services change (Morris, 2002). During the asylum process, for example, there is full entitlement to all healthcare, and some interviewees had registered with GPs during that time in their lives. Once an asylum case is refused, things officially change, although experiences and the consequences of status mobility were uneven. Some people, such as Guang, from China, were able to retain their GP even though their asylum claim had been refused, but others, such as Zilan, had not:

> "I was registered to a GP until the last two years. Then after my [asylum] case was over, my account was deactivated. I go to a private doctor. He is Turkish. He is aware of all my problems." (Zilan, female, Kurd from Turkey)

Bahar lived in London with her husband and young child. In the past they had been registered at a GP practice, based on a letter from the Home Office saying that her visa application was being processed. However, she no longer had a GP, as she explained, and this was a concern, given her husband's health:

> "We are not registered in the GP we used to be. When we changed our address, one of the letters [was] sent back to the GP so they realised that we had changed our address. They deleted our registration and we could not register to the GP in our region because we do not have valid visas. My husband is diabetic. He cannot even go to a GP for examination; he still takes the medication that he was prescribed a few years ago. We need to go to private doctors, which is very expensive. You see how hard a life can be if you are not legal in this country." (Bahar, female, from Turkey)

Some had used health services, but not in their own name, or had strategies in place in order to receive treatment while not being registered with a GP. Being scared was a normal emotion and finding ways of being untraceable and unidentifiable was also part of everyday life. Deniz explains how he deals with medical issues and describes his situation as "helpless", while Roni had a way of getting medical help where necessary:

"[M]y finger was broken and I went to the hospital. I could not even give my own name; I gave my cousin's name. I had a dental operation under someone's name. Even [though] I paid, still I had the operation on someone else's name because you do not exist. I do not have GP registration, my registration is cancelled. I am helpless; my hands are tied." (Deniz, male, Kurd from Turkey)

"I got sick a few times, I went to the emergency; I had infection in my ear. They told me to go to my GP. I said they were not open at the weekends. I lied to them. Now I try to go to the hospitals at the weekends so I can lie about the GP. If I get [a] cold, I buy medicines from Boots." (Roni, male, Kurd from Turkey)

Our interviewees were of a range of different ages and some were well into middle age. What is apparent is that they are likely to experience a number of health problems in the future, but how they will deal with these is unclear. Moreover, there were also issues of women and maternity services. Some of our interviewees had given birth in the UK and others were in age groups where they might decide to have children, or more children. One likely area of concern will be the impact of the 2014 Immigration Act on pre- and post-natal care, as noted earlier (see Grove-White, 2014), as well as on the health of children born in the UK to parents who are undocumented migrants, including their access to immunisation, which will affect not only these children but also the health of the wider population. Excluding undocumented migrants from healthcare thus has consequences far beyond the specific group. It also highlights the tensions between international rights and the nation state and, as such, continues to be a locus of contestation (Chimienti and Solomos, 2015).

Absence of social security

The welfare state as a safety net, while it has been eroded under successive governments as part of the neoliberal agenda, still exists for the majority of those residing in the UK and operates in a diminished form for asylum seekers. While in theory – as noted above – there is access to emergency health provision for everyone regardless of status, the same does not apply for social security payments, and for those without status the safety net does not exist. Previous research has emphasised how exclusion from welfare can potentially further disadvantage those without status within the already segmented labour market (see Wills et al, 2010), leaving them with little choice but to accept the lowest pay and the worst terms and conditions. This lack of welfare therefore attaches an additional layer of pressure on those already marginalised and excluded from finding work(regardless of what it might entail) in relation to their survival and/or it can create dependency on others. Nevertheless, resonating through many of the interviews was a strong sense of our interviewees' resilience and independence. In this section we explore the lack of welfare and what this means for survival during times out of work.

Kadir talks specifically about his situation, and also about the wider relational aspects of being undocumented:

> "I have a family; my wife is pregnant and we don't get any maternity benefits from the government. Not just maternity benefits but we are not getting any type of benefit. This is our situation; we are not entitled to any benefits. If my wife got an opportunity to even get some maternity benefits it would help. I have to pay to get medicine, for example I have to find money to buy paracetamol. Those who are legal get some benefits. There are lots of people here suffering like me." (Kadir, male, from Bangladesh)

While remaining in work was essential, there were of course periods when people found themselves between jobs or unable to work. It was at these points when family and friends helped out or savings were used. While family and friends provided a safety net, in the absence of benefits it was not always straightforward and could, on occasions, leave people feeling uncomfortably dependent and/or like a burden. As we showed in Chapter Six, social networks could also entrap individuals into reciprocal arrangements, ultimately to their disadvantage. In cases where assistance was balanced it seemed to be less problematic. Zilan, a female Kurd from Northern Cyprus, was living with her sisters, who both had status in the UK. While she earned small and ad hoc amounts of money, she had not worked consistently for a number of years since losing her job as an advice worker for a community organisation. She was dependent on the support provided by her sisters, something that was not easy to deal with, especially as she could see no way of making changes to her life, as she explained:

> "I live with my sisters. I do not pay rent. I sometimes accompany some people that I used know as interpreter.

They give me some pocket money. Not much. Sometimes I fill in the forms for some friends. They pay me but it is not very often, rarely. I depend on my sisters, which makes me very upset. Sometimes I even think of suicide. I feel like I am stuck. I cannot get rid of this situation." (Zilan, female, Kurd from Northern Cyprus)

Others too talked about the difficulties of dependency, such as Arjin, a Kurdish woman who could rely on her sister and brother-in-law for support but did not "want to be a burden". Fung, from China, had stayed with relatives and undertaken domestic exchanges, including looking after the children of relatives, during periods out of work and before she had met her husband and had her own children. While it was not explicitly referred to among our interviewees, other research has found that those with precarious status or no status can find themselves in situations of domestic servitude or trapped in exploitative domestic exchanges (Gupta, 2007; Lewis et al, 2014). Nafisa, although not in servitude, felt trapped and described herself as mentally and physically tortured. She was living with the father of a child she had in London, had two daughters in Bangladesh and an ex-husband there with whom she was not in contact. She felt that being an undocumented migrant was largely the reason for her situation because of the associated poverty.

"It's to do with finance. I am basically illegal. Being illegal means I am not entitled to any benefits, I don't have earning capacity. If I had an NI [National Insurance number] now, maybe I could have had a better job … If I had better earnings, I would have been able contribute. I cannot even do that. So these are the issues. I have needs and if I ask for things or I may wish to send something back to my daughters in Bangladesh, I may ask him [the father of her child], but this leads us to have disagreements. I have needs. I have seen that the money [he] earns doesn't really cover everything. Because of me he has to get a place with an extra bedroom. Whatever happens, it is hard for me and I feel tortured by it all. Mental torture is always there; physical is something I didn't expect. I feel if I was earning then I would not have had this happen to me. He is not a bad person. He was a good person but the poverty has affected him and maybe that is why he tortures me. I don't know how long this torture will last, but as I have a child I am in a predicament. It is not possible for me to move." (Nafisa, female, from Bangladesh)

While Nafisa felt trapped in her situation of dependence, so too were others, although without the associated abuse. Those with partners relied on them, and women with children were largely dependent on their partners. Those without family and/or partners had to turn to friends in times of need, although these were often, though not always, more reciprocal relationships, as Dai explained when he described "mutual help" among his social networks, which comprised of other Chinese people. The importance of friends as a safety net during periods of difficulty or hardship was referred to by interviewees. Lok, for example, has had periods out of work with ill-health, and the support of friends has been his only way of surviving:

> "I had a few good friends. They are always there for me when I need them. I didn't have to pay for it. If you have no job, you telephone your friends and tell them about it, they will ask you to come over to stay with them. Since I didn't get any benefits from the government, I had to survive by either staying with my friends or relying on my own labour." (Lok, male, from China)

Relying on others was often seen as a last resort, with savings used first, and so lifestyles were very frugal during difficult financial times. A number of interviewees talked about saving money when working in order to have their own safety net for times out of work. Dai explains how he dealt with periods of unemployment through reducing consumption and being very frugal:

> "I was jobless for nearly three months. When we have no work, no income, we would have to spend money very carefully. We don't waste anything. Some of us, when there is no income, would spend our savings so carefully that we may eat two meals a day only, instead of three. We would eat simple foods, for example, we'd buy pork-bones to make some simple soup for dinner, and in the morning we'd just have bread and milk." (Dai, male, from China)

There is always the anxiety of being out of work, and so money is never wasted. Moreover, the debts accrued in making the journey to the UK added to the pressure that some felt.

"I had to spend each and every penny very carefully. I ate only the very cheap stuff. I did my shopping in the bargain sections of the local market. I tried not to eat meat. I ate mostly vegetables. You know, I was still in debt then. I owed money because I had to borrow a lot of money to go abroad. That was why I wanted to save each and every penny possible. When you have no work, no income, where do you get the money to waste? Where can I get the money to spend? You know, we Chinese always want to save up something for a rainy day." (Fung, female, from China)

This lack of a social security safety net added pressure for those in an already precarious situation, although most people had either savings or someone to turn to. The existing networks or the new ones forged in the UK were invaluable in times of need and were used when necessary.

Police and justice

Among the most significant aspects of being undocumented are the steps taken to avoid the gaze of the state, to be hidden and, in particular, to avoid interactions with the authorities wherever possible (Willen, 2007; Vasta, 2011; Bloch, Sigona and Zetter, 2014). The tactics of irregular migrants are for the most part tied up with the fear of deportation, because contact with the authorities can potentially lead to this. For those who fear persecution in their country of origin, who have accrued debts to make their journey and/or who have made a life in the UK that includes children, the threat of deportation is very real and very frightening. In fact this fear is one of the reasons why refused asylum seekers become undocumented migrants. Instead of adhering to reporting conditions at the local police station, some decide not to sign, with the consequence of becoming undocumented, as we noted in Chapter Three when discussing status mobility. When asylum cases are refused, reporting conditions are imposed, which means regular reporting to and signing at a police station, an act that is considered risky. In the following quote Deniz expresses his everyday anxieties and explains why he decided to stop signing when his asylum case was refused:

"I am even scared when I walk, what if they will catch me and send be back, what will happen to my wife, my children? It is hard to live like that. I need to go to Home Office regularly for the signature, which I do not. If I go

for the signature there is a high risk of being caught and
sent back." (Deniz, male, Kurd from Turkey)

Trying to be invisible, while a strategy to avoid deportation, can produce
'an underclass that is vulnerable on several fronts', argue Goldring,
Berinstein and Bernard (2009: 241). One aspect of vulnerability is the
lack of recourse in the event of a crime, as Bahar explains:

> "[S]omeone physically harassed me one day on my way
> home. I really got disturbed but I could not do anything. I
> could not call the police, I got scared. I do not have a valid
> legal document to present to the police. I should not get
> involved in trouble at all. I might be deported. This thought
> harm[s] me a lot; you get panic[s] about the future. Even if
> I am robbed, what will I do?" (Bahar, female, from Turkey)

Some had experienced contact with the police, not out of choice but
due to events. Guang worked as a motorcycle delivery person for a
take-away shop and had been in two road traffic accidents in the UK.
On both occasions the police had been called, although on neither
occasion did he follow up and try to get compensation, preferring to
avoid all contact with the police due to the risks involved. Exclusion
or vulnerability often has multiple effects. Being a victim of theft or
withheld wages, for example, has to go uncontested, as for the former
going to the police is too risky while for the latter, as we showed in
Chapter Two, employment law rights are denied to those without
documents. In sum, irregular migrants both are excluded and exclude
themselves from access to justice. This has consequences not just for
undocumented migrants themselves, but for wider society, as its effect
is to seemingly condone unlawful activities and to offer no redress.

Status and everyday life

Our focus in this part of the chapter is on the wider consequences
of being an undocumented migrant and how they intersect with and
are managed in everyday life. We begin by exploring experiences of
housing, which is a constant concern for many of those we interviewed
and is topical within policy arenas as it is one of the areas where the
state has extended immigration checks to civil society under the 2014
Immigration Act. Under the Act, landlords have a duty to check the
immigration status of those renting their property. Those without
leave to remain in the UK cannot have a tenancy agreement. The fine

for renting to someone without leave to remain is £3,000 per adult, although there is a right of appeal (JCWI, 2014). While the Act puts emphasis on landlords' checks, the reality is that housing has been identified as a problem area for undocumented migrants, who rarely rent directly from a landlord in any case because renting can often require other documents, such as proof of identity, and it can require references and a bank account for setting up a direct debt.

Housing

Housing is expensive, especially in a global city like London, and a number of our interviewees experienced difficulties in relation to accommodation. For the most part people either lived above the workplace in a shared occupancy room or paid rent for a shared occupancy room in a shared occupancy house, either to a private landlord or as a sub-let. In some cases, people stayed in hostels or rented a bed in a shared room. A minority stayed with family or friends and some at times found themselves without anywhere to stay. Housing could be a major problem, as Afsal (male, from Bangladesh) summed up when he said, "It is bad enough trying to eat but trying to find a place to sleep is an issue". There was a tendency to move around, to look for safe places to stay that would not be targeted by immigration raids, and to be tied into certain jobs as a consequence of the housing provided, however inadequate that housing might be.

On arrival, it was not uncommon to go and stay with a family member, a friend or contact from the same country or area of origin. Staying with people could often be difficult and was a short-term solution for most. Cem, for example, stayed for more than two months with the relatives of a friend with whom he had arrived in the UK, while Hasan had stayed with an uncle. Both the quotes show their efforts to keep out of the way and the difficulties of such an arrangement.

> "I was a single man. It is hard to stay with a family. I was going to their house just for sleeping. I was always going to the centre, the community centre; I was spending my whole time over there. Thank God it was summer time and the weather was good. I was just hanging out until late time, not to disturb any one at home." (Cem, male, Kurd from Turkey)

"I was staying in the living room at my uncle's house. You do not have a separate room in the house. You have to arrange your sleeping times according to them. I was coming home very late, waking up early with uncle. Even if they do not say directly, you do not feel comfortable." (Hasan, male, from Turkey)

Kadir talks about his feelings on staying with his sister-in-law, as well as the difficulties of finding somewhere to rent, which he thinks might be due to his status:

"Housing has been very difficult here. It could be because I don't have legal status. I tried to find elsewhere as I felt bad living with my sister-in-law and being a burden on them. Despite [their] telling me I should not go elsewhere but stay with them, I tried to look for a place of our own, but nobody would rent us a house." (Kadir, male, from Bangladesh)

Moreover, the stigma attached to being undocumented also impacted on family members' willingness to help out, as Naser describes:

"In terms of relatives, I have distant relatives such as aunts and uncles. I first stayed with an uncle, but as you know people are nice at first until your visa expires. After that people are reluctant to have illegal people staying with them." (Naser, male, from Bangladesh)

Being undocumented, while affecting access to housing, was also a major consideration in terms of deciding where to live in relation to reducing the risk of being raided by immigration. Among our interviewees five had actually experienced a raid of their accommodation, and so it was a real threat and finding safe housing was a real concern. Deniz, a Kurdish male, had stayed with his aunt for almost a year, and highlighted the fact that the risk had been low, relative to other housing possibilities, because she owned her own home and was therefore unlikely to be targeted for a raid. Soumen talks about his situation and the threat of raids:

"I don't have a fixed address. They now search people's houses and raid them. Immigration would harass people who give us room, create problems for them. There are instances where they break the door down to get in and search for illegals … I just stay with whichever relative I happen to be with at the time." (Soumen, male, from Bangladesh)

For Soumen, like many others, the pattern of housing was a series of transient places, though he at least had the benefit of having relatives to turn to. Some of our other interviewees were not so fortunate and in their most desperate times had been street homeless. Bik, a woman from China, had stayed in "the hexagonal kiosk" which is the name given to a structure in London's China Town. Piro, a Kurdish male, said: "I slept in [the] train station for two days". Piro was lucky because, through an acquaintance, he found a place to stay in a shared house with women who treated him "like a brother", offering him a new and extended social network to build on.

For most of those whom we interviewed, the cheapest and most viable options for housing were to take a job where accommodation was included, to rent a bed in a multiple occupancy room or to rent a bed on a nightly or weekly basis in a hostel. A number of restaurants and take-away shops provide accommodation for their workers, and for those newly arrived in the UK this offered an immediate and viable solution to their housing difficulties. Nabeel, for example, found work in a restaurant when he first arrived in the UK; board and food were included and he received a cash payment of £60. His decision to work in restaurants was largely based on their provision of free board and lodging. Conditions were not always good in the accommodation supplied with work. Some experienced very poor housing conditions above work premises that included very poor hygiene and inadequate facilities:

> "The illegals stay above the restaurant. They stay there, wake up in the morning, no breakfast or anything, just start work. Some do not have time to bathe. Others have been bitten badly by bed bugs. We do not get fresh bedding. One person goes and another person comes and sleeps in the same bed. And toilets do not get cleaned, not once in a year. There is no cleaning liquid; no hand wash; and most have cold water." (Afsal, male, from Bangladesh)

Moreover, living above the shop could result in the greater exploitation of workers, especially when the employer knew that due to status there was a lack of options, as Shivan describes:

"I had to tell him because he asked. He even attempted to make me work up to 18 hours. Because I was illegal he thought I was in need of him. I could not go anywhere because he also provided me the accommodation. I was even scared to get out of the shop in those days. I was very new, he knew my fear; he misused my condition. He tried to exploit me." (Shivan, male, from Bangladesh)

Even though conditions were often poor and workers potentially vulnerable, there were positives to be found in living above the shop. The close proximity to other workers from the same country background helped to facilitate both friendships and the development of social networks that are so central, as we have seen, to the lives of undocumented migrants:

"As no one of us had any family members we were always hanging around together. We used to stay in the same house, same working hours. They become your relative after a certain period of time, you know." (Hasan, male, from Turkey)

Those not living above the shop usually lived in shared occupancy housing. Among Chinese interviewees, there seemed to be a going rate of £25 a week for a bed in a shared room, with around four or five people sharing a room. Some had found a bed through a co-ethnic internal rental system, with those who had been in the UK longer renting a bed to most recent arrivals, as Li explains.

"I had to pay for a bed to sleep. The cost for a bed was £25 a week. Those who have been here for a longer time would know where and how to rent accommodation and newcomers therefore often have to share with them the accommodation they rented. In most cases, this is just a bed to sleep." (Li, male, from China)

Among Bangladeshi men, hostels offering cheap beds on a daily or weekly basis and two meals were a possibility, as Nasar explains.

"We can go to hostels where they charge £10 for board and lodgings for one night. They feed you twice. You can also give them £40 to £50 and stay for a week ... each room may have 8 to ten people. I need to stay in places like that from time to time; they are Bengali. One room, they have bunk beds and each room may have three or four of them; facilities are shared. The food they provide is sometimes inedible so we go to cheap places to eat." (Nasar, male, from Bangladesh)

As with access to health, the mobility of status impacts on access to housing. Those who had been in the asylum system had received housing benefit or housing for the duration of their claim, but once they were refused, for those who became clandestine, the situation changed and eligibility for housing benefit ended, meaning that they had to find ways to pay their rent or find alternative accommodation. A very small minority rented a property with their immediate family rather than living in a shared occupancy situation. Bahar (from Turkey), for example, who was working as a hairdresser, lived with her husband and child in a sub-let from someone she had met at work. Although Bahar had her own place, she was not renting her property formally from a landlord or through an agent and there were no leases involved.

This section has shown that housing presented difficulties for many of the undocumented migrants whom we interviewed. Accommodation attached to work, while offering a solution, could be very poor and result in greater worker vulnerability, as some unscrupulous employers could take advantage of this additional dependency. In the next section we focus on some of the everyday exclusions experienced by undocumented migrants, which, although seemingly minor in comparison to health, justice and housing, nevertheless limited options and curtailed everyday encounters.

Everyday exclusions and their impacts

Many of the everyday things that are taken for granted by those with a regular status become a major obstacle or impossible for those without status. Our interviewees focused on travel, bank accounts, driving licences and even something as basic as borrowing a book from the library as the areas where they felt the consequences of their status acutely. In this section we consider how these exclusions and barriers are understood and felt. There was a sense of change and a more stringent and punitive environment in recent years, as Zana, who first arrived in the UK in 1988, observes:

"Things were different when I first came. You could get a house from the council even if you do not have status;

171

you could get your driving licence. The opportunities were very good. After 2000s things get changed a lot. We used to work without any fear until there was a report, a complaint to the Home Office. By 2000, they started to raid the factories; before, everybody was free; it is a general state policy. The number of migrants increased so the state changed its policies." (Zana, male, Kurd from Turkey)

Having been in the UK for so long, Zana really feels the exclusions he has been subjected to, as he explains:

"your relatives get married, they have funerals; you cannot go to any of them. Forget about Turkey, I also have many relatives in Europe. I cannot even go to any European countries. You are just locked in Britain; right now you cannot do anything without paper[s]."

Not being able to travel was something that could be experienced with pain, particularly when it involved bereavements. Zilan, living with her two sisters who had 'leave to remain' in the UK, describes the pain she felt over her mother's illness and death, comparing her experiences with those of her siblings, who were able to be with their mother and proactively try to find treatments:

"My mum died in 2011, May 2011. I could not even go to her funeral. My sisters flew immediately but I had to stay here. I was devastated. She was still alive when my sisters went to Cyprus. They changed hospitals a couple of times; private hospitals in Nicosia. When they could not find a cure, my sisters and a brother of mine living in Cyprus took her to Adana [southern Turkey]. They hired a private helicopter. We spent almost all our savings for the treatment. At least they were with her in her last days. I ate my heart out while waiting to hear from them about my mother's state. She died in the end. This just killed all my happiness, hopes. I was away from her for seven years. She died before I could see her for the last time." (Female, Kurd from Northern Cyprus)

Roni also felt pain due to bereavements, and also the loss of engagement in family life and the missing of rites of passage, as he describes:

"due to the status, I feel lonely. I am longing for Turkey a lot. It has been 12 years. I had 15 nephews and nieces since I came here and I have not seen any of them. Two brothers of mine got married, I was not there. Some of my relatives died and I was not there." (Roni, male, from Turkey)

Being unable to travel creates anxiety, fear and loss, as Deniz explains:

"What if something happens to my family in Turkey, how I will go to Turkey? Just imagine, my sister got married last year, I could not go to her wedding. My best and childhood friend also got married a couple months ago, I could not go to his wedding. It is very painful for me. Another brother of mine will get married in December, in Mersin. Again I will not be able to attend his wedding. All these affect my psychology very badly, they are difficult things. Just imagine." (Deniz, male, Kurd from Turkey)

Over a quarter (15 out of 55) had left partners in their country of origin, while more than a third (20 out of 55) had left children behind when they migrated. Jiyan had been in the UK for 12 years and talked about his daughter, who was now a university student:

"When you do not fulfil your plans, you feel some sort of emptiness. I have not seen my family for many years. I have a daughter from my first marriage. First I have not seen her for 10 years. Then we were together for two years, when they deported me. Now it has been another three years that I have not seen her. She stays with my mother." (Jiyan, male, Kurd from Turkey)

In addition to travel, some of the more mundane or ordinary aspects of everyday life were closed or problematic. Arjin, a Kurd from Turkey, was 22 and she had been in the UK for two years, working in the restaurant sector. She describes some of the multiple ways in which being an undocumented migrant has an impact on her everyday life and basic aspirations, while Mahir, from Turkey, who was also working in a restaurant, attributes his lack of happiness to being undocumented:

"I really want to improve my English, if I live in this country. I have to have a good level of English. When I could not sort things out or when I cannot understand what I am told,

I really get very sorry. If I got the status, I would go to a school immediately. There are lots of things that I want to do in this country. I want to get driving licence, I want to improve my English, I want to see all London. I cannot do any of these without the status. I cannot go to Turkey and see my family." (Arjin, female, Kurd from Turkey)

"Of course I cannot be happy in these conditions. If you had status, yes, you might be happy. At least you could travel around or choose the job you want. I do not know, maybe you could go to the school. Now I just go to work and come back home, fear is also something extra." (Mahir, male from Turkey)

Joining the library or opening a bank account was difficult or impossible. Fung was a young woman who lived with her husband and two young children. Most of her day was spent on domestic chores and childcare and she felt she had little chance to use local services, including the library, due not only to her lack of English but also to her status. There were obstacles almost everywhere for those without papers:

"I can't borrow books in the library, because you must have a registration card to borrow books from there. I am told that you must have an NI number or an asylum-seeker card or something like that in order to get a registration card made for you." (Fung, female, from China)

Documents are also required in order to open a bank account and this was particularly problematic, as work within the informal economy tends to be cash in hand, leaving people with nowhere safe to keep their cash or having to trust other people to 'look after' their money:

"A relative keeps £18,000 of my money. I cannot establish a business, cannot save it and keep it with myself. What can I do with that money? I could not wait [until] a thief breaks into my house and fills his or her bag." (Roni, male, Kurd from Turkey)

Li had been in the UK for eight years and had worked for the same contractor in construction throughout that time. The solution he had found, as had his colleagues, was to leave his wages in the contractor's account, as he had never been able to open a bank account. He said that he trusted the contractor because he was "a *xiangqin* [close fellow-villager] of mine". Although Li talks about his trust for the contractor, a fellow villager, the situation nevertheless leaves him vulnerable and dependent. Some employers have withheld wages, and being undocumented means that it can be virtually impossible to contest this. Just doing the simple, practical things in life was made more difficult or impossible by not having status, and among our interviewees everyday life could be a series of hurdles to find a way across.

Conclusion

In this chapter we have focused on the consequences of being undocumented, from the perspectives of those whom we interviewed. We have seen that being undocumented excludes people from those basic services associated with social citizenship, including health and welfare benefits. Access to healthcare does fall within human rights' treaties, although the combination of healthcare provider policy alongside self-imposed exclusion by some from emergency healthcare provision means that access to health services is variable. Many of those whom we interviewed were unclear about entitlements and/or unwilling to risk accessing health services. Instead of statutory provision, alternatives were sought in cases of need, including paying for private doctors or alternative practitioners. The reality was that most just did not access health services, and there was concern about the impact of the 2014 legislation, as noted earlier (see Grove-White, 2014). Not being able to access benefits also had knock-on effects, as we showed in this chapter, most often relating to work and wages, but for those without work it could also create dependency on others. While there was resilience and strategies were in place for those times of need, family and friends were called on as safety nets, although there was a sense of burden in relation to depending on family and the greater reciprocity among friends seemed to be a more comfortable arrangement.

Being in work, having somewhere to live and staying hidden represented the everyday existence of many of those we interviewed. Exclusion and lack of access to basic services leads to vulnerability and greater potential for exploitation both in the workplace and outside of work. The consequences of being undocumented are not isolated from one another. Rather, different exclusions connect to create isolation and marginalisation in almost all aspects of the lives of undocumented migrants.

EIGHT

Grasping life on the margins

"But my experience so far tells me that, for people like us who landed in the UK, once you started out on a certain type of work, you're almost bound to tic yourself there; it won't be easy for you to move away from it. In fact I don't like working in the kitchen; it feels suffocating for me to stay inside the kitchen for too long. This is because of the smoke in there. The noise [that] comes from the extraction fan is horrible. You can't hear anything if you speak in the kitchen like what we are talking now. The fire from the ovens is so fierce. Having worked in the kitchen for this long, I understand why the kitchen is said to be one of the high-risk work environments. Puffs from the steam can cause breathing problems. I actually wanted to change job; because I feel pain in my chest if I stayed in the kitchen for too long without a break." (Cheung, male, from China)

We begin the final chapter of this book with a quote from Cheung, who is 48 years of age and who had arrived in the UK three years earlier. Cheung describes his experiences of working as an undocumented migrant in one of London's many Chinese restaurants. He had been a driver in China and had met people who had already migrated and who had encouraged him to do the same. He came on a tourist visa and was put in contact with a job agent to whom he paid £100, getting work almost immediately. He initially worked outside London in a restaurant, on a 12-hour day for £180 a week, including meals and accommodation. He says that he was treated badly because his employers knew he had no status. A restaurant customer, also from China, advised him to learn cooking skills and gradually he improved his earnings, eventually earning £1,200 a month. However, at the time of the interview he had injured his leg and was out of work. Although his networks have grown and have helped him to get work, he says that there are only a few people, all Chinese, whom he counts as friends and with whom he would socialise. Cheung's story has similarities with many of the accounts of work and of friendships among undocumented migrants.

This concluding chapter returns to some themes discussed in the book, to capture the essence of what makes undocumented migrants like Cheung tolerate such conditions, at the same time questioning whose interests are served; why undocumented migration occurs; what the imperatives are that drive it; and what its effects are on migrants themselves, on their networks, on those who employ them and on society more generally. We do this through a focus on four key themes. First, we reflect on the utilisation, by both undocumented migrants and minority ethnic employers, of resources and networks, taking account of the discussion in Chapters Four to Six. Having reflected on how individuals survive and at what costs, second, we turn to a re-examination of the policy aims and the consequences of migration policies, drawing on Chapters Two, Three and Seven. Third, we consider concepts of risk taking and risk avoidance among undocumented migrants in their economic and social lives, before finally turning to a reflection on the impact of class, gender, language, skills and ethnicity on the lives of those without status.

Networks without influence

Practically all of the migrants whose lives we have touched on in this book spoke of the networks they had on arrival and/or subsequently built, of friends, acquaintances, family or persons with whom they had a shared history, geography, political position or religious affiliation. Their stories were rich in describing how they made and extended their networks and how, in their view, these were essential for basic survival, in their search for work following migration and for help, support and companionship. For nearly everyone, finding people who might be able to help them in some way or another was paramount. Few respondents believed that they could make their way by themselves without assistance, even after months or indeed years of migration. Much time was spent by them in assessing how best to make contacts and how to expand networks, from the limited number of people already known on arrival to the wider groups accessed subsequently, although with caution, given the risks involved as a consequence of being undocumented.

When considering networks, two factors should to be taken into account. First, there is the need to reflect on notions of community networks and identity (Parla, 2007), and in this context it is useful to return to the concept of 'mistrustful solidarity' (Levitt, 2001) discussed in Chapter One. For although we chose as our area of investigation undocumented migrants from three communities already established in the UK and relatively dominant within London, it was not the case that respondents and members of these established communities necessarily expressed themselves as sharing a common identity, had interests in common or had a recognised obligation to offer support. While undocumented migrants might have no alternative but to turn towards these communities, it does not follow that this was done on the basis of trust or because they expected solidarity.

In each of the three national groups, undocumented migrants identified tensions between established communities and new arrivals. In the case of those from Bangladesh, the established community was sometimes perceived as wanting to distance itself from the more recently arrived migrants without documents, so as to draw a line between its own legal status and the undocumented status of the new migrants; and, as Muslim communities increasingly become a target of suspicion (Abbas, 2007; Mandaville, 2009), this too could be a contributory factor in this distancing. Respondents sometimes expressed this distancing in the failure of family members to offer them support when needed, or of Bangladeshi employers to provide decent work. In the case of Chinese origin respondents, while formally they might have a shared national identity with the established Chinese community in London, all of those interviewed had originated from different regions within China to those of the dominant existing Chinese community and most spoke a different language. While the majority of the established Chinese community in London has its origins in Hong Kong, with Cantonese as its first language, the undocumented migrants interviewed mainly came from Fujian and spoke Fujianese. This meant that, as Beck (2007) also found in his study of the established and 'newcomer' Chinese communities, they had almost as much difficulty in communicating with members of the Cantonese community as they did in communicating with English speaking communities. Moreover, their experience of life in China prior to migration was also very different. They had grown up in Mainland China, whereas the established UK Chinese community had come from the British Protectorate in Hong Kong, prior to its reintegration within China.

There were also divisions within the Kurdish/Turkish group of interviewees and between them and the more established Turkish community in London. Twelve of the 20 interviewed identified themselves as Kurdish and as possessing a different culture, ethnic and political identity to that of the Turkish community. They described tensions between Kurdish and Turkish migrants in those cases where they were present in the same workplaces, and also had experienced discriminatory treatment from some Turkish origin employers. These divisions also extended to different religious orientations, notably between Sunni and Alevi. Thus, attempting to categorise individuals simply on the basis of their national origins will always be insufficient in locating communities of interest and, in particular, of trust, as migration trajectories, histories and regional origins can mean that recent migrant groups in actuality have little in common with previous generations of migrants.

A second area of fundamental importance was class and power. Even where identities, as expressed through language, culture and history were shared, undocumented migrants were in a position of disadvantage in relation to the networks of employers who offered them work. Thus, having a linguistic or cultural identity in common could not overcome the divisions of class and power, which they experienced acutely as workers without power facing employers who were only too aware of this fact, a point we return to in the final section of this chapter. Relations with employers were based mostly, although not exclusively, as we saw in Chapter Five, on an economic rationale that enabled the exploitation of those with little power. Even those working for family members were aware of their economic utility and of the fact that their family connection assumed trust and loyalty. They rarely expressed the view that such relationships might be being driven by altruism, reciprocity or solidarity (Engbersen, van San and Leerkes, 2006).

As was noted in Chapter Six, the networks that migrants turned to might indeed assist individuals to find work and/or accommodation; they might provide them with information on how to access services, but this could come at a cost to migrants. Sometimes, this was an obvious and direct cost, in that they were required to pay in return for access to work or other services, but equally there was an even more insidious indirect cost, because networks in general operated more readily as a trap from which there was little opportunity to move on, rather than as a bridge to a wider range of opportunities. The networks that undocumented migrants entered were usually already poor in terms of the resources that they had or that could be accessed through them. A job that paid at half of the national minimum wage might be found through networks, but a job that had the potential to enable individuals to build themselves a decent life, to save money or to contemplate a more secure future was unlikely. The networks that our respondents relied on could not advantage them, beyond ensuring an income to cover basic living expenses and perhaps to pay back debts incurred in migration and/or to send some remittances to family members.

This is not to say that all of the networks used by undocumented migrants were comprised of malign individuals unwilling to share resources; rather, it was the case that the resources that they were able to share were poor. This confirms the reservations already expressed in Chapters One and Six as to the value and application of theories of social capital to the study of undocumented migration, as to theorise the resources derived from the networks they formed or entered as providing advantages is to stretch any definition of the term 'advantage' too far. To argue that Cheung (see the opening quote of this chapter) was 'advantaged' because his social capital, developed through the network of people 'like him', that is, other undocumented migrants, gave him the advantage of a job, as a consequence of which he is exposed to risk to his health, is to take the meaning of social capital beyond any acceptable definition.

Resources have to be judged on the quality and advantage that they permit to individuals. In the context of undocumented migrants, the resources that were at their disposal and that are reported on throughout this book had generally served to imprison them in a cycle of poorly paid work from which it was not just difficult to exit, but which in some cases operated so as to actually prevent exit. Those who worked for family members supplied cheap and compliant labour and, as undocumented migrants, they both were dependent on these family members and also had obligations to them. Migrants in this situation could find that their labour had been exploited and that they were then stuck in circumstances where they were unable to challenge such exploitation, because the network that engulfed them did not permit it. We saw this too even in cases where there was no malice or bad intent, but where simply the only resources that were to be traded left individuals permanently disadvantaged. Networks made up of those who were undocumented could give access only to the resources that the undocumented possessed. They could not provide resources beyond these. Indeed, as discussed below, for those who were able to exercise agency to ameliorate working or living conditions, this was often achieved despite the existence of networks, and here individuals might choose not to utilise networks, in an attempt to move beyond the resources they provided.

Although the main focus of this book has been on the experiences of undocumented migrants themselves, we were conscious of the need to also examine the motivations of some of those who employ them and in Chapter Five we explored undocumented migrants in the workplace from the perspectives of migrant entrepreneurs. Employers rely on social networks to assist their entrepreneurial endeavours. Indeed in some cases their journey into entrepreneurship had been as a consequence of their previous exclusion from the labour market or because they had reached a 'glass ceiling' constructed on the basis of their ethnicity or gender. Some employers had become business owners as a result of their own experiences of discrimination and disadvantage, and this was reflected in the networks they had utilised to guarantee the viability of their businesses. Just as with undocumented migrants, employers demonstrated a heavy reliance on such networks for the capital that was needed to establish or maintain their businesses, as well as in relation to locating appropriate workers, able and willing to work under the conditions that they were able to offer and which were often poor. Many of the employers interviewed (although not all) were in small-scale businesses that were vulnerable to economic downturns. This meant that they had to constantly work to keep labour costs low, but increasingly in a context of labour shortages, particularly as a consequence of the closing of migration channels that had previously enabled them to recruit from origin countries. In the case of a minority, if they had been unable to employ at least some workers without documents, then labour shortages might have led to increased labour costs, but more likely would have led to staffing shortages at a level that made their businesses unsustainable. Thus, having entry to networks that could give access to a labour force willing to accept low pay was essential to the continuance of their businesses on the terms that they wished, or were forced, to operate on.

It was evident that both undocumented migrants and employers were operating within networks whose resources were limited and that provided neither group with the opportunity to move beyond the position that they were in. Migrants moved generally from one poorly paid job to another, while most of the employers managed micro businesses that provided them with little scope for expansion, or indeed for access to networks consisting of useable social capital whose amount and quality might have been sufficient to guarantee them a better life (Portes, 1998).

Gains to the state and profit to employers

The legislative models that governments have established to deal with undocumented migration, which include sanctions on employers, deportations and detentions and the denial of employment rights, can be construed not solely as a response to undocumented migration itself, but rather as deriving from a variety of necessities, not all of which are migration related. Governments may promote policies to exclude migrants on the basis of country of origin, class or professional competency, placing those who enter the territory in a non-compliant way in a position of 'undocumentedness'. However, the relationship between such policies and migration may be tenuous. In fact, measures announced as dealing with undocumented migration may actually have other, wider but unacknowledged aims and, certainly, consequences (Castles, 2004; Bloch, Kumarappan and McKay, 2015).

A public policy that promotes closed borders and restricted and increasing limited opportunities for migration does so in the knowledge that those borders can and will be breached by those seeking to migrate, and indeed it is almost an inevitable consequence of tighter immigration controls that undocumented migrants will continue to arrive, but in a context where there are ever-increasing risks to them and to those who give them support, in whatever form. What such controls cannot do is eliminate undocumented migration. The continuing and indeed growing number of deaths occurring in the Mediterranean sea remain as a grim testimony to the consequences of stricter migrations controls.

Governments have imposed immigration controls even in circumstances where there is an identified need for migrant labour, as currently in the case of skilled restaurant staff, simply because they are responding to other dominant imperatives, such as the need to be tough on migration for electoral reasons. Similarly, placing restrictions on migrants, such as the withdrawal of welfare entitlements, establishes the foundation for subsequent withdrawal from other groups, such as the unemployed. Thus, in the run-up to the 2015 general election in the UK, as we were completing the final sections of this book, the main political parties, regardless of whether they might be classified as more or less to the right or the left, were vying with one another to confirm their support for further restrictions on migration, with no demonstration of concern for their impact on the labour market or the economy more generally.

We would assert that it is governments that create and indeed promote undocumented migration, and that this operates primarily to the benefit of employers (Grasmuck, 1984; Chavez, 2007; Anderson, 2013). The imperative to migrate is a response to many factors that restrictive legislation is not able to counter and that include the necessity to find work, even if that means leaving the country of origin, the need for safety and security where that place of origin is dangerous, and a desire for conditions that might promote greater freedom of thought or of activity, aligned often with the desire to expand horizons (Castles, de Haas and Miller, 2013). Making immigration more restricted does not eliminate any of these factors but instead promotes worsening conditions of employment, together with more insecurity, a condition that, as we have argued, then extends beyond the undocumented. Thus as controls are put in place to detect and remove those without documents, these controls also spread to affect the rights of all who live on the territory, including migrants with a legal right to reside and, indeed, citizens. For example, the collection of biometric data, increased powers for the police to stop and search, and systems for checks on the right to medical care are imposed on all citizens and all may be negatively affected by such restrictions.

At the same time we need to be clear that not everything can be laid at the door of migration policy, as the organisation of the labour market is also relevant. We have demonstrated that those without documents or those using constructed or borrowed documents are nevertheless able to find work, and in part this is because the formal labour market is fundamentally reliant on an informal sector to service it. This is not the product of recent changes in migration law but, rather, it is something that has existed historically, to a greater or lesser extent, in every advanced industrial economy and in every global city (Sassen, 2001). Thus capital has always relied on the existence of an informal labour market as a 'reserve army of labour', a position that is now occupied by migrant labour generally and by undocumented migrants in particular (Reyneri, 2001; Wills, et al, 2010).

For those who employ them, undocumented migrants are most likely seen as low cost and compliant workers, positioned not to question authority nor to demand employment rights or to protest over unfair terms. However, this advantage is extended to employers more generally, including those who employ only workers with the correct documentation, as the presence of a vulnerable labour force enables the reduction of rights to all, including those who are with documents, as well as indigenous workers, who necessarily have to compete on similar terms if they wish to obtain employment. Thus, particularly in periods of high unemployment, it is advantageous to employers to have access to a constant pool of those without documents, ready and willing to work, even if they do not in practice employ them. It is the fear of being undercut that drives workers with rights into work where rights are not respected (Massey and Gentsch, 2014). One outcome of tightening immigration controls has been to alert some migrants to the advantages that resulting tighter labour markets produce. The greater difficulty that migrants generally have in entering the UK means that those who have managed to successfully navigate the barriers have gained an advantage in circumstances where employers need workers. Among our respondents the knowledge of skill shortages, particularly in the restaurant and take-away sector, as a result of the abolition of the sector based scheme for migration, meant that those who were here could (in cases where they had acquired sought-after skills) obtain a higher premium for their work, or at least had access to more secure employment. Thus, while publicly the government shows itself to be acting in opposition to undocumented migration, in reality the presence of undocumented migrants creates the conditions for a more flexible and compliant labour force, advantaging capital over labour. If governments wanted to end this advantage they could promote policies that guaranteed employment rights to all, effectively impeding a 'race to the bottom'.

There are further consequences of government migration policies, outside of the sphere of employment. In Chapter Seven we showed the impact of restrictions on rights to healthcare for those without documents. These exclusions risk not only the health of individuals but also the health of society as a whole, as transmittable diseases cannot be contained when there is no medical support. The measures that the UK government introduced in the 2014 Immigration Act risk a return of diseases that had been generally eliminated, with widespread public health implications across out communities (Grove-White, 2014). Furthermore, they place children born in the UK at risk when their mothers have no access to pre- and post-natal care, and in turn this risk is carried into the general population when children are not immunised. Of course there are the broader issues of human rights in relation to healthcare that should also be considered (Chimienti and Solomos, 2015).

Similarly the new policies on landlords' accommodation checks will encourage overcrowding, risking the return of conditions that had been eliminated for the most part by the early years of the 20th century. They will also drive more people into tied accommodation, with all of its negative features, where the loss of a job results in the loss of a place to live, persuading workers to remain in disadvantageous employment. We demonstrated in Chapter Four the ways in which individuals were constrained to accept very low wages because these were accompanied by a bed in which to sleep, usually above the workplace and almost always in rooms that were shared with two or more others. Placing restrictions on access to rented accommodation will have no other effect than to drive people further into tied accommodation. It also fails to understand the market for housing among undocumented migrants, who, our research shows, do not have lease agreements but instead sub-let if they are not living in accommodation offered either with work or informally by family and friends.

Risk takers, risk avoiders and conceptualising illegality

Migrants, in particular those who arrive without documents or who fall into undocumented status, have been conceptualised as high risk takers (Williams and Baláž, 2012; Hormiga and Bolivar-Cruz, 2014). First, they bear the risk of leaving their own homelands and travelling, sometimes for considerable distances and at considerable cost to them and their families. Second, they exist in marginal lives, with minimal contact with the wider societies in which they find themselves, especially those who have arrived as adults (Abrego, 2011). However, within this they manage risk and, as we noted from the interviews, often differentiate between the illegality of their status and other actions that they associate with illegality. While we have never adopted the term 'illegal' to define those without documents, many interviewees referred to themselves as 'illegal' and attached that identification to their status. However, they made a distinction between their status of illegality and other illegal activities, such as criminal conduct, including the use of false documents and so forth. Thus, some migrants specifically refused to take the risk of obtaining false documents, which might indeed have given them access to better work, simply because to do so would have been, in their eyes, an 'illegal' act.

There were some risks that undocumented migrants had to take and some that they preferred to avoid, which were reflected in their employment and housing choices. Choosing work in sectors and in geographical areas where they thought that the authorities were less likely to investigate was a strategy that some adopted, where they had a choice. Work in construction, retail and in hair and beauty, for example, were thought to be less risky than work in minority ethnic businesses – restaurants and take-aways in particular – where immigration authorities had previously concentrated their investigations. Thus, those who could make a choice for what they understood would be 'safer' types of jobs did so. Living with family members legally resident was another strategy adopted specifically to reduce risk, even where this resulted in tensions inside households, because it was believed that the immigration authorities were less likely to raid private households. Thus, risk takers were also risk avoiders, but above all they were risk assessors constantly assessing and reassessing risks.

Employers too demonstrated that they operated risk limitation strategies. Chapter Five showed that some employers continued to employ those without documents, even though this placed them at risk of ever increasing sanctions. Employing undocumented migrants required them to operationalise the risks they took, through assessments based on the numbers of undocumented workers they might hire at any one time, the times of the day they required them to work and the length of their employment. Hiring one or two undocumented workers in a workforce of ten or more was a risk some were prepared to take, but hiring more than this was too risky. A few workers could be hidden or could be shown how to exit from the back door if a raid took place, but more workers would make this impossible. Hiring for a couple of weeks to cover staff shortages was again another risk that might be taken, on the basis that it would be bad luck indeed if the immigration authorities arrived precisely in those weeks. As with the migrants' calculations, risks were assessed on the basis of sector, hours of work and other elements. Risks also had to be balanced against needs and obligations. Thus migrants who had skills that were in short supply would be employed even when they were undocumented. Obligations based on family membership, or on political or humanitarian principles also meant that risk had to be calculated by different measures. Finally, for employers, trust was as important as it was for the migrants themselves. Employers trusted those accessed through their own networks and with whom they had a shared identity, language, culture or ethnicity more easily than they trusted others and this in turn resulted in their identification of such workers as good, hard working and employable.

Thus the risks of sanctions, whether against employers or against undocumented migrants, are balanced against other factors, including the risk of being found and the risks associated with return. The failure of governments to understand that these calculations have to be made by the individuals themselves means that punitive policies do not change the other sets of factors that these actors take into consideration.

Class, gender and ethnicity

As with migrants generally, the undocumented migrants in our study came from varied social and economic backgrounds. Some had come to the UK with human capital that, were it not for their status, might have been utilisable to their benefit, at least to secure jobs that were more commensurate with their qualifications. Indeed it is palpably the case that undocumented migrants must have had access to financial resources, or at least have had the possibility of a loan of resources, to enable their migration journey, particularly in cases where the distances between origin and destination countries are great and where the costs that have to be paid to smugglers or agents is significant. While we do not know the resources that everyone had prior to migration, we know that the costs of the migration journey could be substantial, as we reported in Chapter Three. Even those who had not paid a third party to facilitate the journey still needed the resources to pay for their travel and to maintain themselves, at least in the first weeks of their migration.

However, class position prior to arrival, among those from more educated backgrounds, did not translate into a resource post arrival. The very fact of being undocumented meant that it was not possible to utilise the human capital they had acquired in the past. Status also meant, in most cases, exclusion from networks made up of persons of a similar class, thus cancelling out the social capital that otherwise they would have had. Thus their class position did not travel with migrants whose status was undocumented. However, it could be observed to some extent in the progress that some respondents had been able to make after their migration and in their use of agency. Thus, although the movements appeared small, some people did manage to progress in their employment, although often hitting a glass ceiling at some point that their status did not permit them to overcome, as we demonstrated in Chapter Four. Those who evidenced these small improvements either had the capacity and confidence to make demands on employers – a product of their social or human capital – or had been able to acquire skills that were needed in order to make incremental improvements to their working lives (Bloch and McKay, 2013). Progression was also related to the type of work that individuals carried out and the extent to which their skills were transferable. Class differences therefore may have had a marginal impact on the working lives of some undocumented migrants in the study, but did not eliminate the disadvantages of status.

The social capital that women utilise appears to lead to fewer job opportunities than that of men and is more likely to decrease women's earnings (Allen, 2009; McDonald, 2011). As we have also suggested, gender and ethnicity influenced access to employment in both negative and positive ways (Reingold, 1999; Martin, 2014). The labour markets in which the respondents operated were segmented and the division of labour into male and female jobs was observable. Females were rarely in kitchen jobs and, if employed in restaurants, were usually working at the front of the house, offering direct customer service when they spoke sufficient English. Employers interviewed in the course of the study made it clear that kitchen jobs were unsuitable for women and that they would not generally employ them in those jobs. Women therefore were segregated in relation to the range of jobs they had access to. Migration did nothing to break down the stereotypes of what work is 'suitable' for men and what is 'suitable' for women, and indeed gender roles were reinforced and absolute among the migrants in the study.

Workplaces were also segregated on the basis of ethnicity. Generally, undocumented migrants worked solely or for the most part with others of the same ethnicity or nationality. This was in part a consequence of the networks they were able to access to look for work, but also came from their own preferences and those of employers. Workers preferred to work with others with whom they shared a language and culture, even though in some cases they did not trust colleagues sufficiently to have revealed their undocumented status. Employers too, as we showed in Chapter Five, made assessments of suitability for work based primarily on ethnic origin, ascribing trust, ability and a willingness to work hard to those sharing their own ethnic identity. In a segment of society to which many of its rules do not extend, the same prejudices and assumptions were made as apply more generally.

Overall, therefore, what do we conclude? We would submit that policies that are stated as having the aim of restricting migration are likely to signify more complex dynamics, the aims of which go well beyond migration controls and are about restricting the entitlements of all citizens or placing them in competition with the undocumented for jobs, in circumstances where wages and working conditions are deteriorating. For those who are present or remain without the legal right to work, there is a direct impact on their working conditions, but indirectly there is at least the potential of worsening working conditions for all workers. The limited data available, covering pay and conditions in those sectors where the undocumented migrants we interviewed had found work, points to these also being sectors in which, since the early years of this century, pay has risen at a slower rate than in other parts of the economy (Bloch and McKay, 2013). This means that it is always unsatisfactory to assess immigration policies purely in relation to their impact on migrant numbers.

We also have argued that the informal economy, where many undocumented migrants find work, displays the same divisions as are present in the formal labour market and that are based on gender, ethnicity and class. Indeed we would argue that being undocumented can reinforce gender, class and ethnic disadvantage. Finally, and returning to the central theme of networks explored in this book, we conclude that being undocumented forces individuals to rely on resource-poor networks and, in so doing, traps individuals into lives of poverty, precarity and marginality from which relatively few ever escape.

Conclusion

We wrote this book in the shadow of the 2015 general election in the UK, which the Conservative party fought and won, arguing for the need for further immigration controls. The rights of those without documents having already been restricted in 2014, as we explored in Chapter Two, the 2015 Conservative election manifesto proposed limiting the numbers who could enter with permission, while extending the policy of 'deport first, appeal later', which has already resulted in increased deportations, to cover all immigration appeals and judicial reviews, apart from those dealing with asylum. It also proposed even tighter border controls, in the futile hope that these would prevent people from entering the UK without the correct documents. The reality is that undocumented migrants will continue to be paraded as scapegoats for the economic crisis that they did not cause and will remain as the excuse for further attacks on welfare. The migrants whose stories we have recounted in this book will mostly stay because they have nowhere else to go, but the conditions under which they live are likely to become even harsher.

Being undocumented does not halt aging, does not stop family formation or the need for healthcare, education or social provision. The longer-term wellbeing of undocumented migrants and their children should be and is a real concern and one that a fully developed country of the global North needs to be mindful of. We began this book with a quote from the US president, Barack Obama, that emphasised the need to be 'reasoned, thoughtful, compassionate' in relation to undocumented migrants. Such an aspiration remains a distant hope in the current UK and wider European context and one that needs to be urgently remedied, not just for the sake of undocumented migrants but for society as a whole.

References

Abbas, T. (2007) 'Muslim minorities in Britain: integration, multiculturalism and radicalism in the post-7/7 period in Western European capitalism', *Journal of Intercultural Studies*, 28(3): 287–300.

Abrego, L. (2011) 'Legal consciousness of undocumented Latinos: fear and stigma as barriers to claims-making for first- and 1.5-generation immigrants', *Law and Society Review*, 45(2): 337–70.

Adams, M. and Campbell, J. (2012) 'Being undocumented and intimate partner violence (IPV): multiple vulnerabilities through the lens of feminist intersectionality', *Women's Health and Urban Life*, 11(1): 15–34.

Ahmad, A.N. (2008a) 'Dead men working: time and space in London's (illegal) migrant economy', *Work, Employment and Society*, 22(2): 301–18.

Ahmad, A.N. (2008b) 'The labour market consequences of human smuggling: "illegal" employment in London's migrant economy', *Journal of Ethnic and Migration Studies*, 34(6): 853–74.

Al-Ali, N., Black, R. and Koser, K. (2001a) 'The limits to "transnationalism": Bosnian and Eritrean refugees in Europe as emerging transnational communities', *Ethnic and Racial Studies*, 24(4): 578–600.

Al-Ali, N., Black, R. and Koser, K. (2001b) 'Refugees and transnationalism: the experience of Bosnians and Eritreans in Europe', *Journal of Ethnic and Migration Studies*, 27(4): 615–34.

Alba, F. (1978) 'Mexico's international migration as a manifestation of its development pattern', *International Migration Review*, 12(4): 502–13.

Aldrich, H.E. and Waldinger, R. (1990) 'Ethnicity and entrepreneurship', *Annual Review of Sociology*, 16: 111–35.

Allen, R. (2009) 'Benefit or burden? Social capital, gender and the economic adaptation of refugees', *International Migration Review*, 43(2): 332–6.

Ambrosini, M. (2012) 'Surviving underground: irregular migrants, Italian families, invisible welfare', *International Journal of Social Welfare*, 21: 361–71.

Anderson, B. (2013) *Us and them? The dangerous politics of immigration controls*, Oxford: Oxford University Press.

Anderson, B. and Ruhs, M. (2010a) Guest editorial: 'Researching illegality and labour migration', *Population, Space and Place*, 16(3): 175–9.

Anderson, B and Ruhs, M. (2010b) 'Migrant workers: who needs them? A framework for the analysis of staff shortages, immigration, and public policy', in Ruhs, M. and Anderson, B. (eds), *Who needs migrant workers? Labour shortages, immigration, and public policy*, Oxford: Oxford University Press, pp 15-52.

Anderson, B., Gibney, M. and Paoletti, E. (2011) 'Boundaries of belonging: deportation and the constitution and contestation of citizenship', *Citizenship Studies*, 15(5): 543–5.

Anderson, B., Ruhs, M., Rogaly, B. and Spencer, S. (2006) *Fair enough? Central and East European migrants in low-wage employment in the UK*, COMPAS, University of Oxford.

Anthias, F. (2007) 'Ethnic ties: social capital and the question of mobilisability', *The Sociological Review*, 55(4): 788–805.

Arango, J. (2000) 'Explaining migration: a critical view', *International Social Science Journal*, 52(3): 283–96.

Arendt, H. (2004) *The origins of totalitarianism*, New York: Schocken Books.

Atkinson, R. and Flint, J. (2001) *Accessing hidden and hard-to-reach populations: snowball research strategies*, Social Research Update, University of Surrey, http://sru.soc.surrey.ac.uk/SRU33.pdf (accessed 6 August 2015).

Bakewell, O. (2015) 'Relaunching migration systems', *Migration Studies*, 3(2): 300–18.

Barbero, I. (2012) 'Expanding acts of citizenship: the struggles of sinpapeles migrants', *Social and Legal Studies*, 21(4): 529–47.

Barrett, A., McGuinness, S. and O'Brien, M. (2012) 'The immigrant earnings disadvantage across the earnings and skills distributions: the case of immigrants from the EU's new member states', *British Journal of Industrial Relations*, 50(3): 457–81.

Beck, S. (2007) 'Meeting on the margins: Cantonese "old timers" and Fujianese "newcomers"', *Population, Space and Place*, 13(2): 141–52.

Betts, A. (2013) *Survival migration: failed governance and the crisis of displacement*, Ithaca, NY: Cornell University Press.

Blitz, B.K. and Otero-Iglesias, M. (2011) 'Stateless by any other name: refused asylum-seekers in the United Kingdom', *Journal of Ethnic and Migration Studies*, 37(4): 657–73.

Bloch, A. (2007) 'Methodological challenges for national and multi-sited comparative survey research', *Journal of Refugee Studies*, 20(2): 230–47.

Bloch, A. (2008) 'Zimbabweans in Britain: transnational activities and capabilities', *Journal of Ethnic and Migration Studies*, 34(2): 287–305.

Bloch, A. (2010) 'The right to rights? Undocumented migrants from Zimbabwe living in South Africa', *Sociology*, 44(2): 233–50.

Bloch, A. (2013) 'The labour market experiences and strategies of young undocumented migrants', *Work, Employment and Society*, 27(2): 272–87.

Bloch, A. (2014) 'Living in fear: rejected asylum seekers living as irregular migrants in England', *Journal of Ethnic and Migration Studies*, 40(10): 1507–25.

Bloch, A. and Chimienti, M. (2011) 'Irregular migration in a globalizing world', *Ethnic and Racial Studies*, 34(8): 1271–85.

Bloch, A. and McKay, S. (2013) 'Hidden dishes – how food gets on to our plates: undocumented migrants and the restaurant sector', *Journal of Workplace Rights*, 17(1): 69–92.

Bloch, A. and McKay, S. (2015) 'Employment, social networks and undocumented migrants: the employer perspective', *Sociology*, 49(1): 38–55.

Bloch, A., Kumarappan, L. and McKay, S. (2014) 'Women migrants today: new directions, no papers, old barriers', *Working USA,* 17(3): 339–55.

Bloch, A., Kumarappan, L. and McKay, S. (2015) 'Employer sanctions: the impact of workplace raids and fines on undocumented migrants and ethnic enclave employers', *Critical Social Policy*, 35(1): 132–51.

Bloch, A., Neal, S. and Solomos, J. (2013) *Race, multiculture and social policy*, Basingstoke: Palgrave Macmillan.

Bloch, A., Sigona, N. and Zetter, R. (2011) 'Migration routes and strategies of young undocumented migrants in England: a qualitative perspective', *Ethnic and Racial Studies* 34(8): 1286–302.

Bloch, A., Sigona, N. and Zetter, R. (2014) *Sans papiers: the social and economic lives of young undocumented migrants*, London: Pluto Press.

Bourdieu, P. (1986) 'The forms of capital' in J. Richardson (ed) *Handbook of theory and research for the sociology of education*, New York, Greenwood, 241-258.

Brettell, C. and Hollifield, J. (eds), (2007) *Migration theory: talking across disciplines*, New York: Routledge, 2nd edition.

Castles, S. (2003) 'Towards a sociology of forced migration and social transformation', *Sociology*, 37(1): 13–34.

Castles, S. (2004) 'Why migration policies fail', *Ethnic and Racial Studies*, 27(2): 205–27.

Castles, S. (2005) 'Nation and empire: hierarchies of citizenship in the new global order', *International Politics*, 42: 203–24.

Castles, S. (2010) 'Understanding global migration: a social transformation perspective', *Journal of Ethnic and Migration Studies*, 36(10): 1565–86.

Castles, S. (2013) 'The forces driving global migration', *Journal of Intercultural Studies*, 34(2): 122–40.

Castles, S. and Davidson, A. (2000) *Citizenship and migration: globalisation and the politics of belonging*, Basingstoke: Palgrave Macmillan.

Castles, S., de Haas, H. and Miller, M.J. (2013) *The age of migration: international population movements in the modern world*, Basingstoke: Palgrave Macmillan (5th edition).

Cederberg, M. (2012) 'Making sense of ethnic inequalities', *Acta Sociologica*, 55: 59–72.

Chaudhry, S. and Crick, D. (2004) 'The business practices of small Chinese restaurants in the UK: an exploratory investigation', *Strategic Change*, 13(1): 37–49.

Chauvin, S. and Garcés-Mascareñas, B. (2014) 'Becoming less illegal: deservingness frames and undocumented migrant incorporation', *Sociology Compass*, 8(4): 422–32.

Chavez, L. (2007) 'The condition of illegality', *International Migration*, 5(3): 192–6.

Chavez, L. (2012) *Shadowed lives: undocumented immigrants in American society*, San Diego, CA: Harcourt Brace Jovanovich (3rd edition).

Chimienti, M. and Solomos, J. (2015) 'How do international human rights influence national healthcare provisions for irregular migrants? A case study of France and the UK', *Journal of Human Rights*, doi: 10.1080 / 14754835.2015.1032225.

Clandestino (2009) *Counting the uncountable: data and trends across Europe*, Clandestino Research Project: Size and Development of Irregular Migration to the EU, October: http://irregular-migration. net//fileadmin/irregular-migration/dateien/4.Background_ Information/4.2.Policy_Briefs_EN/ComparativePolicyBrief_ SizeOfIrregularMigration_Clandestino_Nov09_2.pdf (accessed 6 August 2015).

Clark, K. (2015) 'Ethnic minority self-employment', *IZA World of Labor*, doi: 10.15185/izawol.120.

Clark, K. and Drinkwater, S. (2000) 'Pushed out or pulled in? Self-employment among ethnic minorities in England and Wales', *Labour Economics*, 7(5): 603–28.

Clark, K. and Drinkwater, S. (2007) *Ethnic minorities in the labour market: dynamics and diversity*, York: Joseph Rowntree Foundation.

Cleaveland, C. and Pierson, L. (2009) 'Parking lots and police: undocumented Latinos' tactics for finding day labour jobs', *Ethnography*, 10(4): 515–33.

Cobb, C.L., King, M.C. and Rodriguez, L. (2009) 'Betwixt and between: the spectrum of formality revealed in the labour market experiences of Mexican migrant workers in the United States', *Review of Radical Political Economics*, 41(3): 365–71.

Cohen, R. (2007) 'Response to Hathaway', *Journal of Refugee Studies*, 20(3): 370–6.

Council of the European Union (2008) *European Pact on Immigration and Asylum*, 24 September, http://eur-lex.europa.eu/legal-content/EN/TXT/?uri=URISERV:jl0038

Crisp, J. (2008) 'Beyond the nexus: UNHCR's evolving perspective on refugee protection and international migration', Research paper 155, UN High Commissioner for Refugees: Geneva.

Cuadra, C.B. (2011) 'Right of access to health care for undocumented migrants in EU: a comparative study of national policies', *European Journal of Public Health*, 22(2): 267–71.

Cvajner, M. and Sciortino, G. (2010) 'Theorizing irregular migration: the control of spatial mobility in differentiated societies', *European Journal of Social Theory*, 13(3): 389–404.

da Lomba, S. (2011) 'Irregular migrants and the human right to health care: a case-study of health-care provision for irregular migrants in France and the UK', *International Journal of Law in Context*, suppl. *Health and Human Rights*, 7(3): 357–74.

Daly, M. and Silver, H. (2008) 'Social exclusion and social capital: a comparison and critique', *Theoretical Sociology*, 37: 537–66.

Datta, K., McIlwaine, V., Evans, Y., Herbert, J., May, J. and Wills, J. (2006) *Work and survival strategies among low-paid migrant workers in London*, London: Queen Mary, University of London.

de Genova, N. (2002) 'Migrant "illegality" and deportability in everyday life', *Annual Review of Anthropology*, 31: 419–47.

de Genova, N. (2004) 'The legal production of Mexican/migrant "illegality"', *Latino Studies*, 2: 160–85.

de Lange, T. (2011) 'The privatization of control over labour migration in the Netherlands: in whose interest?', *European Journal of Migration and Law*, 13:185–200.

Dewhurst, E. (2011) 'Right of irregular immigrants to outstanding remuneration under the EU sanctions Directive: rethinking domestic labour policy in a globalised world', *European Journal of Migration and Law*, 13(4): 389–410.

DeWind, J. (2007) 'Response to Hathaway', *Journal of Refugee Studies*, 20(3): 381–5.

Diminescu, D. (2008) 'The connected migrant: an epistemological manifesto', *Social Science Information*, 47: 565.

Düvell, F. (2011a) 'The pathways in and out of irregular migration in the EU: a comparative analysis', *European Journal of Migration and Law*, 13(3): 245–50.

Düvell, F. (2011b) 'Paths into irregularity: the legal and political construction of irregular migration', *European Journal of Migration and Law*, 13(3): 275–95.

Dwyer, P., Lewis, H., Scullion, L. and Waite, L. (2011) *Forced labour and UK immigration policy: status matters?* York: Joseph Rowntree Foundation.

Ellermann, A. (2008) 'The limits of unilateral migration control: deportation and inter-state cooperation', *Government and Opposition*, 43(2): 168–89.

Ellerman, A. (2010) 'Undocumented migrants and resistance in the liberal state', *Politics & Society*, 38(3): 408–29.

Engbersen, G. (2001) 'The unanticipated consequences of panopticon Europe. Residence strategies of illegal immigrants', in Guiraudon, V. and C. Joppke (eds), *Controlling a new migration world*, London: Routledge, pp 222–46.

Engbersen, G. and Broeders, D. (2009) 'The state versus the alien: immigration control and strategies of irregular immigrants', *West European Politics*, 32(5): 867–85.

Engbersen, G., van San, M. and Leerkes, A. (2006) 'A room with a view: irregular immigrants in the legal capital of the world', *Ethnography*, 7(2): 209–42.

Erdemir, A. and Vasta, E. (2007) *Differentiating irregularity and solidarity: Turkish immigrants at work in London*, COMPAS, University of Oxford.

Erel, U. (2010) 'Migrating cultural capital: Bourdieu in migration studies', *Sociology* 44(4): 642–60.

European Commission (2006) *Communication from the Commission on Policy priorities in the fight against illegal immigration of third-country nationals*, COM (2006)402, http://eur-lex.europa.eu/procedure/EN/194507.

European Commission (2011) Communication from the Commission to the European Parliament and the Council (2011), *Evaluation of EU Readmission Agreements*, COM (2011) 76, http://eur-lex.europa.eu/LexUriServ/LexUriServ.do?uri=COM:2011:0076:FIN:EN:PDF.

European Commission (2013) *Study on the situation of third-country nationals pending return/removal in the EU Member States and the Schengen Associated Countries,* http://ec.europa.eu/dgs/home-affairs/e-library/documents/policies/immigration/return-readmission/docs/11032013_sudy_report_on_immigration_return-removal_annex_1_en.pdf (accessed 6 August 2015).

European Commission (2014) *Communication from the Commission to the Council and the European Parliament on EU return policy,* COM (2014) 199 final.

Ewers, M. (2007) 'Migrants, markets and multinationals: competition among world cities for the highly skilled', *GeoJournal,* 68(2): 119–30.

Faist, T. (2000) *The volume and dynamics of international migration and transnational social spaces,* Oxford: Oxford University Press.

Faugier, J. and Sargeant, M. (1997) 'Sampling hard to reach populations', *Journal of Advanced Nursing,* 26(4): 790–7.

Finch, T. and Cherti, M. (2011) *No easy options: irregular immigration in the UK,* London: Institute for Public Policy Research.

Fine, B. (2010) *Theories of social capital – researchers behaving badly,* London: Pluto Press.

Flynn, D. (2014) 'MRN sets out reasons why the *Guardian* should not use the term 'illegal immigrant', http://www.migrantsrights.org.uk/news/2014/mrn-sets-out-reasons-why-guardian-should-not-use-term-illegal-immigrant (accessed 5 January 2015).

Geddes, A. (2005) 'Chronicle of a crisis foretold: the politics of irregular migration, human trafficking and people smuggling in the UK', *The British Journal of Politics & International Relations,* 7(3): 324–39.

Gibney, M. (2008) 'Asylum and the expansion of deportation in the United Kingdom', *Government and Opposition,* 43(2): 146–67.

Gilbert, A. and Koser, K. (2006) 'Coming to the UK: what do asylum-seekers know about the UK before arrival?' *Journal of Ethnic and Migration Studies,* 32(7): 1209–25.

Gill, N. and Bialski, P. (2011) 'New friends in new places: network formation during the migration process among Poles in the UK', *Geoforum,* 42: 241–9.

Goldring, L., Berinstein, C. and Bernard, J.K. (2009) 'Institutionalizing precarious migratory status in Canada', *Citizenship Studies,* 13(3): 239–65.

Goldring, L. and Landolt, P. (2011) 'Caught in the work–citizenship matrix: the lasting effects of precarious legal status on work for Toronto immigrants', *Globalizations,* 8(3): 325–41.

Gomberg-Muñoz, R. (2010) 'Willing to work: agency and vulnerability in an undocumented immigrant network', *American Anthropologist*, 112(2): 295–307.

Gonzales, R.G. and Chavez, L.R. (2012) '"Awakening to a nightmare": abjectivity and illegality in the lives of undocumented 1.5-generation Latino immigrants in the United States', *Current Anthropology* 53(3): 255–81.

Gordon, J. (2007) 'Transnational labor citizenship', *Southern California Law Review*, 80: 503–88.

Gordon, I., Scanlon, K., Travers, T. and Whitehead, C. (2009) 'Economic impact on London and the UK of an earned regularisation of irregular migrants in the UK', Interim Report, London: London School of Economics and Political Sciences.

Granovetter, M. (1983) 'The strength of weak ties' *Sociological Theory*, 1: 201–33.

Grasmuck, S. (1984) 'Immigration, ethnic stratification, and native working class discipline: comparisons of documented and undocumented Dominicans', *International Migration Review*, 18(3): 692–713.

Griffiths, D. (2000) 'Fragmentation and consolidation: the contrasting cases of Somali and Kurdish refugees in London', *Journal of Refugee Studies*, 13(3): 281–302.

Grove-White, R. (2014) 'Immigration Act 2014: what next for migrant's access to NHS care?' http://www.migrantsrights.org.uk/blog/2014/05/immigration-act-2014-what-next-migrants-access-nhs-care (accessed 6 August 2015).

Grzymała-Kazłowska, B. (2005) 'From ethnic cooperation to in-group competition: undocumented Polish workers in Brussels', *Journal of Ethnic and Migration Studies*, 31(4): 675–97.

Gupta, R. (2007) *Enslaved: the new British slavery*, London: Portobello.

Hagan, J. (1998) 'Social networks, gender, and immigrant incorporation: resources and constraints', *American Sociological Review*, 63(1): 55–67.

Hagan, J. (2008) *Migration miracle: faith, hope, and meaning on the undocumented journey*, Cambridge, MA: Harvard University Press.

Hagan, J., Rodriguez, N. and Mullis, B. (2011) 'Social effects of mass deportations by the United States government, 2000–2010', *Ethnic and Racial Studies*, 34(8): 1374–91.

Hamood, S. (2008) 'EU–Libya cooperation on migration: a raw deal for refugees and migrants?' *Journal of Refugee Studies*, 21(1): 19–42.

Hathaway, J.C. (2007) 'Forced migration studies: could we agree just to "date"?', *Journal of Refugee Studies*, 20(3): 349–69.

Holgate, J., Keles, J., Pollert, A. and Kumarappan, L. (2012) 'Workplace problems among Kurdish workers in London: experiences of an invisible community and the role of community organisations as support networks', *Journal of Ethnic and Migration Studies*, 38(4): 595–612.

Holgate, J., Pollert, A., Keles, J. and Kumarappan, L. (2012) 'Union decline and voice among minority ethnic workers: do community-based social networks help to fill the gap?' *Urban Studies* 49(3): 613–30.

Holmes, S. (2007) '"Oaxacans like to work bent over": the naturalization of social suffering among berry farm workers', *International Migration*, 45(3): 39–68.

Holmes, S. (2013) *Fresh fruit, broken bodies: migrant farmworkers in the United States*, Oakland: University of California Press.

Hormiga, E. and Bolivar-Cruz, A. (2014) 'The relationship between the migration experience and risk perception: a factor in the decision to become an entrepreneur', *International Entrepreneurship and Management Journal*, 10(2): 297–307.

Hynes, P. and Sales, R. (2010) 'New communities: asylum seekers and dispersal', in Bloch, A. and Solomos, J. (eds), *Race and ethnicity in the 21st century*, Basingstoke: Palgrave Macmillan.

ICMPD (International Centre for Migration Policy Development) (2009) *REGINE Regularisations in Europe, study on practices in the area of regularisation of illegally staying third-country nationals in the Member States of the EU*, Final report, Vienna, Austria.

Inghammar, A. (2010) 'The employment contract revisited: undocumented migrant workers and the intersection between international standards, immigration policy and employment law', *European Journal of Migration and Law*, 12(2): 193–214.

International Organization for Migration (2010) *World Migration Report 2010*, Geneva: International Organization for Migration.

Iskander, N. (2007) 'Informal work and protest: undocumented immigrant activism in France, 1996–2000', *British Journal of Industrial Relations*, 45(2): 309–34.

JCWI (2014) *Immigration Act 2014 Summary of provisions*, http://www.jcwi.org.uk/sites/default/files/Immigration%20Act%202014%20Summary%20Provisions_0.pdf (accessed 6 August 2015).

Jones, T., Mascarenhas-Keyes, S. and Ram, M. (2012) 'The ethnic entrepreneurial transition: recent trends in British Indian self-employment', *Journal of Ethnic and Migration Studies*, 38(1): 93–109.

Jones, T., Ram, M. and Edwards, P. (2006) 'Ethnic minority business and the employment of illegal immigrants', *Entrepreneurship and Regional Development: An International Journal* 18(2): 133–50.

Jones, T., Ram, M., Li, Y. and Edwards, P. (2014) *The contribution of new migrant entrepreneurs in the UK*, Centre for Entrepreneurs, www.centreforentrepreneurs.org.

Jones, T., Ram, M., Li, Y., Edwards, P. and Villares, M. (2015) 'Super-diverse Britain and new migrant enterprises', *IRiS Working Paper Series*, No. 8/2015, Birmingham: Institute for Research into Superdiversity.

Jordan, B. and Düvell, F. (2002) *Irregular migration: the dilemmas of transnational mobility*, Cheltenham: Edward Elgar Publishing.

Judge, J. (2014) 'Making claims for migrant workers: human rights and citizenship', *Citizenship Studies*, 18(1): 29–45.

Khattab, N., Johnston, R., Sirkeci, I. and Modood, T. (2010) 'The impact of spatial segregation on the employment outcomes amongst Bangladeshi men and women in England and Wales', *Sociological Research Online*, 5(1)3, doi:10.5153/sro.2082.

Khosravi, S. (2010) 'An ethnography of migrant "illegality" in Sweden: included yet excepted?' *Journal of International Political Theory*, 6(1): 95–116.

Kilner, H. (2014) 'Hostile health care – why charging migrants will harm the most vulnerable', *British Journal of General Practice*, 64(626): 590–2.

King, R., Thomson, M., Mai. N. and Keles, Y. (2008) *'Turks' in London: shades of invisibility and the shifting relevance of policy in the migration process*, Working Paper No. 51, Sussex Centre for Migration Research, University of Sussex.

Kitching, J., Smallbone, D. and Athayde, R. (2009) 'Ethnic diasporas and business competitiveness: minority owned enterprises in London', *Journal of Ethnic and Migration Studies*, 35(4): 689–705.

Kloosterman, R., van der Leun, J. and Rath, J. (1999) *Mixed embeddedness: (in)formal economic activities and immigrant businesses in the Netherlands*, London: Blackwell.

Knight, J. (2015) 'Migrant employment in the ethnic economy: why do some migrants become ethnic entrepreneurs and others co-ethnic workers?', *Journal of International Migration and Integration* 16: 575–92.

Koser, K. (2005) 'Irregular migration, state security and human security', paper prepared for the Policy Analysis and Research Programme of the Global Commission on International Migration (GCIM), September.

Koser, K. (2008) 'Why smuggling pays', *International Migration*, 46(2): 3–26.

Koser, K. (2010) 'Dimensions and dynamics of irregular migration', *Population, Space and Place*, 16(3): 181–93.

Kraler, A. (2009) *Regularisation: a misguided option or part and parcel of a comprehensive policy response to irregular migration?* Austria: IMISCOE Working Paper No. 24, ICMPD.

Kraler, A. (2011) 'Fixing, adjusting, regulating, protecting human rights – the shifting uses of regularisations in the European Union', *European Journal of Migration and Law*, 13(3): 297–316.

Lammers, E. (2005) 'Refugees, asylum seekers and anthropologists; the taboo on giving', *Global Migration Perspectives*, No. 29, Geneva: Global Commission on International Migration.

Lancee, B. (2012) 'The economic returns of bonding and bridging social capital for immigrant men in Germany', *Ethnic and Racial Studies*, 34(4): 664–83.

Levie, J.D. (2007) 'Immigration, in-migration, ethnicity and entrepreneurship in the United Kingdom', *Small Business Economics*, 28(2–3): 143–69.

Levie, J.D., Smallbone, D. and Minnitti, M. (2009) 'Immigration, ethnicity and entrepreneurial behaviour', in J.D. Levie, D. Smallbone and M. Minnitti, *Perspectives on entrepreneurship, 1*, Praeger Publishers, pp 157–80.

Levinson, A. (2005) *The regularisation of unauthorized migrants: literature survey and country case studies*, Centre on Migration, Policy and Society, University of Oxford.

Levitt, P. (2001) *The transnational villagers*, Berkeley: University of California Press.

Lewis, H., Dwyer, P., Hodkinson, S. and Waite, L. (2013) *Precarious lives: experiences of forced labour among refugees and asylum seekers in England*, Leeds: University of Leeds and University of Salford.

Lewis, H., Dwyer, P., Hodkinson, S. and Waite, L. (2014) *Precarious lives: forced labour exploitation and asylum*, Bristol: The Policy Press.

Light, I., Sabagh, G., Bozorgmeh, M. and Der-Martirosian, C. (1994) 'Beyond the ethnic economy', *Social Problems*, 41(1): 65–80.

Logan, J.R., Alba, R.D. and Stults, B.J. (2003) 'Enclaves and entrepreneurs: assessing the payoff for immigrants and minorities', *International Migration Review*, 37(2): 344–60.

Lucas, R. and Mansfield, S. (2010) 'The use of migrant labour in the hospitality sector: current and future implications', in Ruhs, M. and Anderson, B. (eds), *Who needs migrant workers? Labour shortages, immigration, and public policy*, Oxford: Oxford University Press.

McDonald, S. (2011) 'What's in the "old boys'" network? Accessing social capital in gendered and racialized networks', *Social Networks*, 33: 317–30.

McGregor, J. (2007) '"Joining the BBC (British Bottom Cleaners)": Zimbabwean migrants and the UK care industry', *Journal of Ethnic and Migration Studies*, 33(5): 801–24.

McIlwaine, V., Datta, K., Evans, Y., Herbert, J., May, J. and Wills, J. (2006) *Gender and ethnic identities among low-paid migrant workers in London*, London: Queen Mary, University of London.

McIlwaine, C. (2014) 'Legal Latins: creating webs and practices of immigration status among Latin American migrants in London', *Journal of Ethnic and Migration Studies*, doi: 10.1080/1369183X.2014.931803.

McKay, S. (2009) *'The relationship between status and rights', Themes on Migration and Ethnic Studies*, Linkoping University, http://liu.diva-portal.org/smash/record.jsf?searchId=1&pid=diva2:275412.

McKay, S. (2014) 'Why are the most vulnerable denied employment rights?' in Anderson, B. and Keith, M. (eds), *Migration: the COMPAS anthology*, Oxford: COMPAS, University of Oxford.

McKay, S., Markova, E. and Paraskevopoulou, A. (2011) *Undocumented workers' transitions: legal status, migration and work in Europe*, London: Routledge.

MacKenzie, R. and Forde, C. (2009) 'The rhetoric of the "good worker" versus the realities of employers' use and the experiences of migrant workers', *Work, Employment and Society*, 23(1): 142–59.

MacKenzie, R., Forde, C. and Ciupijus, Z. (2012) 'Networks of support for new migrant communities: institutional goals versus substantive goals', *Urban Studies*, 49(3): 631–47.

Mandaville, P. (2009) 'Muslim transnational identity and state responses in Europe and the UK after 9/11: political community, ideology and authority', *Journal of Ethnic and Migration Studies*, 35(3): 491–506.

Mantouvalou, V. (2006) 'Servitude and forced labour in the 21st century: the human rights of domestic workers', *Industrial Law Journal*, 35(4): 395–414.

Maroukis, T., Iglicka, K. and Katarzyna, G. (2011) 'Irregular migration and informal economy in Southern and Central-Eastern Europe: breaking the vicious cycle?' *International Migration*, 49(5): 129–56.

Martin, N. (2014) 'Spaces of hidden labor: migrant women and work in non-profit organizations', *Gender, Place & Culture: A Journal of Feminist Geography*, 21(1): 17–34.

Massey, D. and Gentsch, K. (2014) 'Undocumented migration to the United States and the wages of Mexican immigrants', *International Migration Review*, 48(2): 482–99.

Menjívar, C. (2006) 'Liminal legality: Salvadoran and Guatemalan immigrants' lives in the United States', *American Journal of Sociology*, 111(4): 999–1037.

Morris, L. (2002) 'Britain's asylum and immigration regime: the shifting contours of rights', *Journal of Ethnic and Migration Studies*, 28(3): 409–25.

Morris, L. (2007) 'New Labour's community of rights: welfare, immigration and asylum', *Journal of Social Policy*, 36(1): 39–57.

Munck, R., Schierup, U.C. and Delgado Wise, K. (2011) 'Migration, work and citizenship in the new world order', *Globalizations*, 8(3): 249–60.

Nakhaie, R., Lin, X. and Guan, J. (2009) 'Social capital and the myth of minority self-employment: evidence from Canada', *Journal of Ethnic and Migration Studies*, 35(4): 625–44

Nash, K. (2009) 'Between citizenship and human rights', *Sociology*, 43(6): 1067–83.

Nash, K. (2015) *The political sociology of human rights*, Cambridge: Cambridge University Press.

Nawyn, S., Gjokaj, L., de Brenna, L., Agbenyiga, L. and Breanne, G. (2012) 'Linguistic isolation, social capital and immigrant belonging', *Journal of Contemporary Ethnography*, 41: 255–82.

Nee, V. and Sanders, J. (2001) 'Understanding the diversity of immigrant incorporation: a forms-of-capital model', *Ethnic and Racial Studies*, 24(3): 386–411.

Oelgemoller, C. (2011) '"Transit" and "suspension": migration management or the metamorphosis of asylum-seekers into "illegal" immigrants', *Journal of Ethnic and Migration Studies*, 37(3): 407–24.

Papademetriou, D.G. (2005) *The 'regularization' option in managing illegal migration more effectively: a comparative perspective*, Washington: Migration Policy Institute.

Parla, A. (2007) 'Irregular workers or ethnic kin? Post 1990s labour migration from Bulgaria to Turkey', *International Migration*, 45(3): 158–80.

Pécoud, A. and de Guchteneire, P. (2006) 'International migration, border controls and human rights: assessing the relevance of a right to mobility', *Journal of Borderlands Studies*, 21(2): 69–86.

Pero, D. (2014) 'Class politics and migrants: collective action among new migrant workers in Britain', *Sociology*, 48(6): 1156–72.

Phung, V. (2011) 'Ethnicity, migration and employment disadvantage under New Labour: reviewing the evidence from the United Kingdom', *Policy Studies*, 32(5): 497–513.

Poelemans, M. and de Sèze, S. (2000) 'The regularisation of clandestine immigrants in France', *European Journal of Migration and Law*, 2: 309–36.

Portes, A. (1981) 'Modes of structural incorporation and present theories of labour immigration', in Kritz, M., Kelly, C.B. and Tomasi, S.M. (eds), *Global trends in migration: theory and research on international population movements*, pp 279–97. Staten Island, NY: Centre for Migration Studies.

Portes, A. (1998) 'Social capital: its origins and applications in modern sociology', *Annual Review of Sociology*, 24: 1–24.

Portes, A. (2001) 'Introduction: the debates and significance of immigrant transnationalism', *Global Networks*, 1(3): 181–93.

Portes, A. (2009) 'Migration and development: reconciling opposite view', *Ethnic and Racial Studies*, 32(1): 5–22.

Portes, A. and Bach, R.L. (1985) *Latin journey: Cuban and Mexican immigrants in the United States*, Berkeley: University of California Press.

Putnam, R. (2000) *Bowling alone: the collapse and revival of American community*, New York: Simon & Schuster.

Raj, A. and Silverstone, J. (2002) 'Violence against immigrant women: the roles of culture, context and legal immigrant status on intimate partner violence', *Violence against Women*, 8(3): 367–98.

Ram, M., Sanghera, B., Abbas, T., Barlow, G. and Jones, T. (2000) 'Ethnic minority business in comparative perspective: the case of the independent restaurant sector', *Journal of Ethnic and Migration Studies*, 26(3): 495–510.

Reeskens, T. and Wright, M. (2012) 'Nationalism and the cohesive society: a multilevel analysis of the interplay among diversity, national identity, and social capital', *Comparative Political Studies*, 46(2): 153–81.

Reeves, M. (2013) 'Clean fake: authenticating documents and persons in migrant Moscow', *American Ethnologist*, 40(3): 508–24.

Reingold, D. (1999) 'Social networks and the employment problem of the urban poor', *Urban Studies*, 36(11): 1907–32.

Reyneri, E. (2001) 'Migrants' involvement in irregular employment in the Mediterranean countries of the European Union', *International Migration Papers*, Geneva: International Labour Organisation.

Reynolds, T. (2012) 'Birds of a feather stick together? Negotiating community, family and intimate relationships between established and newcomer Caribbean migrants in Britain', *Community, Work & Family*, 15(1): 69–84.

Roggeveen, S. (2013) 'Beyond community: an analysis of social capital and the social networks of Brazilian migrants in Amsterdam', *Current Sociology*, 61(7): 1078–96.

Rosenblum, M. and Meissner, D. with Bergeron, C. and Hipsman, F. (2014) *The deportation dilemma: reconciling tough and humane enforcement*, Washington: Migration Policy Institute.

Rutherford, B. and Addison, L. (2007) 'Zimbabwean farm workers in northern South Africa', *Review of African Political Economy*, 114: 617–33.

Ryan, L. (2011) 'Migrants' social networks and weak ties: accessing resources and constructing relationships post-migration', *The Sociological Review*, 59 (4): 707–24.

Ryan, L., Sales, R., Tilki, M. and Siarra, B. (2008) 'Social networks, social support and social capital: the experiences of recent Polish migrants', *Sociology*, 42(4): 672–90.

Sahin, M., Nijkamp, P. and Suzuki, S. (2014) 'Contrasts and similarities in economic performance of migrant entrepreneurs', *Journal of Migration*, 3(7): 2–21.

Sales, R. (2007) *Understanding immigration and refugee policy: contradictions and. continuities*, Bristol: The Policy Press.

Samers, M. (2002) 'Immigration and the global city hypothesis: towards and alternative research agenda', *International Journal of Urban and Regional Research*, 26: 389–402.

Samers, M. (2008) 'At the heart of migration management: immigration and labour markets in the European Union', in Gabriel, C. and Pellerin, H. (eds), *Governing international labour migration: current issues, challenges and dilemmas*, London: Routledge, pp 128–44.

Sanders, J., Nee, V. and Sernau, S. (2002) 'Asian immigrants' reliance on social ties in a multi ethnic labor market', *Social Forces*, 81(1): 281–314.

Sassen, S. (2001) *The global city: New York, London, Tokyo*, Princeton: Princeton University Press.

Scheel, S. (2013) 'Autonomy of migration despite its securitisation? Facing the terms and conditions of biometric rebordering', *Millennium: Journal of International Studies* 41(3): 575–600.

Schrover, M., van der Leun, J. and Quispel, C. (2007) 'Niches, labour market segregation, ethnicity and gender', *Journal of Ethnic and Migration Studies*, 3(4): 529–40.

Schuster, L. (2011) 'Turning refugees into "illegal migrants": Afghan asylum seekers in Europe', *Ethnic and Racial Studies*, 34(8): 1392–407.

Sequeira, M. and Rasheed, A. (2006) 'Start-up and growth of immigrant small business: the impact of social and human capital', *Journal of Developmental Entrepreneurship*, 11: 357–75.

Sigona, N. (2012) '"I have too much baggage": the impacts of legal status on the social worlds of irregular migrants', *Social Anthropology/Anthropologie Sociale*, 20(1): 50–65.

Smallbone, D., Kitching, J. and Athayde, R. (2010) 'Ethnic diversity, entrepreneurship and competitiveness in a global city', *International Small Business Journal*, 28(2): 174–90.

Solomos, J. (2003) *Race and racism in Britain*, Basingstoke: Palgrave Macmillan.

Tackey, N., Casebourne, J., Aston, J., Ritchie, H., Sinclair, A., Tyers, C., Hurstfield, J., Willison, R. and Page, R. (2006) *Barriers to employment for Pakistanis and Bangledeshis in Britain*, Research Report No. 360, London: Department for Work and Pensions.

Triandafyllidou, A. and Ambrosini, M. (2011) 'Irregular immigration control in Italy and Greece: strong fencing and weak gate-keeping serving the labour market', *European Journal of Migration and Law*, 13(3): 251–73.

Triandafyllidou, A. and Ilies, M. (2010) 'EU policies on irregular migration', in Triandafyllidou, A. (ed), *Irregular Migration in Europe. Myths and Realities*, Aldershot: Ashgate, pp 23–41.

Valdez, Z. (2008) 'The effect of social capital on white, Korean, Mexican and black business owners' earnings in the US', *Journal of Ethnic and Migration Studies*, 34(6): 955–73.

Van Hear, N. (2014) 'Reconsidering migration and class', *International Migration Review*, 48(1): 100–21.

van Liempt, I. and Doomernik, J. (2006) 'Migrants' agency in the smuggling process: the perspectives of smuggled migrants in the Netherlands', *International Migration*, 44(4): 165–90.

van Meeteren, M. (2010) *Life without papers: aspirations, incorporation and transnational activities of irregular migrants in the Low Countries*, Rotterdam: Erasmus Universiteit.

van Meeteren, M. (2012a) 'Living different dreams: aspirations and social activities of irregular migrants in the Low Countries', *Journal of Ethnic and Migration Studies*, 38(10): 1643–59.

van Meeteren, M. (2012b) 'Transnational activities and aspirations of irregular migrants in Belgium and the Netherlands', *Global Networks*, 12(3): 314–32.

Vasta, E. (2011) 'Immigrants and the paper market: borrowing, renting and buying identities', *Ethnic and Racial Studies*, 34(2): 187–206.

Vasta, E. and Erdemir, A. (2010) 'Immigrant work strategies and social rights: the construction and circulation of myths', *Die Erde*, 141(1–2): 15–29.

Vertovec, S. (2007) 'Super-diversity and its implications', *Ethnic and Racial Studies*, 30(6): 1024–54.

Vine, J. (2014) *An inspection of the use of the power to enter business premises without a search warrant*, October–November 2013, Independent Chief Inspector of Border and Immigration.

Vollmer, B.A. (2011) 'Policy discourses on irregular migration in the EU – "number games" and "political games"', *European Journal of Migration and Law*, 13(3): 317–39.

Wahlbeck, O. (1998) 'Community work and exile politics: Kurdish refugee associations in London', *Journal of Refugee Studies*, 11(3): 215–30.

Wahlbeck, O. (2007) 'Work in the kebab economy: a study of the ethnic economy of immigrants in Finland', *Ethnicities*, 7(4): 543–63.

Waldinger, R. and Lichter, M. (2003) *How the other half works: immigration and the social organisation of labor*, Berkeley: University of California Press.

Waldinger, R., Ward, R. and Aldrich, H.E. (1990) *Ethnic entrepreneurs: immigrant business in industrial societies*, California: Sage Publications.

Willen, S. (2007) 'Toward a critical phenomenology of "illegality": state power, criminalization, and abjectivity among undocumented migrant workers in Tel Aviv, Israel', *International Migration*, 45(3): 8–38.

Williams, A. and Baláž, V. (2012) 'Migration, risk and uncertainty: theoretical perspectives', *Population, Space and Place*, 18(2): 167–80.

Williams, C. and Renooy, P. (2013) *Tackling undeclared work in 27 Member States and Norway*, Dublin: European Foundation for Living and Working Conditions.

Wills, J., Datta, K., Evans, Y., Herbert, J., May, J. and McIlwaine, C. (2010) *Global cities at work: new migrant divisions of labour*, London: Pluto Press.

Woodbridge, J. (2005) *Sizing the unauthorised (illegal) migrant population in the United Kingdom in 2001*, London: Home Office.

Wright, T. (2007) 'The problems and experiences of ethnic minority and migrant workers in hotels and restaurants in England', *Just Labour*, 10: 74–84.

Wright, T. and McKay, S. (2007) *United Kingdom country report*, Undocumented Worker Transitions, EU Sixth Framework Programme, Contract Number: 044272.

Zetter, R. (2007) 'More labels, fewer refugees: remaking the refugee label in an era of globalisation', *Journal of Refugee Studies*, 20(2): 172–92.

Zetter, R. and Pearl, M. (2000) 'The minority within the minority: refugee community based organisations in the UK and the impact of restrictionism on asylum-seekers', *Journal of Ethnic and Migration Studies*, 26(4): 675–97.

Zhou, M. (2004) 'Revisiting ethnic entrepreneurship: convergences, controversies and conceptual advancements', *International Migration Review*, 38(3): 1040–74.

Zolin, R., Chang, A. and Steffens, P. (2014) 'The role of the ethnic enclave in facilitating immigrant business performance and social integration', in Davidsson, P. (ed.), *Australian Centre for Entrepreneurship Research Exchange Conference 2014 Proceedings*, Sydney: Queensland University of Technology, pp 1212–24.

Index

References to tables are in *italics*